Peter S. Fisher
Weimar Controversies

Culture & Theory | Volume 224

For Alessandro and Valeria

Peter S. Fisher received a doctorate in European history from Harvard University. His research interests lie at the intersection of history and popular culture. He has published on German visionary interwar literature.

Peter S. Fisher
Weimar Controversies
Explorations in Popular Culture with Siegfried Kracauer

[transcript]

I would like to thank Michael Ermarth for having introduced me to the works of Siegfried Kracauer long ago at Dartmouth College. Another excellent teacher of mine in the history department was Henry Roberts, who had collaborated with Kracauer at Columbia University.

It is a blessing to be able to do research in Germany where libraries and archives are easily accessible and staffs are friendly and helpful. I wish to thank the Hauptstaatsarchiv Stuttgart, the Literaturarchiv Marbach, the library of the Friedrich Ebert Gedenkstätte (Heidelberg), the Bundesarchiv Berlin, and the Saarländische Universitätsbibliothek. My „home library" at the Technische Universität Kaiserslautern provided much essential support, especially with interlibrary loans.

On the private side, my friends John and Wulf hosted my stays in Stuttgart. Valuable technical assistance came from my children Alessandro and Valeria. Many thanks also to Fiammetta for her support. Clint helped with preliminary editing and Seth returned the document when it was done.

At transcript, I benefited from the guidance and coordination of Annika Linnemann. She managed the publication process in a smooth and gentle manner.

Bibliographic information published by the Deutsche Nationalbibliothek
The Deutsche Nationalbibliothek lists this publication in the Deutsche Nationalbibliografie; detailed bibliographic data are available in the Internet at http://dnb.d-nb.de

© 2020 transcript Verlag, Bielefeld

All rights reserved. No part of this book may be reprinted or reproduced or utilized in any form or by any electronic, mechanical, or other means, now known or hereafter invented, including photocopying and recording, or in any information storage or retrieval system, without permission in writing from the publisher.

Cover layout: Maria Arndt, Bielefeld
Cover illustration: Strongman Act and Audience – Berlin 1928 (Underwood and Underwood)
Typeset by Justine Buri, Bielefeld

Print-ISBN 978-3-8376-5146-1
PDF-ISBN 978-3-8394-5146-5
https://doi.org/10.14361/9783839451465

Table of Contents

Introduction 11

Chapter One. Occultism: Empowerment or Menace? 17

Chapter Two. Colportage:
Harmless Pleasure or Dangerous Diversion? 67

Chapter Three. The Schund Law:
Defending Morality or Undermining Freedom? 99

Chapter Four. Detective Pulps:
Modeling Justice or Glamorizing Crime? 143

Chapter Five. Nudism:
Weimar Renaissance or National Degeneration? 173

Epilogue 213

Bibliography 227

Index 233

Illustrations

1.1 Psychic detective August Drost and medium Marie Neumann
1.2 *Lachen Links* lampoons August Drost
1.3 Psychic detective Elsbeth Günther-Geffers at work
1.4 Crowds of faithful wait for admission in Konnersreuth
1.5 Parish priest exploits Therese Neumann and affluent tourists
1.6 Gregor Strasser on the cover of *Die Zukunft*
1.7 Jan Erik Hanussen on the cover of a Nazi book

2.1 Secretaries dream of liaisons with the wealthy in Weimar film
2.2 Popular actor Harry Piel
2.3 Cover of installment novel *Grossstadtmädel*
2.4 Cover of installment novel *Schwarze Natascha*
2.5 Cover of installment novel *Mein Sonny-Boy*
2.6 Two illustrations from *Mein Sonny-Boy*
2.7 Cover of *Ihr Junge* on *Illustrierter Film-Kurier 1556*
2.8 Cover of Pinkert's installment novel *Ihr Junge*

3.1 An antisemitic illustration in the installment novel *Der Fetzer*
3.2 Outdoor *Schinderhannes* performance in Vockenhausen
3.3 Illustration of a popular highwayman in an installment novel
3.4 Cover of installment novel *Der Hiesel*

4.1 SPD advertisement for a "trashy literature" bonfire
4.2 Film still covers for the detective series *Harald Harst*
4.3 Film still cover for the detective series *Harald Harst*

5.1 Cover of the nudist journal *Die Schönheit*
5.2 Cover of the nudist novel *Ist Nacktheit Sünde?*
5.3 Cover of the nudist novel *Die Insel der Nackten*
5.4 Cover of the nudist book *Das Nacktkultur-Paradies von Berlin*

Epilogue 1.1. Elsbeth Günther-Geffers in the film *Somnambul*

Abbreviations

BArch	Bundesarchiv Berlin
HStA	Hauptstaatsarchiv Stuttgart
PS Berlin	Prüfstelle Berlin
PS Munich	Prüfstelle München
OPS Leipzig	Oberprüfstelle Leipzig
RSR	Reichstag Stenographic Reports

Introduction

Siegfried Kracauer lauded film director Fritz Lang for the masterful build-up of suspense in the opening scene of his crime thriller M (1931).[1] A mother, busy with household chores, shows increasing concern as she notices that her daughter Elsi has not returned from school at the regular time. A door-to-door salesman slowly climbs up the staircase and distracts Elsi's mother from her worries. He is a colporteur delivering the next installment of a subscription novel. For many lower class housewives, the colporteur was a welcome visitor who interrupted the monotonous routine of cooking, cleaning, and mending. The ten-penny subscription stories that he sold transported the reader into a world of innocent Cinderellas, dashing Prince Charmings, and evil villains with enough energy to pursue and terrify heroines over the course of one hundred installments or more than two thousand pages. Colportage's cheap thrills served to break momentarily the pattern of daily *tristesse*. So, too, did crime films like Lang's drama. Was the appearance of the colporteur in M merely a device to heighten suspense, or did his presence pay homage to the penny dreadfuls that were the forerunners of moving picture thrillers?

Kracauer did not mention the brief appearance of the colporteur in M. He often, however, liked to focus exactly on these minor, overlooked figures. He was attracted to them and they became an important part of his analysis of Weimar culture. One such figure was the Nummernmädchen or "number girl" at a Berlin variety theater: "In the Scala, a girl appears every evening who, as far as I know, has never been the subject of an article."[2] Kracauer described the job of the "the number girl" as simply crossing the stage between acts with a large numbered card to signal the next act. Admitting that her job was minute, he, nevertheless, was enchanted by her smooth pirouette from one end of the stage to the other: "And then the smile – this beaming smile… that accompanies her numerical message. It is as if she is fulfilling a delicate mission that ought not to be trumpeted out loud. This smile is so flirtatious and personal. In a word, I mean that this triviality deserves mention merely on account of her evocative presence."[3] This apparently insignificant girl captured Kracauer's fancy and led him to philosophize: "A number girl, why the big deal? Yet, some so-called historical events have only left behind the numerals of a date, and the marginal not rarely turns out to be the main thing."⁴ Kracauer's interest in the marginal was not simply an idiosyncrasy: it was the core of his method of social analysis. A seemingly insignificant figure, an obscure, anonymous place, or a popular fad might be the means for discovering something important about a social process that normally was difficult to detect. Taking a cue from Kracauer, I will explore what seemed at the time to be three marginal phenomena of Weimar culture.⁵ The subjects broadly described are occultism, nudism, and colportage. Each of these three components of Weimar's popular culture were subjects of controversy and heated debate. Here and there, in his Frankfurter Zeitung articles of the 1920s and early 1930s, he would discuss them.

Weimar occultism, nudism, and colportage had their roots in the Wilhelmine period and were tied in one way or another to Weimar's most dynamic form of popular culture: the movies. It was no accident that Kracauer, as a film reviewer, was exposed to and interested in these facets of Weimar culture. Nudism he first discussed in a film review of the propagandistic Wege zu Kraft und Schönheit (Paths to Strength and Beauty, 1925).⁶ 1920s society, he observed, wanted a healthy body through physical education, dance, and sport. He wrote about occultism in a review of Somnambul (1929), a film that featured the famous medium and psychic detective Elsbeth Günther-Geffers.⁷ The film tried to illustrate telepathy's usefulness in fighting crime. Kracauer expressed his opinions about colportage and detective thrillers in various reviews of action films, like those of Harry Piel (whose screen popularity led to the publication of a pulp adventure series). As a sociologist Kracauer focused on the formation of a rapidly growing white-collar class and explored its habits and proclivities, including its reading tastes. The myriad subjects covered in his articles and reviews shed light on many aspects of Weimar culture, not only on the behavior of the new white-collar class. Kracauer's writing explored a dynamic society that he himself found more intriguing than the distant, exotic worlds which, he complained, received far too much coverage in Weimar's flashy magazines and illustrated journals.

Kracauer's generally liberal and open-minded analysis of Weimar culture contrasted sharply with that of a host of conservative cultural critics who derided the Republic and expressed contempt for Germany's dizzying postwar culture of diversion and pleasure. They detested Weimar's pluralism and tolerance and regretted the passing of the patriarchal Wilhelmine order. Wherever possible, they called for state controls and sanctions against what they considered the egregious manifestations of popular culture. They wanted to forge a conservative, nationalist hegemony to restore a moral order that would oversee the country's cultural activities and decide what was and was not suitable for public consumption. The conservative critics saw themselves as defenders of a civic code that had been severely shaken and needed to be restored. Their efforts were flanked and supported by the Catholic and Protestant Churches which felt threatened by such popular phenomena as occultism, nudism, and the reading of colportage. Colportage was often called "trashy and filthy literature" [Schund und Schmutzschriften]. The word Schund originally referred to the wood pealings left from a craftsman's carvings. During the Industrial Age it began to mean any mass-produced article of poor quality intended to reap profits at the customer's expense. Church organizations in the 1920s were among the most actively involved in the Schundkampf [the battle against trashy literature], which reached a climax in 1926 as parliament debated and finally passed a law restricting the proliferation of this literature.[8]

The Catholic Church took a consistent position in opposing all three forms of popular culture discussed in this study. Weimar's political parties had more varied, ambiguous positions and sometimes even suffered internal splits over questions regarding popular culture. Calls for control by conservative cultural critics showed an intolerance and a deep suspicion of popular culture, accompanied by a willingness to sacrifice individual freedom for an enforced system of national ethics. Conservative and church demands clashed with the liberal spirit of Weimar democracy. Generally, Social Democrats and liberals opposed censorship and restrictive legislation.

Concerns about suitable degrees of governmental control and curtailment of individual freedom sparked lively debates in parliament and the press. When exactly did governmental control impinge on vital individual freedoms? When was it needed to protect citizens? To what extent should official authorities act to prevent the public's exposure to the supposed dangers emanating from occultism, nudism, or the distribution of "trashy or filthy literature?" Differences of opinion on how to deal with these issues revealed deep rifts within German society and helped widen them. Kracauer did not completely oppose state intervention, but generally he felt that government tutelage and an unsolicited protection of the citizenry were inappropriate.

The Weimar Republic was, in this case, no different from other modern democracies that debated when and where it was appropriate for the state to intervene or to restrict cultural activities. What kind of media should be denied to youth? When did soothsayers, clairvoyants, stigmatics, or natural healers cross the border into fraudulence and possible exploitation of the public? What sorts of behavior undermined or upset the customs that a society shared and that helped glue it together? General questions of this nature played a part in the cultural conflicts that polarized Weimar society and eventually helped break it apart. In the end, the Weimar Constitution itself would become an object of political debate and cultural conflict.

This study takes into account that Weimar's cultural discourse was largely shaped by elites and often left out the people most affected by government intervention. Rarely, if ever, can one hear the voice of a youthful reader of detective pulps, or the retired couple devoted to occultism, or the proletarian family enjoying a lakeside nudist retreat on the outskirts of Berlin. Many of the people engaged in these contested activities were members of disempowered subcultures. They were either undereducated, poor, young, or female. William Christian in his study of 1920s Spanish visionaries referred to such people as cultural underdogs.[9] Antonio Gramsci would have included them in what he defined as a mute subaltern class. The views and aims of these people, largely hidden from history, must be teased out of the actions and the political and moral discourse that was often carried on over their heads and against their will.

In chapter one, I will examine how state and church authorities confronted the supporters of two types of occultism. The first type was called "criminal telepathy" [Kriminaltelepathie]. Its advocates thought crimes could be investigated and solved by supersensory methods. The second type involved the stigmata or bearing of wounds, similar to those of Christ, supernaturally imposed on certain exceptional individuals. In "criminal telepathy," people claiming special psychic abilities, gained widespread attention in the 1920s by uncovering crimes and sparked numerous controversies about truth and fraudulence, and whether or not supersensory experience was a hoax or a reality. Two trials in the provincial towns of Bernburg and Insterburg tried to determine whether psychic detectives were guilty of fraud. Should these "supernatural criminologists" be incarcerated as charlatans or were they to be applauded as auxiliary policemen? The trial verdicts left an air of unsatisfying ambiguity, while the press misinterpreted them as occultist victories.

In Weimar's main experience with stigmatic occultism, institutional religious authority was called into question by a supernatural event in rural Bavaria. In a remote village near the Czech border, a young woman relived the Passion of Christ and suffered stigmata in weekly interludes. A horde of pilgrims descended on the holy place, much to the consternation of church and state. Should they stand by and condone the fervid, gory display?

Chapter two focuses on the battle over popular "trashy literature." Self-proclaimed guardians of German culture as well as parliamentary delegates scrutinized installment novels and detective pulps in an endeavor to protect German youth from the nefarious pens of hack writers and the profits of greedy, assembly-line publishers. Supposedly, this popular literature undermined young people's morals and even threatened their sanity. Should the state intervene with censorship?

The works of one of Weimar's most prolific colportage or installment novel writers are used to illustrate the complexities of this conflict. The parliamentary debate over the Schund law, its passage, and the fight over its application are discussed in chapter three. This chapter also elaborates an interpretation of a particular subgenre of the colportage novel: the story of the highwayman and how he paradoxically restores law and order.

The controversy about new pulp detective series (viewed as particularly dangerous for youth) is discussed in chapter four. The "German detective" Harald Harst's popularity extended over the entire period of the Weimar Republic. Tolerated by the Republic, he met his demise at the hands of "trashy literature" censors in 1934. A hardening intolerance towards some types of popular culture manifested itself with the Nazis in power.

Chapter five examines the debate over nudism. If the founding coalition of Weimar democracy had great difficulty overseeing the thorny issue of popular literature, how could Social Democracy and the Catholic Center Party compromise on the divisive subject of nudism? In the Rhine Valley, weekend urban bathers enjoyed nude swimming sometimes in the immediate proximity of religious processions. The questions of Scham [shame] and Schund ["trashy literature"] vexed and plagued the embattled Republic. The book's epilogue draws the cultural conflicts together within the context of the final political attack on the Republic. Siegfried Kracauer's essays about Berlin's modern avenue of splendor, the Kurfürstendamm, emblemize the deadly finale of Weimar culture.

Endnotes

1   Siegfried Kracauer, "Neue Filme," in Kleine Schriften zum Film 1928-1931 (Frankfurt: Suhrkamp, 2004), 509.
2   Siegfried Kracauer, "Berliner Figuren," in Schriften 5.2 Aufsätze 1927-1931 (Frankfurt: Suhrkamp, 1990), 348.
3   Ibid., 349.
4   Ibid.
5   For an interesting, critical view of Kracauer's methodology during Weimar, see Michael Ermarth, "Girls Gone Wild in Weimar: Siegfried Kracauer on Girlkultur and the Un-Kultur of Amercanism," in Modernism/modernity (Vol.19, No.1, Jan.2012), pages 1-18. Ermarth relates that new phenomena like Kino, Konsum Kosmetik and Körper were viewed by Kracauer "as surface ciphers or cryptograms of an inverted, inhuman 'brave new world' of reifying rationalization." (p.7) Kracauer's goal was "to observe and correlate surface manifestations in order to attain an ulterior understanding... The ultimate aim was to move beyond them and their own blinkered viewpoint to something better, more progressive, more wholesome, more humane: their ultimate redemption would follow upon their ulterior understanding..." (p.14).
6   Kracauer, "Wege zu Kraft und Schönheit," in Kleine Schriften zum Film 1921-1927 (Frankfurt: Suhrkamp, 2004), 143-147.
7   Kracauer, "Ein Hellseher-Film," in Kleine Schriften zum Film 1928-1931 (Frankfurt: Suhrkamp, 2004), 231-232.
8   For the history of the Schundkampf see Kara L. Ritzheimer, "Trash," Censorship, and National Identity in Early Twentieth-Century Germany (New York: Cambridge Univeristy Press, 2016).
9   William A. Christian Jr., Visionaries: The Spanish Republic and the Reign of Christ (Berkeley: University of California Press, 1996), 162 , 252.

Chapter One. Occultism: Empowerment or Menace?

On a cold, overcast November afternoon, Siegfried Kracauer left his apartment in the Sternstrasse, just a couple blocks north of Frankfurt's downtown and made his way to the edge of the city, where the Sarrasani Circus had set up its beckoning, illuminated tent. An expectant crowd waited for admission. Kracauer observed: "Rows of light bulbs trickle down the façades and shine like stars on the massive canvas dome."[1] What brought an intellectual like Kracauer to visit the circus? In the decade prior to Hitler's takeover, Kracauer worked as editor for the Frankfurter Zeitung, first in Frankfurt and then, from 1930 to 1933, in Berlin. He wrote hundreds of articles for the paper in which he both diagnosed modern society's malaise and found signs of its possible redemption. He had a particular penchant for observing the crowd in its fleeting moments of entertainment and leisure activity. His expert eyes uncovered patterns of interaction and social or cultural trends that otherwise remained invisible.

The opening parade of performers and animals in the Sarrasani show was led by Mr. Sarrasani himself and the circus band played a military march, much to the audience's delight.[2] The ensuing acts of racing Japanese stilt men, Moroccan daredevil acrobats, and Cossack horse-back riders followed one another with such precise timing that the crowd could hardly gasp. Kracauer noted that the technical skills of the individual acts were subsumed in the circus's own organizational perfection. Rationalization permeated the circus experience from the manipulated audience to the performing animals that acted "according to the idea which they did not think."[3] Kracauer asked, "is their more rationalization in the factory or in the circus?"[4] Within seconds the bulky circus carpet was rolled up and stowed away. The changing show seemed to be timed by stopwatch. The density of exciting acts bedazzled the crowd. There was not a free moment.

So much perfection could, however, also be stifling. The critical visitor noted the absence of a genuine clown routine, "There is no time for the clowns, we must rationalize too much. Soon improvisation won't be granted any place to unfold." For Kracauer, the clown represented more than a breath of fresh air. In an article about the acclaimed clown Grock, Kracauer noted that the master clown's act was a product of improvisation, born from a creative tension between audience and performer.⁵ Clowns were not just society's escape artists, potentially they could provide a glimpse of freedom, an indication to a richer alternative life.

In a 1932 performance of the Andreu-Rivel clowns at the Scala Variety Theater in Berlin, Kracauer witnessed a clown routine that opposed and transcended the ubiquitous grid of rationalization. Remarkably, the Andreu-Rivels did not "produce individual acts [Einfälle] wedged between a wild animal number and a rodeo performance," but, instead, built a whole structure, a complete piece with a beginning, a climax , and an end.⁶ "Doesn't such a construction contradict the usually imposed need for the clown to improvise," Kracauer asked. "What distinguishes the Andreu-Rivel's composition is that it actually consists of a sequence of accidents that miraculously transform themselves into a single entity." The clowns first decide, on a lark, that they should become acrobats. Next they get caught up in the idea of building a bridge. "The trick is that the bridge will be built only by taking all sorts of detours, and these are of more importance than the end-product itself." Kracauer was awed by the clowns' scintillating, seemingly scurrilous performance, and what he detected as its underlying meaning. "The clowns could not fulfill their mission in a more conscious and dialectical manner. What is this mission? Proving that the thing we normally consider to be most important is, in reality, of minor consequence. There is no genuine clowning which does not take it upon itself to turn the world's normal relations upside down."⁷ Kracauer pointed to Grock's fooling around at the piano or Chaplin's tribulation with machines as examples. "Deepest significance of clowning: to transcend those life coordinates that we accept and take for granted, and to question the hierarchy of values which we subject ourselves to in our daily lives."⁸

The Andreu-Rivel's way to build a bridge reveals a logic that is not normal but rather pertains to the realm of fairy tales. Their clowning goes beyond breaking apart the false seriousness and individual isolation [Verschlossenheit] that typifies modern society.⁹ Kracauer viewed these clowns as metaphorically creating "a dizzying bridge bolder than the one they actually build" and across which, with "a little acrobatic practice," men could find their way to freedom. The Andreu-Rivel performance hints at the possibility of an alternative life. Kracauer claimed it evokes a reality not identical with ours, a world that stands in "the same relation to our quotidian reality as that of fairy tales or some dreams."¹⁰

This taste of utopia that Kracauer discovered in the Andreu-Rivel act contrasts with the repeated observations of the leisure crowd's attraction to militaristic music, parades, and activities offered up by an entertainment industry that was itself ever more subjected to rationalization. Kracauer's Frankfurter Zeitung articles were meant to be more than individual snapshots of Weimar society; they were an ongoing project to illuminate a modern society's oscillations between poles of emancipation and enslavement, between self-discovery and regimented, external control. In the snapshots one senses that either development was possible: this was a society in flux and it was Kracauer's achievement to pick out neglected moments and to analyze experiences that cast a light on problems and qualities that shaped the Weimar period.

Kracauer preferred to view his essays as mosaic pieces that, if fitted together, revealed a larger composition of society's potentials and predicaments. We can use single stones and motifs in this mosaic to investigate particularly revealing features of Weimar society. Thus we can follow a path that might have tempted Kracauer himself if he had had time to leave his newspaper office and daily duties to indulge in a more sustained form of "rag picking," as his friend Walter Benjamin endearingly called his ventures into the realm of cultural detritus.

In one such area of popular culture, Weimar crowds were magnetically drawn to performances by psychics claiming powers of clairvoyance and telepathy. The clairvoyant Kara-Iki boasted many years of occult studies in India and other Asian countries. In a Berlin appearance witnessed by Kracauer, Kara-Iki collected scraps of paper upon which members of the audience jotted down the time and place of some significant event in their lives.[11] After focusing on a pendulum to reach a heightened level of consciousness, Kara-Iki took each scrap and correctly related what the given person experienced on that date. To this he added some vague, consolatory comment about the person's future. "More interesting than the prophesying is the audience which eagerly absorbs each proclamation. It consists largely of members of those strata that today passionately hope for a miracle."[12] Kracauer described the audience as men and women of the middle class: with a bit of irony, he called them people of independent means. "They flee from a state of desperation to one of delirium, pushing reason aside because it only pains them. They would rather place their trust in a clairvoyant so that they themselves do not need to see clearly."[13]

At the Scala, Kracauer observed a 1932 performance by Hanussen, Weimar's most celebrated clairvoyant. Skillfully building suspense, Hanussen won the crowd's confidence with some lesser tricks before he blindfolded himself and demonstrated his seeing abilities. "I have rarely seen such an expectant audience... one can practically hear it listening while Hanussen silently concentrates and it begins to rumble with delight as Hanussen delivers his answers. A sultry excitement that indicates how the waiting for a miracle has been amplified by the crisis. As if the crisis could be overcome by a miracle! But holding out in the shadows seems, for many, more comfortable than the planned improvement of conditions which would be the only legitimate miracle."[14]

Kracauer's varieté reports of Kara-Iki and Hanussen performances showed a society crumbling away toward dictatorship. The articles appeared as the lights went out for the Republic. The fascination with the occult had gripped German society even before the turn of the century, but had garnered ever more interest and support after the war and defeat. The occult arts included astrology, graphology, telepathy, clairvoyance, spirit encounters, hypnosis, magnetic healings (to name only a few popular subtypes) and offered a seemingly endless array of new experiences, insights, and seductive possibilities to a population hungry for amusement, but also for escape, hope, and a new sense of empowerment. Occultists claimed remedies for all sorts of private and public ills. While such popular stars, as Kara-Iki and Hanussen were known chiefly as multitalented occultist entertainers, others offered more specific, practical services.

1.1 Psychic detective August Drost and medium Marie Neumann

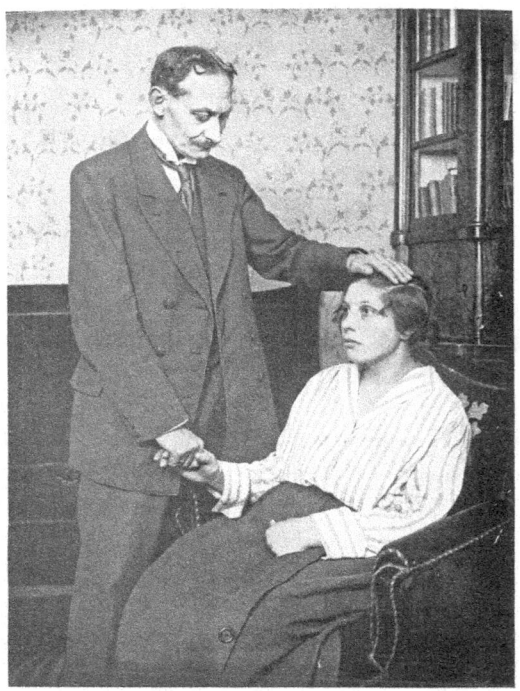

Abbildung 8 (zu S. 209 ff.). Lehrer Drost mit seinem berühmtesten Medium, Fräulein Marie Neumann. Er ist im Begriff, das Medium einzuschläfern, um es zur Verbrechensaufklärung zu befähigen.

Hellwig, Okkultismus, Bg. 16, S. 240/241.

1.1 Psychic detective August Drost working with his favorite medium Marie Neumann. Prosecuted in Bernburg for fraud and for falsely accusing innocent people of crimes, Drost was found "not guilty." Occultists used the trial to vindicate their movement. Albert Hellwig, *Okkultismus und Verbrechen* (Berlin: Hanseatischer Rechts und Wirtschaftsverlag, 1929), illus.8.

The new field of criminal telepathy [Kriminaltelepathie] promised to harness occult forces in the battle against crime. The years after the war had seen an explosive growth in both petty and serious forms of crime. Clairvoyant mediums and psychic detectives were the occult's answer to this social malaise that the state seemed incapable of addressing adequately. Erosion of the public's confidence in the police was part of a larger disillusionment in a state whose once rock-solid authority during the Kaiserreich had been severely tested by war, defeat, and Weimar's unstable political and economic aftermath.

From 1919 to 1924, the Bernburg schoolteacher and occultist August Drost had hypnotized a number of mediums. While in a trance state, they provided clues and information about various crimes ranging from theft to homicide. Drost acquired notoriety after ostensibly solving a local case of homicide in 1921. From then on, victims of crime in the Bernburg area sought his assistance. Marie Neumann, a young woman in her twenties, eventually became his favorite medium. Together they helped retrieve not only pilfered money, but stolen keys, watches, clocks, silverware, clothing, furs, sausages, a stamp collection, missing animals, and bags of grain.[15]

Through her clairvoyant powers, Neumann described suspects who had been involved in serious crimes, such as firing a gun at a police officer, murdering a Magdeburg railway man, or setting fire to a castle in the town of Biendorf.[16] In the last case, Drost had been contacted by the police commissioner of Dessau for assistance. This increased his reputation as a serious crime fighter.

For their services, Drost and Neumann were paid either in currency or in kind. Remuneration for hunting criminals got them in trouble with the law. They were charged with fraud and creating a public nuisance (grober Unfug.) State prosecutors argued that fraud applied because the para-police's clients expected and paid for a service which in all likelihood could not be delivered. The legal challenge to the state authorities lay in proving that the psychic detectives either did not themselves believe in their supernatural abilities or used trickery to mislead clients into believing that they possessed extrasensory capacities applicable to the field of crime.[17] The second charge could be initiated whenever the psychic detectives mistakenly identified "perpetrators" with alibis that proved their innocence. These could in turn hire lawyers to initiate charges of libel. An earlier conviction of two other Bernburg psychic detectives established a precedent that would lead to the widely followed Drost and Neumann trial.

On December 18, 1924, the two former variety artists Paul Hildebrecht and Erich Möckel, who had briefly worked as psychic detectives, were found guilty of fraud in the Bernburg court. Möckel had confessed to the police that Hildebrecht pretended to hypnotise him and then, in a simulated state of hypnosis, preferred all kinds of information pertinent to the examined cases. Möckel admitted that he either simply invented names and activities or if Hildebrecht had garnered and conveyed some actual information about the crime, Möckel would use it to confabulate a plausible unrolling of events.[18] Unusual about the Hildebrecht-Möckel trial was that both men admitted to having deceived their clients and were thus easily convicted for fraud. The Drost case proved more complicated because he and his mediums confidently insisted that they were capable of harnessing extrasensory powers to help solve cases of burglary, arson, and homicide. In contrast to Hildebrecht and Möckel, whose shady social background as variety artists, cast them in an unfavorable light, Drost was a school teacher with an impeccable reputation vouchsafed by the local superintendent. Although Drost lacked academic credentials, he had read a considerable amount of occultist literature and showed a genuine interest in parapsychology. In addition, the court could not ignore a large number of Drost followers and victims of crime who were convinced that he had helped them retrieve stolen goods or provided the police with essential clues.

The trial took place from October 12 to October 17, 1925, in the provincial town of Bernburg (Saxony-Anhalt). Prominent legal reporter Paul Schlesinger, who signed off as "Sling" in the Vossische Zeitung, arrived from Berlin and entitled his first article "the Clairvoyant of Bernburg: Hypnotiser or Swindler?" He noted great popular interest and every seat in the visitor's gallery was occupied when the trial began. Sling explained that the prosecution's goal was to prove Drost guilty of profiting from his medium's clairvoyant utterances, even though he did not believe in her extrasensory powers. But Sling quickly added, "There are people in Bernburg who think the trial is not so much about Drost, but rather about whether or not there really are clairvoyant phenomena. It is – so they say – occultism itself that wants to fight this battle...."[19] What Sling did not realize as the trial opened was that he himself would become enmeshed in the wider cultural conflict that framed the Bernburg trial.

Each day, witnesses paraded in, giving testimony as to how the psychic detective and his medium had offered their unusual services. Sausages, geese, goats, pigs, bicycles, clocks, jewelry, clothes, blankets, shoes were among the many stolen items that the hypnotist and his clairvoyant partner attempted to retrieve. In many instances, neither stolen goods, nor culprits were found. Yet, there were also successes that, Sling felt, showed the uncanny perceptions of the medium. In November, 1922, a Dr. Danziger had asked Drost and Neumann to shed light on a burglary in his Ballenstedt home. Neumann, in trance, described the break-in and mentioned that a checkbook had been taken from Danziger's desk. Until that point, Danziger had not even been aware that his checkbook was gone. To Sling, who noted that two policemen corroborated the story, this seemed pretty solid proof of clairvoyance. Two of the three experts hired by the court as consultants, agreed that in this instance there was a high probability of clairvoyance.[20] The third expert, however, disagreed.[21] Albert Hellwig skeptically maintained that the medium had probably seen a list of stolen items which included a missing checkbook.[22]

In Dingelstedt, in the summer of 1922, jewelry had been pilfered from a closet of the Kunkel family's apartment. The medium first named a maid of the Kunkel household and then a local gold merchant as the robbers. Sling reported that Neumann, in trance, had envisioned a sick boy and that, strikingly, the jewels were recovered four months later in a drawer under the child's clothing. Mrs. Kunkel declared she had opened the drawer daily without noticing anything but clothes until she unexpectedly found the jewelry. This case further convinced Sling of Neumann's special parapsychological gift.[23] Another corroborating case concerned laundry stolen from the Rockmann family in Kalbe an der Saale. Drost's medium offered a detailed account of the burglary and listed the missing goods, including a red-striped tablecloth that the Rockmanns had not yet noticed as lost. In her vision, Neumann also located where the laundry was hidden and identified "Edde" and "Äfer" as the thieves.[24] Although the laundry was later found in another place, two men named Ende and Schäfer were eventually accused and convicted of the crime. Sling was impressed by the fact that farmer Rockmann explicitly said the tablecloth had not been taken, yet it was among the recovered laundry. By the third day of the trial, Sling was convinced that Marie Neumann possessed supernatural powers and Drost knew how to tap them.[25]

Sling not only felt increasing sympathy for "the little schoolmaster," as he condescendingly called Drost, but also anger at the state prosecutors. They, he pointed out, had first asked for Drost's collaboration in solving criminal cases, then, when they realized possible legal complications, had turned against him and called for prosecution. Sling was also dismayed by Albert Hellwig, the Potsdam judge and expert who, Sling insisted, simply wanted to help the prosecution frame Drost for fraud so as to score a victory in his own personal crusade against occultism.

Furthermore, was it appropriate for a Prussian judge to be serving as an expert witness at a trial? "Does Prussia's judicial administration prefer to have him occupied with occultism rather than things relevant to his position," Sling angrily asked.[26]

In his next article, published on October 16, Sling resumed the attack on Hellwig. A defense lawyer asked Hellwig how he would explain some of the curious findings presented to the court. Sling quoted the Potsdam judge as saying, "I have no explanation. But these cases all lack the required precautions of scientific experiments."[27] In fact, Hellwig repeatedly discussed how subjective and misleading witness observations could be, how long ago the events had taken place, how incomplete the written reports were, how previous knowledge might have influenced the medium, and how Drost might have willfully elicited self-serving responses. In other words, Hellwig rejected any testimony that failed a strict empirical test. Sling propounded that Hellwig applied a double standard. He credited his consultant colleagues as sincere in their beliefs in the existence of clairvoyance and supersensory phenomena. He respected them because of their academic credentials, but what he allowed them, he denied the humble Drost. "Or should one maintain that only the scientific conviction of the expert has validity, but the same conviction in the mouth of a son of the people [Volkskind] is equivalent to fraud?"²⁸

At first it may appear surprising that the prestigious Vossische Zeitung's reporter was taking the part of the accused psychic detective and attacking the skeptical Potsdam judge. But the quarrel revealed a deep fissure in Weimar culture and society. On the one side, vox populi proposed a radically altered perception and experience of reality, a discovery of new, hitherto unknown truths, and on the other side, an establishment maintained the status quo and determined to draw a clear line between fact and fiction, proven data and wild speculation. As many observers of the Bernburg trial had sensed, the agitation in the provincial courtroom had a significance that transcended the fate of the "little schoolmaster" and his medium. Who would win this battle? The occultists and their "son of the people," or the state prosecutor assisted by an anti-occultist, academic mandarin? The battle also revealed tears in Weimar's frayed social fabric: the lesser educated versus those with university diplomas; the lower middle class versus the Bildungsbürgertum; the Republic's disenchanted, anxious outsiders versus those with secure, high-paying jobs, prestige, and power.

Perhaps Sling sympathized with the outsiders because he himself was not an academic. He had somehow stumbled into his career without formal training in either journalism or law. Art interested him more than science and he liked presenting his court reports as subjective, literary dramas. He was interested in "the psychological motivation" [seelische Beweggründe] of the accused and the witnesses; he wanted, as he put it, "to peer into the hearts of the prosecutors and judges." For Sling, there was "no such thing as objectivity. Neither in science, nor in the court."²⁹ In venting his anger at Hellwig, Sling revealed a growing popular desire to embrace a supersensory realm in which the hitherto unexplainable was entwined with previously unreachable divine forms of power. Sling was elated when the Bernburg trial ended on October 17, 1925, and the court found Drost not guilty of either of the two charges of fraud or creating a condition of public nuisance. "The main thing: the would-be Grand Inquisitor has been brought down," crowed Sling.³⁰ For the Berlin reporter, when a free Drost walked out of the court to the cheers of the crowd, it was a triumph of David over Goliath.

All the Potsdam judge's efforts to steer the court's attention to fraudulent remuneration, all his doubts about the supernatural talents of the psychic detective and his mediums, all his allegations that Drost himself did not believe in what he was doing had left Sling furious. For him, Hellwig was a "humorless bureaucrat who imagined that occultism would be dead if he could get Mr. Drost of Bernburg convicted."³¹ Sling wondered why all strange phenomena required an explanation.

Why could Hellwig not allow for the existence of the supernatural? "There is nothing more beautiful on earth than a miracle," Sling remarked. But, according to the reporter, Hellwig hated miracles. "A miracle is disorderly [unordentlich].

Miracles contradict an orderly administration of justice, or should a village witch really know more about a set of circumstances than someone who has passed a whole battery of legal exams? Hellwig won't stand for it."³²

Three weeks later Hellwig struck back with a public letter and a statement signed by himself and the other two court experts hired for the Bernburg trial. The Vossische Zeitung published them on November 6, 1925, along with a rebuttal by Sling. Hellwig claimed he had been attacked in a most exaggerated, despicable manner. While the personal attacks left him cold, he was not indifferent to these attacks if they hurt the cause for which he stood. He implied that Sling's reports had been colored by a pro-occultist hysteria [Massensuggestion] that gripped the town of Bernburg during the trial. In the statement signed by the three consultants (they were, besides the Potsdam judge, the director of the Bernburg insane asylum and a local ophthalmologist), the psychiatrist and the medical specialist parted ways with Hellwig in reiterating their belief in the existence of clairvoyance. Important for Hellwig's argument, however, was their unanimous agreement that "not in a single one of the cases presented at the hearings could it be scientifically proven that Drost's mediums were capable of clairvoyance."³³ The experts underlined the damaging effects of some of the psychic detective's allegations. The statement continued, "we also agree that in many cases the mediums provided false information. Innocent people were accused of theft. On account of information given by the mediums, home searches and arrests of innocent people were made."³⁴

In his rebuttal Sling noted that he "did not arrive in Bernburg as an occultist, nor did he drive home as an occultist."³⁵ He had anticipated a trial in which the prosecution would present concrete evidence that Drost had manipulated information to make himself seem omniscient and had presented his customers with extravagant bills. Instead the trial revealed a complete lack of hard evidence against the psychic detective. If anyone was at fault, it was the police and prosecutors who helped Drost get his original clientele and perhaps contributed to making him feel unnecessarily sure of himself. Sling accused Hellwig of doing whatever he could to coach and assist the prosecution in its efforts to find Drost guilty, regardless of the evidence. The reporter for the Vossische Zeitung thought Hellwig merited the media's harsh attacks because, as he put it in a self-congratulatory manner, "the press has a sensitive feeling for what is appropriate in the courtroom."³⁶

Sling addressed Hellwig's concern that "the cause" for which he stood ought not to be damaged. "Was the cause anti-occultism?" Sling asked, "No, you fight against superstition, or as I once already expressed it, against the miraculous. But why? A lawyer, who is a friend of mine, told me that indeed 'the miracle' is not so harmless as I thought. If its existence could be proven, it would mean turning the world upside down: we would all have to change our ideas and start from scratch.

Right. Is that so bad? Have we not experienced in an extreme form the disgrace of everything that had been taught and learned? Should we not welcome a chance to start fresh again? Would it not be fitting and nice? Could there be, in a time like this, anything more exhilarating than a 'miracle?'"[37] In this passage, Sling revealed that same longing that Kracauer detected in the expectant Berlin audience of the clairvoyant entertainer Kara-Iki.[38] Was this a society prepared to throw overboard all previously acquired rational norms of knowledge and scientific laws so as to ride an irrational wave into a magically imbued future? The "disgrace" that Sling felt burdening the country was the war and its humiliating Versailles aftermath. His words and his reactions to the Bernburg trial indicate that, indeed, there was more at stake here than the fate of a wayward Catholic school teacher practicing dark sciences. The trial was a minor earthquake that momentarily revealed a crack in the crust, a potential civilizational shift that was not yet clearly discernible to contemporary eyes. At the very end of his response to Hellwig's complaints, Sling seemed to catch himself in the middle of his reverie and partly to deny it. "And if -unfortunately- I did not believe it [the miracle], should I fight it? No, Mr. Court Superintendant, we all have more important things to do. I, and you too!"[39] Hellwig disagreed. For him, the struggle against occultism, psychic detectives, or "the miracle," as Sling summed it up, deserved highest urgency. "It is a tragedy that a large part of public opinion carelessly passes over the dangerous consequences of an uncritical addiction to miracles and, itself addicted, begins to search everywhere for new miracles."[40] Hellwig called on the press to discharge its duties and to have an enlightening effect, to "exercise objective and sober criticism." The Prussian judge saw it as his duty to resist the occult storm which had engulfed Germany after the lost war.[41] He observed that one needed strong nerves to stand up to "the unscrupulous methods used by a part of the occultists against their irksome opponents." "I, luckily, have such good nerves," he declared and notified his adversaries that "nothing will stop me from...resisting this unholy, mass hysteria [Massensuggestion] that threatens our nation [Volk]."[42]

There were no shades of gray in Hellwig's position. By the late twenties, the Potsdam judge had evolved into the nemesis of Weimar's psychic detectives. His meticulously researched volume Okkultismus und Verbrechen (Occultism and Crime) was published in 1929 and became the standard reference in the field, a study that would make any police inspector or prosecutor think twice about turning to mediums or parapsychology for help in solving criminal cases. Reaffirming the position taken at the Bernburg trial, Hellwig determined to reveal all psychic detectives' claims as either outright fraud or, at least, as not worthy of scientific approval. He discussed the Drost case at length and caustically mentioned that Marie Neumann had previously served as a medium for Hildebrecht and Möckel, the psychic detectives who admitted they had rigged their investigations.

In his book, Hellwig repeated his claim that Drost originally believed in his ability to "lead" and channel the clairvoyant powers of his mediums, but, over time, recognized the absence of such forces in the light of repeated failures.[43] Instead of giving up his enterprise, he had decided to take advantage of a vulnerable, easily exploited population and proceeded to fill his pockets. For Hellwig, Drost was a con artist not lacking "a certain natural slyness. Even newspapers that passionately supported him in the trial spoke of a 'fox face' and one reporter at the trial, a good judge of character, told me already on the first day that Drost was the 'slyest' one in the whole court room."[44] Although the court agreed with Hellwig that Drost was a skilled businessman (especially during the Inflation when he requested payments in kind rather than devalued money), they did not think he unduly profited from his customers. Like Sling, the court placed blame on public authorities who either requested Drost's investigative help or recommended him to the victims of crime.[45]

1.2 Lachen Links lampoons August Drost

1.2 August Drost was lampooned on the cover of SPD satire journal Lachen Links (January 1, 1926). For Weimar's left, occultism was a dangerous form of brainwashing.

The tribunal further reasoned that, when in doubt, it should favor the innocence of the accused, especially in light of the praise he received from the local school superintendent.[46] The court also believed that the trial would have a salubrious effect in discouraging people from seeking further assistance from psychic detectives.

Hellwig considered the court's views naïve. He knew Drost's acquittal would be trumpeted in the press as a great victory for occultism and that a large part of the public would misinterpret the trial's outcome as giving an official stamp of approval on the veracity of parapsychological phenomena. Hellwig heard reports after the trial that Drost received so many requests from Germany and abroad that he could not answer them all.[47] Police offices informed Hellwig that when they failed to solve a burglary case, the victims would often request Drost's address. When serious crimes were not resolved in a short time, people and press suggested that the famed psychic detective from Bernburg should be summoned. A major publishing house purchased the rights to Drost's future publications and a film company planned to make a documentary of the psychic detective at work.[48]

The world of politics could also not fail to show interest. A cover of a Social Democratic publication showed a goggle-eyed Drost hypnotizing a comic figure symbolizing the socialist humor magazine Lachen Links.[49] Cartoons inside illustrated questions posed to "the medium" and the answers. In one, the question "where is Germany's savior?" showed a table of beer-drinking patriots seated below a portrait of Hindenburg. The accompanying answer showed an idealized worker in a heroic pose clenching a hammer, implying that only the sober proletariat, not inebriated nationalists, could save Germany.[50] Right-wing newspapers launched a false story telling that Drost had been introduced to Berlin high society after giving a parapsychological performance in the home of Gustav Stresemann, Germany's Foreign Minister. Hellwig received a letter from Stresemann explaining that the story was a fabrication and part of a smear campaign meant to undermine his foreign policy.[51]

Hellwig's hunch that the outcome of the Bernburg trial would be grossly distorted by the press proved accurate. Two months after the court experts had denied any evidence of verified clairvoyance on the part of Drost's mediums in the Vossische Zeitung, the popular magazine Uhu introduced an article by Drost stating that "the legal proceedings revealed that, in fact, Drost managed to unmask numerous criminals and, through his mediums, described events that lay far back in the past, unknown to anyone."[52] While the introduction admitted that the question of clairvoyance was not "fully scientifically resolved," it erroneously informed the reader that two of the three court experts agreed that Drost delivered enough evidence to prove his mediums were clairvoyant.

What infuriated Hellwig about the article was that Drost distortedly quoted him at length, and did so in a manner that completely cancelled his demolition of Drost's claims to having solved a murder case in 1921.[53] Hellwig made an analogy to World War I propaganda in which the enemy used snippets of carefully edited texts to turn events and observations upside down. Indeed, it is unlikely that many readers referred to Hellwig's meticulous research and point-by-point refutation of each criminal case involving Drost and his mediums. The public, more likely accepted Sling's views and Uhu's appealingly simple endorsement of the psychic detective.

In the Uhu article, Drost told of his family's sufferings and his personal martyrdom. The police had arrested him in his classroom in April, 1924. He had spent months in jail and lost his job. Once the trial began, Drost recounted, he had the feeling that "I and my personal destiny were only side issues in what was a larger event – a battle between world views [Weltanschauungen]."[54] Interestingly, he framed this battle as one between idealism and realism. The restoration of his honor, Drost argued, would also mean the rehabilitation of a new branch of science whose value had been underestimated. This linkage of personal honor with the procurement of a heightened status for occultism revealed how a social stake was being claimed, in proxy, for the hard-pressed lower middle class. This new field was to a considerable degree their knowledge, their experience, their new means of empowerment; they were not going to let the university-educated Bürgertum deny them what they had explored and deservedly acquired. Whenever the academic community stubbornly rejected occultism as a science, its defenders would claim a higher, divine status for it.

At the end of the Uhu article, Drost suggested that the other-worldliness of occultism made it impervious to scientific investigation, leaving him in a paradoxical and contradictory position that characterized other occultists too: science should verify parapsychic phenomena whenever possible; when not, science ought to recognize its limitations and agree that these phenomena lay in a region beyond its reach. "I have no explanation for what powers bring about the clairvoyance of my mediums," Drost ventured. "I also can't say if this mysterious power slumbers in me or if it is only through my gift that it is triggered in my mediums. Still less will I venture a judgment whether this power can ever be explained or measured by the rational means and formulas of science."[55]

These heady gyrations typified another aspect of Weimar culture: the trope of the common man picked by destiny unexpectedly and miraculously to deliver the German people from its Fall. Drost tied the knot between humble stature and the quest for something exceptional at the beginning of the Uhu article: "I am merely a simple teacher in a little provincial town – but maybe it was meant to be me who would contribute to the progress of human knowledge and make it possible for the so-called occult sciences to be viewed with less mistrust and more objectivity."[56]

Drost's self-aggrandizement continued in his reflections on how he had been chosen for a divine mission. Each one of his criminal inquiries, he humbly maintained, had been preceded with a quiet prayer and handled with great seriousness.

"That's why I don't feel guilty of transgressing into God's omniscience. After all, I'm a victim of destiny and my innate powers I steadfastly sought to apply only for pure purposes."[57]

Another "victim of destiny," psychic detective Elsbeth Günther-Geffers, faced similar charges of fraud in the town of Insterburg (East Prussia). While Drost needed a medium to penetrate the supersensory world, Günther-Geffers was both medium and psychic detective. In her defense plea Günther-Geffers told the court about her life. She recounted that already in childhood her clairvoyant abilities had been recognized by family and friends, who nicknamed her "strange Else." A Gypsy fortune teller told her, "You are a white Gypsy. You see the same things I can see."[58]

Günther-Geffers claimed to have accurately predicted that Germany would lose the war once America intervened. She had prophesied that crowned heads would fall, and she had even foreseen the fate of individual soldiers, naming those who would survive the carnage and return from the front.

1.3 Psychic detective Elsbeth Günther-Geffers at work

1.3 Psychic detective Elsbeth Günther-Geffers in a trance picks up the crime trail. Like Drost, she ended up in court, was also judged "not guilty," and became more popular than ever. Albert Hellwig, *Okkultismus und Verbrechen* (Berlin: Hanseatischer Rechts und Wirtschaftsverlag, 1929), illus. 5.

It was at the beginning of the Great Inflation that she first used her supernatural abilities to earn an income to support her unemployed husband and their three children. At first, she read palms, then she began answering customer questions about their future while she was in a self-induced state of trance. She earned between 200 and 400 marks a month.[59] In 1922 she expanded her activities into the field of criminal investigations.[60] Similar to Drost's story, sometimes it was the authorities themselves who had requested Günther-Geffers' help and who designated her a "detective with special aptitude."[61] Whoever called her to the scene of a crime, was picked to act as a "guide" and asked questions while she was in a self-induced trance state. After she awoke from the trance, she said she had no consciousness of what had just transpired. In her estimation, success depended heavily on the skills of the "guide" and on the quality of the questions directed at her.

When asked to describe the trance state, she said, "I feel as if clairvoyance is an inner spiritual process. You are a completely different person then, you seem to lose your earthliness."[62] She blamed failures in her investigations on the lack of a good "guide" or on the disturbing presence of skeptics. A gentle calling of her name or simply having cigarette smoke blown in her face would end the trance state.[63]

The East Prussian judge confronted Günther-Geffers by noting that several witnesses declared she left a trance state whenever things "got too hot." He elaborated how people accused her of intentionally giving vague information so she could not be pinned down and that they felt it was all a charade. But, as in the Drost case, the psychic detective could rely on numerous witnesses who testified that she had helped them identify culprits and resolved crimes. As in Bernburg, the psychic detective had usually been summoned to help regain all kinds of stolen property: sheep, cows, horses, eels, laundry, shoes, beets, straw, lard, wine, watches, jewelry, and a photo camera were among the long list of belongings missing in largely rural East Prussia.

She was also asked to resolve cases of arson and murder. Like Drost's medium, Günther-Geffers astonished victims of crime by identifying lost items that they had not yet noticed as missing. Thus she explained to a teacher in Pissanitzen that the burglar had taken a desk clock in addition to his missing briefcase.[64] The jeweler and clockmaker Wilhelm Preugschat of Königsberg related how Günther-Geffers went directly from the scene of the crime to the home of the thief who had stolen laundry and shoes from him. At first the accused woman denied that she was guilty but later confessed to the police. In return for Günther-Geffers' help, Preugschat repaired several broken clocks in her home.[65]

The case of a missing farmhand generated a lot of positive publicity for the psychic detective. Farmer Migge of Woymans reported that one of his laborers, a team driver named Kaschnitzki, had disappeared one evening after attending a local veterans' celebration. The police assumed that the inebriated man had fallen into a nearby lake and drowned. Migge wanted to know more and asked the psychic detective for help. She came and quickly made her way to the lake. She conjectured that Kaschnitzki had been fatally injured by a passing automobile and that the driver had thrown his body into the lake. Migge said she described the position of the corpse, adding that a hat still covered the victim's head, and she declared that the body would soon be found. According to the farmer, a few months later, as reeds were being cut along the lake's shore, the corpse was recovered in exactly the position described by Günther-Geffers, and most remarkably, the skull was crowned with the remains of a hat.[66]

In 1928 East Prussian police detective Carl Pelz published a booklet in which he reviewed the case of the missing farmhand and other supposedly successful interventions of the acclaimed psychic detective. Pelz took apart her theory of the car accident and speculated that when the corpse was discovered, someone had probably remarked that it lay just like Günther-Geffers had foreseen, but he noted there was no written record of her original hypothesis. Instead, Pelz argued, the idea that she had correctly identified the body's posture and referred to the hat simply galvanized the popular imagination and confirmed her prophetic acumen. Pelz felt that his rebuttal was particularly pertinent because he had once acted as "guide" for the psychic detective.

Rudolf Lambert, a high school teacher and author of numerous scholarly articles on the occult, agreed with the policeman that practically nothing of Günther-Geffers' version of the story remained intact once one carefully reviewed the facts. The corpse revealed no injuries and the stiffened hands still grasped clumps of grass, making Günther-Geffers' theory of an automotive accident untenable.[67] Also, one local inhabitant said he thought he had heard cries for help coming from the lake on the night of Kaschnitzki's disappearance. "Yet the Migge family immediately believed Günther-Geffers' explanation of his fate. When the body was found still wearing the hat, it was nothing but a miracle," Lambert reported. For him it was clear that Günther-Geffers had concocted her story from whatever she had read in the newspapers and embellished it with a few details from her own imagination.[68] He found it hard to believe that court consultant Dr. Walter Kröner could credit this case for the psychic detective.[69]

In May 1922, Günther-Geffers was invited to investigate the murder of a retired man in Schmalleningken. When asked to help identify a killer, she gave all sorts of information, but first tried to evade a specific answer and finally named a man who was suspected in another homicide.[70] According to Pelz, the information she provided was useless. He mentioned that he had peered through the keyhole of Günther-Geffers' hotel room and had seen her leafing through a notebook which, he believed, contained her notes on the case.[71] Pelz implied that, in contrast to her requests not to be given any information beforehand, she actually studied each case thoroughly before visiting the scene of a crime. Like a professional detective, she had developed a trained eye for significant clues and small, incriminating details.

After the case of the retired man, she was asked to help resolve a burglary in which a valuable fur had been stolen among other things. Moments after leaving the car at the crime scene Günther-Geffers pointed to a window explaining, "The criminal climbed through this window." The homeowner confirmed the point of break-in much to the astonishment of everyone present. Eyewitness Pelz, however, observed that if one looked carefully, one could see that only this window's glass had been resealed with new putty. The owner had immediately replaced the glass after the burglary.[72] Lambert reported another case of theft of 2,000 marks where Günther-Geffers sent her assistant Radtke to gather information prior to her arrival. On the next day she took a stroll with Radtke. To Lambert this seemed "suspicious since he probably discussed the results of his investigation and she proceeded to use these facts once in trance."[73] Lambert also noted that her Königsberg office kept her informed on current crimes and suspects. In addition to her assistant Radtke, her husband and one of her sons helped manage the office and collected information.[74] When farmer Hartmann's barn burned down in Walterkehren, suspicion was cast on Communists because Hartmann was a member of the anti-Communist Heimatwehr (Homeland Guards). The village constable called Günther-Geffers and told her whom he suspected. In trance, Günther-Geffers proclaimed "Kroll was sent by Communist headquarters in Insterburg to start the fire...he came by bicycle."[75] But Kroll, who lived in a nearby village, had a solid alibi. The other suspect proved that he was away in Königsberg. Lambert thought it was pretty obvious that Günther-Geffers simply used suggested suspicions, found out where the few local Communists resided and then used this information to elaborate her charges while in a faked trance state.[76]

Pelz admitted that he and his police colleagues in the Memel region had originally been amazed by Günther-Geffers. But their initial endorsement of her work changed to disapproval when they observed her more closely. She eventually considered Pelz to be her "greatest adversary."[77] And it was the Nemesis of occultism, Albert Hellwig (the Prussian Minister of Justice did not give him permission to attend the Insterburg trial) who recommended Pelz to the prosecution.

They chose him as their primary witness. When it was his turn to speak at the trial, a reporter for the Königsberger Allgemeine Zeitung wrote: "the accused, who until then had remained calm, became very agitated during his remarks and repeatedly sought to interrupt Pelz."[78] Pelz may not have had Hellwig's academic credentials, but as an experienced police detective who had acted as Günther-Geffers' "guide" and had seen her in action several times, he proved to be a tough witness against the defense. Like Hellwig, he sought to deflate the psychic detective's reputation by explaining how she could have deduced information that later proved to be accurate and he also cataloged her many deliveries of false information.[79] He argued that her presence at an investigation caused more confusion than clarity.

In his book <u>Die Hellseherin: Betrachtungen eines ihrer 'geistigen Führer' zum Insterburger Hellseherprozess</u> (The Clairvoyant: Observations by One of Her 'Spiritual Guides' on Occasion of the Insterburg Trial, 1928), Pelz noted how Günther-Geffers usually let several weeks pass before she appeared on the scene of a crime. He then listed ways that the psychic detective could acquire information that prepared her for an investigation. She received reports from assistants who visited the crime site. She read newspaper articles and official police bulletins. Names of possible perpetrators might be familiar to her from previous cases or might be mentioned by people around her. The skillful sounding out of clients could produce useful bits of information as could a talkative, curious crowd of onlookers who Günther-Geffers always welcomed to gather around her. Pelz noticed a key part of her trance method. If she uttered a syllable in an attempt to identify a perpetrator's name, a bystander inclined to believe in her might complete the sound of the name and thus suggest a possible suspect. "One has to have experienced and observed, as I have, the curious and expectant people (especially the unenlightened rural population) follow the seer as she wanders about in her trance state. They have never seen a clairvoyant and imagine in her a supernatural being much more readily than one would normally think possible. They stare at her as if transfixed. Through the strange sight of the medium in trance, with closed eyes, contorted face, the outstretched arms and groping hands, all these people find themselves as if under a spell in which they, largely unconsciously, take over the actual role of 'guide.' They look at or nod to each other, or they shake their heads, and so serve as a means to an end."[80]

In a March, 1923, case of stolen sugar and flour in Tilsit, Lambert described how Günther-Geffers visited a neighborhood, followed by a host of curious onlookers. The crowd named three men who, on the following day, confessed to the crime. The court felt that this case showed in exemplary fashion "the unconscious reactions of an unrestrained audience."[81] Yet such cases only magnified Günther-Geffers' reputation and made her ever more believable, especially when the newspapers focused attention on her and announced in bold print that the famed psychic detective from Königsberg had solved another crime.

While rural East Prussia was considered a particularly backward part of Germany whose inhabitants were easily inclined to believe in the supernatural, their credulity was also conditioned by the unusually hard times according to Pelz. He felt that occultists thrived in these anxious times: "Before the Great War, one actually heard little about such people. In contrast, after the war, in this age of misery and increasing nervousness, we see them on the scene. Like mushrooms they grow on the ground. They know how to gain the admiration and astonishment of society through amazing achievements of all kinds. And so they manage, to an incredible extent, to spread the ancient belief of the occult in all its variations, further and further."[82] Yet not all of Günther-Geffers' followers were uneducated, rural folk.

Physician and court consultant Walter Kröner thought that Günther-Geffers possessed the sixth sense and found it remarkable that she could speak in foreign languages when in trance. Witnesses reported that Günther-Geffers sometimes talked in Polish, Yiddish, or Lithuanian but could not speak these languages in a normal state of consciousness. Pelz pointed out that saying a few phrases in languages that were commonly spoken in Eastern Prussia was hardly sensational.[83] But Günther-Geffers' supporters insisted that her foreign utterances were a further sign of supersensory abilities and compared her to Therese Neumann, the stigmatized seer of Konnersreuth, who supposedly spoke ancient Aramaic when in trance.[84]

Kröner expounded at length on what he believed were Günther-Geffers' special gifts stemming from a transcendental, unconscious power.[85] Like all genuine mediums, he concluded, she could not be held legally responsible for what she said while in a trance. Another consultant Max Dessoir took issue with Kröner's views and, in a book published in 1931, wrote that Kröner's "arguments could only convince those who already were convinced."[86] Dessoir, who created the term "parapsychology," had been invited by the court to attend as expert, but arrived only on the ninth day of the trial because he was busy examining his philosophy students at the University of Berlin. Dessoir had been investigating parapsychology for over thirty years and kept an open mind about the subject without abandoning an empirical, scientific approach. At Insterburg, he experienced firsthand the heated atmosphere of a clairvoyant trial. As in Bernburg, agitated occultists compared the trial to a witch hunt. Dessoir, unlike Hellwig and Pelz, thought of himself as a neutral observer inclined neither to attack nor to defend Günther-Geffers. He soon learned that in this conflict there was no neutral ground.

Upon entering the court hall, he noticed that the defense made sure that everyone was given a pamphlet espousing the successful activities of Günther-Geffers. Dessoir judged these press references as highly prejudiced for Günther-Geffers; they described at length anything that seemed to favor her case while giving short notice to anything contrary.[87] When Dessoir failed to agree with a portion of chief defense lawyer Richard Winterberg's arguments, he found himself being pushed involuntarily into an adversarial position. Winterberg wanted Dessoir to agree with him on the value of certain parapsychological experiments and definitions.[88]

Refusing and replying that the supposed evidence presented by Winterberg amounted only to unconfirmed reports and not facts, the defense lashed out and paired Dessoir with the anti-occultist doyen Albert Hellwig. Contemptuously, Winterberg berated the philosopher: "Professor Dessoir has been committed to the same position for forty years, just as Dr. Moll and Dr. Hellwig have become rigidified in their views."[89] Dessoir countered, "For forty years it has been my position to test the truth."[90]

Winterberg angrily contended that Dessoir's knowledge was out of date and his position not objective. When Winterberg's attack became more personal and acrimonious, the judge issued a reprimand and silenced him. In the meantime, the accused Königsberg psychic detective became agitated and hardly able to contain herself. When Dessoir contradicted a statement she made, she broke out in sobs, "All you want is to take from me the way I earn my daily bread!"[91] The astonished Berlin professor sought to mollify the crying suspect. The judge closed the day's proceedings, but the outraged audience lingered and refused to leave the courtroom. The writer for the Königsberger Allgemeine Zeitung reported: "Many of the ladies have tears in their eyes. After several minutes, in which the excited audience releases angry outbursts, the judge has the court cleared."[92] In traveling from Berlin to Insterburg, the professor had exchanged his ivory tower for the lion's den.[93]

Outside the court, the bristling crowd discussed the day's proceedings. With their heroine in tears and her defense attorney receiving a reprimand from the judge, occultist outrage was reaching a boiling point. The trial in this remote town in the provincial backwater of East Prussia evolved into a challenge for the Republic and its values. An usually invisible part of Weimar society was crystallizing around a clairvoyant martyr and her cause for occultism. They were what Antonio Gramsci would have termed a subaltern group. These assembled, angry people wanted to contest and challenge the hegemonic culture represented in the trial by a university professor, a retired police detective, and a state prosecutor.[94] When defense attorney Winterberg attacked Dessoir for clinging to antiquated views, he was articulating the occultist belief that they had overcome the tightly defined, scientific world practiced by a stultified academia and an old, brittle establishment. In Insterburg, the occultists challenged the guardians of reason, science, and Western civilization. The Republic was very much a part of this Western heritage. In the time after the Treaty of Versailles, when many Germans felt mistreated and victimized by the Allies, this tie to Western democracy would be one of the Republic's predicaments and a source of ongoing hostility for those subaltern groups that espoused anti-establishment, anti-republican views.

The Insterburg court found plenty of evidence that Günther-Geffers was not dealing in good faith and that her investigations were a charade. Whatever relevant information she gave, the court believed, came from prior knowledge, not extrasensory contact with a spirit world. Even the friendly occultist researcher Rudolf Lambert was only willing to classify one fifth of the cases under examination as showing proof of extrasensory ability by Günther-Geffers (he contrasted this figure with Dr. Kröner's estimate of two thirds).[95] But all this empiricism meant little to the occultists. They believed in her and nothing could rock their faith. Those rallying around Günther-Geffers wanted to be rid of the old rationalist truths embodied by professors and judges. Those truths, that view of reality, had failed them, and they wanted something radically new and different.

When Sling, in his articles on the Bernburg trial, peremptorily asked why one could not acquiesce and allow oneself to be pulled into the realm of "the miraculous," he was echoing a widely felt Weimar sentiment that anything was better than muddling along in a dreary and depressing status quo. When August Drost hypnotically glared into the eyes of his favorite medium, when Elsbeth Günther-Geffers slipped into trance and began her somnambulant peregrinations, or when, at about the same time, the young Bavarian stigmatic Therese Neumann rhapsodized about encounters with Christ in her hometown of Konnersreuth, a seemingly alternative world was opening itself for exploration – a world that canceled out the uninspiring, cold reality of the Weimar Republic.

Beyond the Bernburg and Insterburg courts' questions of whether or not Drost and Günther-Geffers were guilty of fraud, loomed the larger question of whether or not <u>Hellsehen</u> or clairvoyance was real. When both psychic detectives were found not guilty, a large part of the popular press misleadingly reported the court decisions as official verifications of the reality of clairvoyance. The occultists proclaimed victory for their cause, despite the fact that the more sober and accurate news reports showed the cases had not given ultimate proof either way concerning the reality of clairvoyance. The courts themselves declared that they were not the appropriate venues to confirm or refute the existence of parapsychological phenomena. Their job was simply to determine whether or not the psychic detectives had handled their cases in bad faith.

Academics like Hellwig and Dessoir repeatedly called on mediums and parapyschological "guides" to subject themselves to lengthy laboratory tests where usable results could be produced.[96] Rarely would they be able to find volunteers. Most occultists could not understand the need for such rigor; they felt that intuition and spiritual experience taught them what a laboratory could only confirm after a tedious battery of experiments. In <u>Vom Jenseits der Seele</u> (<u>From Beyond the Soul</u>, 1931) Dessoir explained how the occultists considered themselves less prejudiced than the "official" exponents of science: "They see us as limited. On the one hand, so they say, we have become overly refined through our studies. On the other, we are ill-disposed toward anything new because we are committed to accepted doctrine and because we belong to the academic clique. True enlightenment consists of having an open mind, and openly registering, undistracted by official opinion [<u>Schulmeinung</u>], the facts of spiritualism. I would not deny that we too, sometimes, lapse into one-sidedness. Yet, in the essence of science there lies no restriction to abide by certain facts or laws. If that were the case, then the Republic of Letters would be nothing more than a sect. In truth, science is not a sum of dogmas, but an approach and a method of analysis. If we are expected to acknowledge things that fly in the face of all human experience and all heretofore accepted scientific knowledge, all we ask for is the compelling evidence."⁹⁷

In a curious analogy, occultist teacher Otto Seeling viewed the struggle against the anti-occultists as similar to arguing with antisemites, "Just like when an anti-Semite drops one ground of his principally anti-Jewish approach and immediately has two new ones at hand, so the enemy of parapsychology, who lacks the gift of parapsychological research, will always raise new grounds for rejection. The methods of the battle have become all too familiar: disparaging the opponent, suspicions, insults..."⁹⁸ What Seeling failed to realize was that occultism, like antisemitism, turned its back on accepted scientific methods and knowledge, and took a leap of faith into a supposedly higher realm than the modern material one. The antisemites were, in fact, another subaltern group challenging the western, rationalist tradition embodied in the Weimar Republic and supporting supposedly new forms of science.

The occultists acted as an inadvertent ally in the process of breaking the Weimar state and the connected principles of reason, empiricism, and scientific proof. Beneath the battle of mentalities, one can also see, in Seeling's frustrated comments, a social component of conflict. He and other occultists felt belittled and slighted by those who had attained the diplomas and titles bequeathed by the state and its institutions. Günther-Geffers liked embellishing her name with fraudulent titles and wanted to be addressed as Frau Doktor or Frau Direktorin.⁹⁹ Drost's defenders were outraged and hurt when he was referred to as "the little schoolmaster."

The fact that Drost's supernatural detective services were paid for in kind during the Inflation caused court advisor Hellwig to raise his eyebrows. He interpreted this behavior as part of a criminal pattern of sly business acumen and fraudulent exploitation of his clients. But maybe the Potsdam judge was a little unkind and insensitive in taking this position. He failed to see how difficult it was for lower middle class families to make ends meet during the Inflation. Max Dessoir was also stunned by Günther-Geffers' tearful, melodramatic outburst in which she claimed that he was simply seeking to deny her her "daily bread." What for him was an interesting epistemological debate, for her was a battle of survival. In the Bernburg and Insterburg courts two worlds were colliding that normally had little contact with one another. The clash of mentalities, beliefs, or "world views" was also a social clash and a conflict over power.

As a common enemy of established science and religion, occultism drew these two previously contrary forces together in an alliance that sought to secure their own custody over questions concerning the material and the theological worlds. Corinna Treitel in A Science for the Soul has shown how this unanticipated constellation already developed in the period preceding the war.¹⁰⁰ Occultism questioned these boundaries and mocked both religion and science as having a limited and inadequate understanding of holistic reality. After the war, a weakening Protestant church faced an additional challenge from a host of self-styled saviors and prophets who managed to attract sizeable numbers of disgruntled, mainly Protestant adherents. Friedrich Muck-Lamberty the "messiah of Thuringia," Ludwig Christian Hauesser, "the spiritual monarch," and Joseph Weissenberg, founder of the "Evangelisch-Johannische Kirche nach der Offenbarung St. Johannes" were among a throng of religious rebels.[101] Weissenberg tapped into the spirit world during sermons by placing selected converts into a trance state and using them as mediums.[102] But it was not only the Protestant establishment that faced occultist challenges in the interwar period.

In 1926 the Catholic Church was compelled to examine the visionary claims of a young stigmatic peasant woman from the northern Bavarian hamlet of Konnersreuth. She was attracting many followers. More and more were joining the pilgrimage to her home in the hope of witnessing one of her trance state experiences of the Passion of Christ. During these visions, it was said, she shed tears of blood.

Word soon spread that sick pilgrims had returned from Konnersreuth miraculously cured of their illnesses. In addition to her healing abilities, the faithful believed that Therese Neumann had clairvoyant and prophetic powers. News reports asserted that she subsisted on one communion host per day. Michael O'Sullivan in his study of Therese Neumann notes that "in a cultural landscape that increasingly gravitated towards miraculous explanations," Neumann's prophesy "helped pilgrims process a seemingly senseless world...."[103] He also explains: "Many Germans sought non-conventional and sometimes occult avenues for comfort in frightening historic times, but Catholics felt most at home with Neumann forging a new and more personal spirituality from within the confines of their religious tradition."[104] Her physically dramatic form of unmediated popular religion would be hotly contested by Catholic institutions and medical doctors in particular.

Her fame spread beyond the borders of Germany and drew international visitors to the remote village. One of these was Paramhansa Yognanda, a Hindu founder of yoga teaching in the United States. Touring Europe in the summer of 1935 he gave high priority to a Konnersreuth visit. In his autobiography, he summarized Therese Neumann's story: "The stigmata, or sacred wounds of Christ appeared in 1926 on Therese's head, breasts, hands, and feet. On Friday of every week thereafter, she has passed through the Passion of Christ, suffering in her own body all his historic agonies."[105] Authorized by the Church to meet the stigmatic, he expressed to her his amazement that she could survive by eating only one "paper thin wafer." Therese replied, "I live by God's light." The Hindu visitor became an immediate believer, "How simple her reply, how Einsteinian!"[106] Yogananda felt honored to receive official Church permission to witness one of her Friday ordeals and recorded the shocking sight: "Blood flowed thinly and continuously in an inch-wide stream from Therese's lower eyelids...the cloth wrapped around her head was drenched in blood from the stigmata wounds of the crown of thorns... Therese's hands were extended in a gesture maternal, pleading...."[107]

1.4 *Crowds of faithful wait for admission in Konnersreuth*

1.4 Crowds assemble in the village of Konnersreuth waiting to see the stigmatic Therese Neumann. The Catholic Church skeptically observed the uncontrolled outpouring of faith in the remote Bavarian countryside. (1920s postcards)

These extraordinary happenings raised the same question that had been central to media interest in the Bernburg and Insterburg trials: was modern science being disproved by the unexplainable experiences and supersensory insights of selected extraordinary people who lived far away from German cities? Would science open itself and expand its horizons to include what the occultists and the pilgrims to Konnersreuth believed to be a new, more truly encompassing, deeper version of reality? Or would church and state act together to crush those who dared to claim access to a special knowledge that by-passed sanctioned and accepted forms of institutional approval and control? Could the courts, the universities, and the churches tolerate an alternate reality? "As a subaltern cultural force," observes O'Sullivan, "...Konnersreuth supporters understood this sacramental mission differently from their formal religious leaders, seeking public affirmation of otherworldly occurrences, God's comfort from personal hardship, and direct access to their higher power."[108]

Catholic newspapers were warned to report about Konnersreuth carefully and to avoid labeling the seer as holy or miraculous. Some papers diplomatically referred to the events as "the riddle of Konnersreuth," but others could not resist the temptation to speak of miracles. A reporter for the Düsseldorfer Tagesblatt prefaced a series of articles by reassuring his readers that he was skeptical and not predisposed towards mystical or miraculous explanations. He asked if "volatile souls" might see miracles where things did not exist or could be explained by science?[109] Like the journalist Sling at Bernburg, who also described himself as a sober, objective reporter, the anonymous reporter for the Düsseldorfer Tagesblatt quickly drifted into the orbit of the believers once he reached the scene of events. Like his colleague from the Vossische Zeitung, he found himself disagreeing with the skeptical experts who were determined to stake out the boundaries of what was real and what was not, and who wished to subject clairvoyants and mystic visionaries to controlled tests.

The respected Munich newspaper editor and historian Fritz Gerlich published Die Stigmatisierte von Konnersreuth (The Stigmatic of Konnersreuth, 1929), a two volume study professing the truth of the miracle at Konnersreuth and denying the skeptics' views, particularly those regarding Therese Neumann's astonishing medical history.[110] His work immediately aroused the ire of Catholic medical doctors and university professors who condemned it as highly flawed and misleading. Josef Deutsch, surgeon, gynecologist, and head doctor of Lippstadt's Trinity Hospital, recognized Gerlich's efforts as serious but strongly disagreed with his study and felt that it had sown much confusion among the faithful. He explained that his criticism of Gerlich was meant to protect the Church's stature from damaging external attacks as well as from internal strife. In Konnersreuth in Ärztlicher Beleuchtung (Konnersreuth Seen From the Perspective of a Medical Investigation, 1932), he took apart Gerlich's account of Neumann's illnesses arguing that the historian lacked the necessary professional knowledge to explain, in a convincing, scientific manner, the many extraordinary rebounds and medical developments that Neumann's body had undergone: these included unexplained recoveries from paralysis and blindness and a long term absence of food intake.[111] Deutsch found it strange that Gerlich gave no thought to the possibility that he lacked the medical qualifications to examine the stigmatic's complex medical history. The Catholic surgeon discounted Gerlich's claim that he had proven Therese did not suffer from hysteria. The hysteria thesis remained popular both among the stigmatic's non-Catholic detractors as well as the more scientifically inclined Catholic skeptics. They saw it as a possible way to bring her many symptoms together into one whole explanation based on natural laws.

Deutsch let it be known that doctors were made particularly suspicious when they learned that Neumann had received a disability pension for hysteria for a number of years.[112] Gerlich had slighted and reinterpreted some of Neumann's medically diagnosed hysterical attacks as mere fainting spells.[113] For Deutsch, it was highly plausible that the seer's paralysis was caused by hysteria. Gerlich's argument that all her ills were of an organic nature and not psychic in origin seemed extremely unlikely to the medical professional. For him, Gerlich was "naïve," "uncritical," and lacking the necessary "objectivity" to present an accurate picture of Neumann.[114] "He is only satisfied when he finds something that speaks on her behalf. This is not the standpoint of a doctor who with cool level-headedness must weigh the pros and cons as he judges the possible reasons for an illness. His [Gerlich's] standpoint is more that of an advocate who, help what may, is defending his charge."[115]

Deutsch asserted that Neumann's claim to have abstained completely from eating was unbelievable and impossible to explain in a natural way. He thought if this assertion could be medically proven, it would revolutionize the way people looked at the world and the beyond. "Without much effort one could break through natural law in a manner that the world has not seen before. God's omnipotence could be shown incontestably to millions of people. And why does it not happen? Because Therese Neumann and her parents don't want to and because they deem such a test as too burdensome."[116] Here Deutsch almost seemed disappointed, as if he too would have welcomed a chance to join Neumann's believers. Instead he reminded the reader that practically all Catholic medical practitioners viewed "the riddle of Konnersreuth" with grave doubt.[117] They wondered why Neumann's family and supporters blocked every effort to subject her to thorough medical tests. "Does not the Catholic have reason to push for a fitting clarification? If they refuse, well, then the Catholic Church can set this straight. At any rate, the Church can prevent the Konnersreuth apostles from trying to associate their cause with that of Catholicism."[118] By the end of his proposed invalidation of Gerlich's theses, Deutsch drew together religion and science into, what for him and the majority of his Catholic medical colleagues, was the only acceptable synthesis: "Aren't natural laws God's work? Isn't the fact that through natural laws we recognize that the world is not a confusing chaos, but a well-ordered whole, one of the strongest pillars of our belief in God?"[119] Deutsch continued that, to some extent, we could penetrate these laws but never completely comprehend them. In a concluding rejection of Konnersreuth and all it stood for, he rhetorically asked if the Almighty "would find it necessary to change his laws at every moment?"[120]

Reality would not be bent at Konnersreuth, no matter how hard Neumann and her supporters mistakenly believed in miracles.

Gerlich and his circle of supporters, who were called the Konnersreuther Kreis, responded aggressively to the attacks issuing forth from Catholic hospitals and universities. One of their targets was Georg Wunderle, Professor of Religious Psychology at the University of Würzburg and the first academic teacher to take a serious interest in Konnersreuth. He had visited Konnersreuth in July, 1926, and like most witnesses had been amazed by Neumann's blood-letting and visionary revelations. Wunderle was convinced that what he saw was neither act nor fraudulent display. But this did not mean he was immediately willing to accept the stigmatic's physical wounds and visions as a miracle. He found it peculiar that some overzealous clergymen opposed any scientific attempts at clarification, thereby prematurely taking a stand when the Church itself had not yet reached its own binding opinion on the matter.[121] Wunderle declared approvingly that the Church did not jump to conclusions but built its own case thoroughly, carefully including the essential scientific component.[122] He noted that he would neither take the position of a dogmatic materialist who denied any possibility of a miracle, nor slip into the role of a credulous, uncritical believer who rejected any need for a scientific explanation.

In Der Kampf um die Glaubwürdigkeit der Therese Neumann (The Battle for the Credibility of Konnersreuth, 1931), Gerlich contrasted the positions of the Konnersreuther Kreis with those of Wunderle and Alois Mager, a skeptical Catholic philosopher, as if the two sides had confronted each other in a trial.[123] Wunderle's and Mager's criticism implied, according to Gerlich, that the Konnersreuther Kreis was falsifying facts in order to bolster their preconceived beliefs that Therese's stigmas were God-given. The credibility and trustworthiness of the Konnersreuther Kreis was at stake. Gerlich wanted to show that his opponents' arguments were riddled with holes. Their claims that they had been denied access to Neumann were false, as were their innuendos that the Konnersreuther Kreis tried to cover up any evidence that might indicate that Therese did indeed suffer from hysteria. Marshaling together quotations from numerous letters and newspaper articles, many written by Wunderle and Mager themselves, he sought to reveal contradictions and statements that undermined their positions. But what seemed especially to exasperate Gerlich was that these two Catholic academics had at first gravitated to the position of the Konnersreuther Kreis and then drifted away toward an increasingly skeptical standpoint. Thus the proponents of the miracle theory had lost two important academic allies who could have proved essential in advancing their cause.

As with the pro- and anti-occultist polemics manifested at the Bernburg and Insterburg trials, the fight within Catholicism deteriorated to the level of personal attacks and insults. The anti-Konnersreuth investigators were portrayed as arrogant academics with very inflated views of themselves: they seemed to think everything depended on their imprimatur. Their behavior, Gerlich argued, disagreed with the humility that Neumann prized and believed Jesus himself embodied and wished his faithful to imitate.[124] Instead of approaching the seer with respect, they treated her like some sort of odd specimen requiring inspection in a laboratory setting. Neumann said she felt uncomfortable around them; she sensed they had dishonest intentions.[125]

1.5 Parish priest exploits Therese Neumann and affluent tourists

1.5 While the stigmatized Therese Neumann bleeds, affluent tourist voyeurs eagerly wait for admission. The parish priest happily looks at his collection pot. Cover of leftist <u>Freidenker</u> booklet by "AST," *Das"Wunder"von Konnersreuth* (Wien: Freidenkerbund, 1928).

She distrusted Wunderle who "looked at her in such a strange way, she did not know how."[126] Even intimate parts of her body were subject to their investigations. Was such conduct necessary or appropriate, Gerlich asked.[127] He also felt that it was understandable that Neumann and her father had become increasingly unwilling to allow intrusive examinations or clinical tests, which the skeptics insisted were essential to uphold claims of a supernatural status.[128] And so there would be no satisfactory resolution to the problems posed by the seer at Konnersreuth. The believers continued to believe, though the river of pilgrims trickled down as the church instituted controls and stymied the flow by requiring permits for visitors. The skeptics continued to advance vague, not particularly convincing theories of hysteria to explain Neumann's intriguing condition.

Weimar's leftist forces had no qualms about voicing their opinions on Konnersreuth: it was a clear case of mass brainwashing (Volksverdummung). The socialist freethinkers published a series of three pamphlets ironically titled Das "Wunder" von Konnersreuth (The "Miracle" of Konnersreuth, 1928).[129] The cover illustration showed a crowd of wealthy miracle tourists goggling a bandaged and bleeding Neumann, while a chubby priest happily walks off with a loaded pot containing the day's charitable offerings. The pseudonymous writer AST saw it all through the spectacles of class conflict: "Last summer it was considered good form in Karlsbad, Marienbad, and Franzensbad [popular thermal springs in nearby Czechoslovakia] to pass by Konnersreuth along with other places of interest. The 'stigmatic' Therese Neumann could be neatly scheduled between a five o'clock tea with a famous jazz band and a visit to a pastry shop."[130] When AST himself visited Konnersreuth and dared to suggest to the inhabitants that Neumann was victim of a serious illness, he faced angry disapproval from the villagers.[131] For them, Konnersreuth was home to a miracle, not a charade.

AST witnessed the weekly transformation from sleepy backcountry hamlet to center of excitement that took place weekly between Thursday and Friday. He counted fifty parked automobiles on Friday morning.[132] Buses and even trucks transported eager visitors to the tiny market crossroad. Approximately eight hundred people lined up to catch a brief glimpse of the seer reliving the Friday Passion. AST was convinced that behind the official pronouncements of cautious reserve, the Church was already planning to build a second Lourdes here. To bolster his thesis he explained that in similar cases, the Church proceeded step by step to embrace "the miracle" and make the most out of it for its own selfish purposes. Such chicanery is what infuriated him the most: a sick person was being exploited for a religion's sake and thousands were misled. He had sympathy for the hysteric stigmatic, but none for her Church or for the voyeurs who streamed past her, gawking at her agony. After a one and a half hour wait, each person was granted a few seconds to see the transfixed martyr until the local constable told them to move on.

Afterwards, curiosity satisfied, the visitors found themselves at the market place and discussed what they had seen.[133] Their perceptions, according to AST, were shaped by the lies spread in the books about Konnersreuth and the Catholic newspapers. Everywhere the same talk of a miracle. AST saw himself as a lone exponent of enlightenment in a backwater of darkness. He watched as the cars got cranked up and readied for departure. It reminded him of the commotion that took place after a horse race or a circus performance. Talking away and sharing their thoughts, those who came on foot slowly marched off in long lines. The freethinker AST's articles were intended to make sure that his readers would themselves not fall victims to the spell cast by the Catholic pilgrims returning home from Konnersreuth. Whether he was successful or not remained uncertain. The simple dichotomy that he proposed – here the light of marxism, there the darkness of Christianity – would hardly have helped him reach out to those whom he considered as the brainwashed crowd manipulated by a conniving Church and misled by a poor, hysterical peasant.

Lacking the ideological blinders of AST, Rudolf Olden went to Konnersreuth in 1927 on assignment for the Berliner Tageblatt. Olden's series of articles were among the best on the delicate subject because he approached the stigmatic and her flock with a questioning but open and unprejudiced mind.[134] Olden felt neither compelled to join the forces advocating a supernatural interpretation or those expounding a medical or psychiatric explanation. To him, those writers who subsumed the bleeding wounds, the trance states, and the fasting all under the sweepingly imprecise term of hysteria seemed to beg the question as much as the other side's attribution of everything to a miracle. What interested Olden more was the cultural setting, the peculiar theatrical framework in which the stigmatic's weekly drama unfolded. It all reminded him of crude scenes he had seen depicted on old devotional paintings.

Like other visitors, Olden was moved by the dramatic physical display of holy suffering. Tracks of dried, dark blood ran down from Neumann's eyes across her cheeks. She looked like "a wax figure" or seemed to have been "painted over like a wood carving."[135] Yet, Olden exclaimed, as if surprised, she was alive. Her face tightened in anguish, or relaxed, depending on what part of the Passion she experienced. He was fascinated by the brutal drama and the manner in which it was staged: "I would like to take a moment to say a word about the picture from an aesthetic viewpoint. Everyone has seen in a traditional farmhouse room or a shop filled with religious relics or keepsakes, one of those unartistic oil prints that illustrate some biblical scene in brown, white, and red, and that is intended to impress primitive eyes. This is the style of this living picture. The style... has grown out of the surroundings. It is an old-fashioned farmer's style: raw, bloody, gruesome, and horrible."[136] Olden described the sacred presentation's audience: the lower middle class predominated with women outnumbering men. This social profile resembled that of the vocal supporters of the psychic detectives at Bernburg and Insterburg. Olden patronizingly labeled the Konnersreuth pilgrims as travelers of the third class, though he, like AST, also noticed a contingent of bourgeois and upper class spa tourists from Karlsbad, Marienbad, and Franzensbad.

A sizeable number of visiting priests were present too. Olden studied the faces of these people trying to find the effects of the ghastly, other-worldly event. "There is little more to see than shock, a thirst to satisfy curiosity, even some fear. I can tell that the rapture has not been contagious; there are no signs of it among the onlookers. No one is crying or screaming, no one sinks to his or her knees on this Friday."[137] Olden was puzzled, even perturbed by the contrast between the bleeding visionary, curling in pain, supplicating the Lord, and a silent stream of seemingly detached guests: "A priest admonishes to keep going, a constable makes sure the procession moves along... The twitching, grimacing face, the twisting body of the pale, waxen, holy image – and the prosaic marching past of the colorful crowd, chatting before and after, munching pretzels, unmoved, at least outwardly."[138]

These were not the kind of emotional faithful who, roughly at the same time, were reporting multiple sightings of the Virgin Mary in northern Spain and partaking in what William Christian calls "a subculture of religious excitement."[139] But in Spain, as in Germany, society was divided about mystic phenomena and the Catholic Church too was split into skeptics and mystic enthusiasts. Konnersreuth resembled Ezquioga in that a cooperative allegiance developed between an educated few who could publicly articulate and defend the seer's insights, and the numerous underprivileged seers and their supporters, who Christian aptly describes as "cultural underdogs."[140] He notes, too, that the Spanish seers were mainly women, youths, and children – people who lacked power in a society run by adult men.[141] In transporting and publicizing their visions, these cultural underdogs seized what Christian calls "the power of divine privilege."[142]

Therese Neumann fits with the Spanish pattern even if her mass following did not demonstrate the signs of contagious excitement displayed by the pilgrims crisscrossing the visionary landscape of Spain. As one of ten surviving children of a country tailor who also did some farming, she was part of Germany's rural underclass. Yet this uneducated woman, inhabitant of a remote Fichtelgebirge village, was able to attract thousands of onlookers and pilgrims and to draw the attention of educated men as well. Some of these she was even able to convert thanks to her dual gift for delivering an authentic experience of revelation and for being able to understand intuitively the deepest needs of disenchanted people struggling to find meaning in a modern society that Siegfried Kracauer described as quintessentially "empty."

When Olden edited a collection of essays about Weimar's "prophets of the German crisis," he picked Benno Karpeles to write about Konnersreuth.[143] A Jew and disaffected Social Democrat, Karpeles was one of those visitors who instantly fell under the spell of Neumann. Chaplain Helmut Fahsel accompanied Karpeles on his visit to Konnersreuth. During a conversation with Neumann, Fahsel noticed his Jewish companion's hand trembling. She motioned toward Karpeles and announced, in Bavarian dialect, "Do you know, there stands someone who doesn't have the Savior yet. But he is good, he wants to go to the Savior. And the Savior wants him too."[144] When the two men left the room, they descended a staircase.

Karpeles, shaking, gripped the railing. They returned to see Neumann after she underwent the weekly Passion. When the Jewish guest touched her hands, she said, "You search and search and brood, but you are not satisfied. If you want the Savior, then you will find great joy. Then you have everything."[145] Karpeles, much agitated, asked her how he could find faith. She replied, "Don't worry. The Savior will take care of it. I have taken on suffering for you...." On the next day, the new convert told his chaplain friend that never in his life had he felt such certainty: "A miracle has happened."[146]

Karpeles, inspired by his wondrous conversion, would seek to find a way to reconcile Catholicism with Social Democracy. Fritz Gerlich's conversion from Protestantism to Catholicism provided a second example of how an educated man could be transformed by an encounter with the seer of Konnersreuth. Before the war, Gerlich had been a supporter of the militant right Pan-German League. After 1918, he saw Germany's greatest enemy in Communism and believed that Hitler might be Germany's anti-Bolshevik savior; but since he witnessed Hitler's politics close-up in his hometown Munich, he turned from friend to foe and became one of Hitler's most ardent and vocal opponents. Gerlich published hundreds of anti-Nazi articles in the Munich press. He founded the newspaper Der gerade Weg (1932-1933) that consisted mainly of biting articles condemning Hitler and warning Germans of what disasters lay ahead if the Nazis ever gained power.[147] Gerlich was arrested after the Reichstag fire in 1933 and murdered on Hitler's orders in a concentration camp the following year. That two highly educated men as different in political and religious backgrounds as Gerlich and Karpeles found lasting inspiration and redirected their lives after visiting Konnersreuth, bears testimony to the power of the stigmatic peasant woman.

Writing the preface to Propheten in deutscher Krise: das Wunderbare oder die Verzauberten (Prophets in the German Crisis: the Miraculous or the Enchanted, 1932), Rudolf Olden struggled to explain the irrational wave sweeping across Germany. The ascendancy of what he called das Wunderbare (the miraculous) in politics was having a dramatic impact on the country: "In the short history of the German Republic, there has been such an incredible swing from the rational to the irrational that even a blind person can see it."[148] Instead of focusing on the obvious case of Hitler and his followers, he wanted to show how the drift away from reason was also taking effect in a multitude of smaller movements. By examining them, he thought one might illuminate and help make more comprehensible the larger movement. Olden's book included chapters on the followers of occultism, anthroposophy, the spiritualist philosopher Krishnamurti, Therese of Konnersreuth, and "the godly master" Joseph Weissenberg. He also showed how charlatans like Franz Tausend, who claimed to have discovered a chemical process for making gold (whose adherents included General Erich Ludendorff), and how a quack doctor like Valentin Zeileis, who treated all illnesses with electrotherapy, gained thousands of followers. The manifold topics covered were meant to illustrate the scope of the mass attraction to the world of wonders and miracles. A distinct weakness of Olden's pioneering work was that it was heavy in description but light in explanation.

The opposite could be said of Carl Christian Bry's Verkappte Religionen (Disguised Religions, 1925). Bry also embraced a dizzying number of movements in his critical interpretation of what he loosely called "disguised religions." Everywhere he saw new ideas fermenting and attracting fanatical believers who were bent on "world conquest."[149] He examined everything from communism to antisemitism, occultism, psychoanalysis, and the temperance and youth movements. All of these espoused messianic visions of change. All claimed to have uncovered a previously hidden truth that if applied socially and politically, would transform and shape an unequivocally better world. Bry believed that true religion expanded an individual's horizons and enriched one's life. It defined the individual as an incomplete project. In contrast, the proliferating verkappte Religionen tended to blind and diminish experience. They saw everything from one angle only, and from this unique vantage point, they claimed, everything could be understood and explained. Such reductionism created compelling monomaniacal views of reality from which believers could only escape with difficulty.

Occultist practitioners of phrenology, chiromancy, and graphology claimed that they could understand an individual completely by either examining the shape of the head, interpreting lines on the palm, or studying the idiosyncrasies of writing styles.[150] Sarcastically, Bry predicted that such exaggerations would eventually lead to claims that the essential qualities of a man were revealed in the way he held his cigar.[151] Bry was willing to concede that close observation of a special characteristic might lead to an insight, but "the disguised religions" did not content themselves with modest claims. In their method of understanding, they believed they possessed a key to man's hidden mysteries. Bry wrote, "They must bring light to what he wants to hide or does not himself know. One does not just formulate impressions, like we all do every day, and just lift them into consciousness. No, here details are interpreted. The secret, the most secret quality must be revealed, man must be deciphered entirely. This is the expectation one wants to fulfill by getting into these practices: one wants to know something special, something hidden and not something normal."[152]

The monomaniacal method and its absurd outcomes characterized such diverse "disguised religions" as psychoanalysis, the youth movement, and antisemitism. By dissecting their exaggerated claims, Bry uncovered their intellectual narrowness and danger. Instead of limiting itself to those therapeutic situations where psychoanalysis appeared successful, it was proceeding to claim that it could unravel the workings of all human development, individual as well as collective. Instead of enjoying the self-evident rewards of hiking and camping in nature, the youth movement claimed that mankind's redemption depended on its success. The antisemite, Bry scoffed, could not look at a salt shaker without launching into a diatribe about how, in ancient times, Jews cheated Phoenicians in the salt trade and how far too many Jewish merchants were still involved in the salt business.[153]

Bry also pointed to glaring contradictions made in the "disguised religions." For example, the antisemite's charged that Jews tried to accommodate themselves to all different surroundings, while also objecting that Jews held on tenaciously to their traditional, separate ways.[154] Bry's main point, however, was to show that the many examined "systems of thought" were self-defeating in the end: "The method of the 'disguised religion' is more important than what it pretends to achieve. It destroys what it seeks to accomplish through the broad arbitrariness of its attempts at explanation. The para-world swallows up the world, the interpretation of dreams swallows the dream."[155] The proliferation of these "disguised religions" took place in a general climate of wild exaggeration, inflated ideas, and intellectual pretentiousness.

"Our time suffers from a sickness," Bry complained, "that even the most modest thought promptly is transformed into a world view."[156] Siegfried Kracauer similarly lamented that in Germany one could not even buy a toothbrush without receiving, as a bonus, an accompanying world view.[157] All of this bombast covered a profound insecurity, a spiritual emptiness, a desperate search for new bearings.

Bry pointed out that the followers of "disguised religions" defined themselves to a large extent by what they opposed. Animosity for an opponent helped crystallize a new identity and with it a sense of meaning. The socialist hated the bourgeois, the vegetarian hated the meat-eater, the Nazi hated the Jew, the occultist hated the proponent of empirical science, the Konnersreuth faithful despised those who denied miracles or argued that Therese Neumann suffered from hysteria. Bry felt they were all dangerous and deserved condemnation: ".....the wish to be a scientific pioneer can just as easily lead one astray as the wish to conjure spirits..."[158] The occultists, Bry declared, had "not achieved a breakthrough to a great world" but had merely opened "a rather laughable cabinet of horrors."[159] They had failed miserably in their goal to overturn natural laws.[160]

Bry maintained that neither the occultists nor the believers in other "disguised religions" could be talked out of their views through rational discourse. They would stubbornly defend a belief that gave them a feeling of superiority over others.[161] Why give up a secret knowledge with which one could decipher everything, the visible as well as the invisible? "In a thousand forms that continually change," Bry explained, "they put one idea in the middle and seek to form man from it and through it."[162] Just gaining a few adherents would not satisfy their messianic ambitions: "They do not just want their part of the world, however small it may be. They want, with all their might, to give the entire world and the universe too a new sense of meaning."[163]

Through a plethora of their own publications and much popular attention, the occultists had succeeded in spreading their ideas in the postwar years. Like a worsening fever, occultism became more and more evident as the Republic neared collapse. Popular journals and magazines high-lighted occultism as a theme worthy of special attention in the waning months of the Republic in 1932. The Süddeutsche Monatshefte, in August, 1932, printed two editions of an issue entitled Weissagungen (prophecies). The September, 1932, issue of Die Woche carried the title "Wunderglaube der Gegenwart" ("Contemporary Miracle Beliefs"). It included the report "Are There Spirits?" by Walter Kröner, who had helped defend Elsbeth Günther-Geffers at Insterburg. There were articles discussing the power of divining rods, magical stones, and heretofore unknown earth rays. The miracle healers Joseph Weissenberg and Valentin Zeileis were presented along with photographs of Weimar's leading clairvoyants: Erik Jan Hanussen, Max Moecke, Raphael Schermann, and Elsbeth Günther-Geffers. Foreign mediums such as "the Persian messiah" Shri Meher Baba and the famed Indian spiritualist Krishnamurti added exotic and international stature to the occultist cause. The December, 1932, issue of Der Querschnitt was entitled "Querschnitt durch den Okkultismus" ("Highlights of Occultism") and discussed topics like "teleplasma, a mysterious substance," "visits to the fourth dimension," and "a view into the year 1933."

While occultist prophets, clairvoyants, and esoteric healers garnered much interest from Weimar society, they faced increasing difficulty once the Republic was overthrown and a competing "disguised religion" began reshaping the German world according to its ideas. By hammering away at long-accepted notions of reality, at the laws of cause and effect, at the standards of proof set by the scientific method, at normally acknowledged conceptions of time and space, of life and death, the occultists unintentionally helped bring down a Republic whose laws, values, and ideas were based on Western civilization. What Bry had feared now happened: one "disguised religion" ushered victorious. In the form of National Socialism, Germany was revolutionized and a new hegemony established. Although there were certain underlying affinities between National Socialism and occultism, their versions of reality were fundamentally incompatible and bound to collide. The new hegemony of the Nazi state would prove far less tolerant for the occultists than the old "system," as the Nazis disparagingly referred to the Republic.

The occultists' penchant for making political forecasts drew a harsh response. Even favorable predictions were unwelcome. The Nazis rejected occultist elaborations as to when and where political decisions were in harmony with the stars or the forces of destiny. Astrologist Elsbeth Ebertin was one of many who liked mixing politics and occultism. Her catalogs of annual predictions were bestsellers. She prided herself on having accurately foreseen Hitler as Germany's savior already in 1923. Ebertin also claimed to have warned Hitler that he was undertaking the Munich Putsch at an astrologically inopportune moment. Ostensibly, at that time, the Nazi leader had impertinently quipped, "What do I care about women and stars!"[164]

This expression of double contempt surely did not sit well with Ebertin. As an experienced occultist though, she had heard it all before, usually from the lecture halls of the academic mandarins. She admonished skeptics "not to pass judgment too quickly on things they did not understand or had not examined."[165] The occultist belief system deserved respect and not the censure it all too often received from the unknowing and uninitiated. "Those gentlemen," Ebertin shot back, "who perhaps lack the time to orient themselves as to the essence of astrology, don't understand that the truly learned reader, the spiritually more developed person, as well as the simple man of the people, are shocked deeply into their souls when their belief in the stars is profaned by some smart alecks."[166]

With the onset of the Depression, Ebertin's popularity grew and she found herself assailed by more and more people worried about the future.[167] An article entitled "Meeting with Elsbeth Ebertin" in a Munich daily created a record flood of requests and unmanageable quantities of mail. While many of Weimar's citizens lost their jobs, Weimar's astrologists could hardly meet their professional obligations.[168]

On weekends the automobiles came to Heilbronn from Munich and Augsburg and parked in front of Ebertin's house. All wanted a chance to discover what the near future had in store for them. Seeking to protect her privacy, she traveled to Munich to meet her clients. Large crowds lining up at her hotel from morning until night. Later, she proudly recalled, "They all waited in the hotel lobby: the high and the low, young people hoping for some particular good fortune, and others with intentions to commit suicide, the employed and the unemployed, private businessmen and civil servants, mediums, dancers, milkmaids, occultists, and homeless people. But sometimes it happened that an elegant automobile snatched Elsbeth Ebertin away from them and took her to a private audience."[169]

Her more affluent clients were chiefly interested in the nation's fate. One group wished to know "if a world war would break out in 1932."[170] Ebertin's occultist colleague Günther-Geffers, a few years earlier, had also been asked to outline future events for a curious and nervous crowd. She had prophesied an imminent Lithuanian invasion of East Prussia in 1925 and when asked about Germany's fortune, she said she anticipated the making of a large and mighty empire.[171] A medical doctor who witnessed these predictions considered her outlook for East Prussia an example of telepathic sensitivity and insight. The local population, he recalled, was in a state of heightened excitement because, shortly before, the Memel area had been occupied by Lithuanian forces and many people feared another invasion. "In my view," reported the doctor, "it was a case of telepathic relaying of the population's fears."[172]

Günther-Geffers' pronouncements reflected popular sentiments as well as her own narrow political views and prejudices. In uncovering crimes of property she commonly envisioned minorities such as Gypsies, Jews, and Poles as the perpetrators. When asked to investigate some crimes of arson, she repeatedly construed local Communists as the culprits. These accusations mirrored a widespread belief illustrated in many of Weimar's anti-Communist political posters. On these posters a stereotyped proletarian, wearing a puffy baker's hat, was shown torching a farmer's barn or setting fire to the country as a whole.

Some social characteristics and mental dispositions of occultists and Nazis bore resemblance or were even identical: the lower middle class environment in which both flourished; the feeling of anxiety and damaged self-esteem brought about by defeat and postwar turmoil; the quest for a new orientation and sense of meaning and purpose; the monomaniacal belief system that Bry described; and the hopes placed in a special German destiny and a miraculous turn for the nation. Although occultist ideas could be spread in a myriad of popular or specialized publishing houses and newspapers, occultism, unlike antisemitism, lacked a political organization. It had no direct access to or influence on politics. The seemingly endless number of clairvoyants, astrologers, psychic detectives, palm readers, mystic visionaries, and cult leaders could not equal the power that converged in the single antisemitic prophet. Once in control of the government, the Nazis clamped down on occultist programs that clashed with their own views.[173] As Bry noted in his Verkappte Religionen, one common quality of the 'disguised religions' was their extreme intolerance. For Hitler, Germany's destiny lay in the struggle of races, not in the movement of stars.

The kind of near-future predictions that two Querschnitt political astrologists offered the magazine's readers in December, 1932, were, in the last days of the Republic, a risky business. One of the writers, Harald Keun von Hoogerwoerd, projected a positive period for Germany as the zodiacal constellation shifted from Capricorn to Aquarius.[174] Germany's domestic and foreign position was bound to strengthen. This was a promising moment to reform the country. The opportunities offered early in 1933, he advised, should not be squandered because the planetary position of Jupiter, later in the year, would have an inhibiting effect. The political astrologer proceeded to examine individual horoscopes of Weimar's leaders to show how they and their programs would fare in the coming months. Chancellor Franz von Papen and General Kurt von Schleicher faced constellations blocking their efforts, but former chancellor Heinrich Brüning and Otto Braun, Governor of Prussia, would be helped by planetary movements. Hoogerwoerd warned Hitler to stop acting in crass opposition to the constellations. Instead of using favorable planetary conditions in August, 1932, Hitler had foolishly rejected the acting government's offer of the vice-chancellorship and two cabinet posts for the Nazi Party.[175] With vague optimism, the astrologer ended his forecast suggesting that whoever led the next regime would utilize the more propitious heavenly alignments coming about in 1933. Overall, he painted the prospect for a new and lasting national ascendance.

1.6 Gregor Strasser on the cover of Die Zukunft

1.6 Political astrology reached its heyday in 1932. Gregor Strasser, a popular Nazi leader who fell out of favor with Hitler, on the cover of *Die Zukunft* (June 1932).

The second writer, Artur Schumacher, admitted that political astrology required much more research and study to become an established field.[176] He cautioned readers that his prognosis only worked within certain limits of probability. For 1933, he saw astrological signs of economic improvement on the world market. On the other hand, politically, the new year would bring one of the worst crises for the German Republic. The tensions would reach their zenith by May and June and could include "eruptive turmoil of the radical masses." Such predictions of civil war contributed to growing fears in Weimar society that increased the citizenry's willingness to replace an ever more unstable, explosive democracy with a dictatorship that promised national unity and domestic peace.

But Schumacher foresaw 1933 as a gloomy year for Hitler because the constellations were positioned against him. He would face tough situations that he simply was unable to master. The Nazis would be severely weakened and the year was singularly unsuitable for a Hitler chancellorship. Like the other Querschnitt political astrologer, Schumacher suggested that Hitler's widely known failure to listen to astrological advice predestined him to political defeat. The writer echoed Ebertin's criticism that in 1923 Hitler had staged a rebellion when his horoscope indicated probable failure. In 1932 he demanded the position of chancellor at a moment that was completely mismatched for such a step. In May and June, Schumacher ominously asserted, a battle for power would take place that would decide the Republic's fate. The Querschnitt's unfriendly anti-Nazi forecasts revealed the kinds of tension and conflict that could pit occultists against Nazis. Each espoused a secret knowledge that construed different and contrary forces as the true movers of history and shapers of reality. While both moved in murky, unreal worlds of pseudo-scientific notions, they moved in worlds that were not concordant.

Even more off the mark then Querschnitt's political astrologers, were the predictions made in the June, 1932, issue of the occult magazine Die Zukunft: Monatsschrift für moderne Astrologie, Graphologie, Charakterologie und neue Lebensgestaltung (The Future: Monthly for modern Astrology, Graphology, Characterology and new Lifestyle). The magazine featured several articles about the rising Nazi star Gregor Strasser who was portrayed on the cover with the premonitory caption "Hitler's Ministerpräsident" (Hitler's Governor). The author of one article entitled "Physiognomic Judgment of the Picture" viewed Strasser's striking forehead as evidence of an ability for "realistic thinking, a constant dealing with facts and thus excellent observation of given relations unperturbed by gray theory."[177] A second graphological article discussed how Strasser's handwriting revealed that he was "true to himself."[178] Detailed horoscopes studied by the magazine's editor indicated that despite some conflicts, Strasser's career as a political leader would achieve major successes in the months that lay ahead. According to the magazine's editor, Strasser possessed a "strong political gift," "a deep identification with socialism," and "a rare sense of foresight which allows him to detect approaching developments with a single-minded instinct."[179]

Were such sycophantic descriptions and forecasts meant to position the magazine in a favored spot should the Nazi takeover be imminent? If so, the horoscopic and political calculations of these astrologers failed miserably. At the peak of his political career in December, 1932, Gregor Strasser came close to becoming German Vice-chancellor and Prussian governor in a plan arranged by Chancellor Kurt von Schleicher. When Hitler rejected the deal, Strasser angrily resigned his party functions and began a precipitous fall that would end with his execution in 1934. Inaccurate, unflattering political forecasts placed Die Zukunft astrologers, like their Querschnitt colleagues, in a vulnerable position once their Nazi subjects gained power.

Within the Nazi leadership, opinions about occultism were not uniform. Some Nazis, like Rudolf Hess and Heinrich Himmler, flirted with occultist ideas. On the other hand, Joseph Goebbels associated occultism with superstition, with popular brainwashing (Volksverdummung), and with the fraudulent exploitation of the uneducated and the poor. Alfred Rosenberg, a rival of Goebbels in the realm of the new state's cultural policies and a more radical advocate of ideological transformation, influenced Nazi cultural policies through the publishing house Deutsche Kultur-Wacht. This publisher sponsored a sustained attack against occultism in its book Vampyre des Aberglaubens (Vampires of Superstition, 1935).

The book's author, writing under the pseudonym Fred Karsten, was Carl Pelz, chief witness against psychic detective Günther-Geffers in the Insterburg Trial. The book's cover displayed a well-known photographic portrait of Erik Jan Hanussen in an eerie pose as hypnotist. In a sinister way the cover and title claimed that this clairvoyant (most people knew he was of Jewish origins and had been killed, in mysterious circumstances, in 1933) had been a dangerous vampire taking advantage of a superstitious population. Inside, the publisher declared it was not enough to fight occultism with ordinances and laws. This book was meant to be part of a Nazi campaign to educate and enlighten the public. The publisher announced that the new state intended to protect society from the occultist abuses it had suffered in the profligate Weimar Republic: "The system regimes of the Jewish Weimar Republic [Weimarer Judenrepublik] allowed no limits to be set on the con artists who profited from clairvoyance, telepathy and other supernatural powers. There was a method to the brainwashing: the more confused people's views and opinions became, the more fully the Republic's ruling class could fill its pockets."[180]

Detective Pelz began his diatribe by lamenting the corruption that, like "a creeping poison," trickled down from Weimar's ruling class to the people. He asked, "What did concepts like decency, honor, and cleanliness count for? Nothing!"[181] Crime and fraud characterized the day. Poverty and spiritual decline together set the stage for the innocent public's victimization.[182] A society living in fear of its future, Pelz continued, naively hoped for salvation in the world of superstition: "Everywhere in the German lands appeared miracle-makers, fortune tellers, palm readers, faith healers, and other charlatans.... Most of all it was clairvoyants and telepathists who appeared everywhere and enjoyed popular success."[183] All these occultists smartly took advantage of a disoriented, gullible population. Pelz blamed Weimar democracy's constitutional right to freedom of speech for shielding the nefarious activities of the occultists. Newspapers, Pelz implied, used freedom of press laws to increase their sales by inundating the public with misleading, catchy headlines. Thus the Weimar Constitution, according to this crude Nazi argument, promoted an occult conspiracy against the people. Variety halls were part of the problem as they took advantage of the troubled audience's penchant for the mystical and occult.¹⁸⁴ To increase attendance and "purely for business interests," Pelz scolded, variety directors included more and more occultist tricksters in their programs: "No, my dear variety hall and cabaret directors, it won't continue this way in the new dawn that is breaking." Pelz's shrill attacks corresponded with the Ministry of Propaganda's measures to purify popular entertainment according to Nazi tenets.

Fitting in with Pelz's theory was the fact that Hanussen had been one of the entertainment world's biggest drawing cards. The Nazi writer cited a newspaper that called Hanussen a "Czech Jew" and "a swindler of greatest proportions."¹⁸⁵ Hanussen, Pelz contended, was a man without scruples bent only on making as much money as possible through his cunning shows in Berlin and the provinces. His performances elicited many spectators (Kracauer had described them as "the expectant audience") to request an expensive, personal visit with the clairvoyant. After a show, Hanussen's fans ran to his hotel, where they formed long lines, and, to Pelz's outrage, " could hardly wait to throw away their hard-earned money."¹⁸⁶ All this swindling and profiteering, Pelz reported with barely disguised envy, allowed Hanussen to employ private secretaries, own a grand apartment, rent office space on the Kurfürstendamm, drive a luxury limousine, and sail about the Baltic Sea in a yacht.¹⁸⁷ To complete his harangue, Pelz described how Hanussen, aided by "superstitious fools," rose up to occupy the position of chief prophet in the capital city. He was even able to start a newspaper, the <u>Hellseherzeitung</u>, in which, Pelz mockingly related, Hanussen wrote "along the lines of National Socialism, probably thereby hoping to rescue himself into the Third Reich."¹⁸⁸ For Pelz, Hanussen was a striking emblem of the hated Weimar Republic. In him, he contemplated "a single rascal and national double-dealer" who "revealed an entire epoch."¹⁸⁹

The "bleeding miner Diebel" was a popular performer who Hanussen included in his shows, much to Pelz's chagrin. The media proclaimed Paul Diebel the secular counterpart to Therese Neumann of Konnersreuth. Supposedly, he could produce stigmata through autosuggestion and, for a while, succeeded in fooling the public.

One newspaper announced, "He Outdoes Konnersreuth." Diebel performed his thrilling, bloody act in cafés on the <u>Friedrichstrasse</u> and even in Berlin's renowned <u>Wintergarten</u>. For a substantial fee, offered by a wealthy admirer, he finally revealed his tricks, showing how, in a deftly concealed manner, he cut himself with a needle or put red chalk around his eyes so that he could cry bloody tears like those of the Catholic stigmatic. Pelz declared that the new state would show no tolerance for such skullduggery. In sharp contrast to the Republic, which not only endured charlatans, but gave them support, "today's state of order, authority, and discipline" was set on "eradicating professional criminals by root and branch."

1.7 Jan Erik Hanussen on the cover of a Nazi book

1.7 Weimar's most famous hypnotist and clairvoyant Erik Jan Hanussen appeared in a characteristically ominous pose on the cover of an anti-occultist, Nazi tract. Cover of Fred Karsten, Vampyre des Aberglaubens (Berlin: Verlag Deutsche Kultur-Wacht, 1935).

Pelz complained that in 1930 he had been denied air time on Berlin radio when he proposed a program to criticize the clairvoyant menace.[190] Instead, the famed radio reporter Alfred Braun was given plenty of time to conduct a live interview with Hanussen during a show at the Scala Variety Hall. Times had changed, however, and Pelz thanked Hitler for having done away with the conditions that promoted mass fraud and brainwashing [Volksverdummung]. He applauded recent police ordinances, like the one issued August 13, 1934, in Berlin. It effectively clamped down on fortune telling, clairvoyance, and telepathy. New laws were putting an end to the making of horoscopes, the reading of cards, and the interpretation of dreams. Referring to a report in the Völkischer Beobachter of April 14, 1934, Pelz showed how the police had requested and been granted authority to eradicate an ever-increasing amount of harmful occult activity in Berlin.

In a grandiloquent conclusion, Pelz contrasted the National Socialist community of honest, hard-working Germans with Weimar's crooked society that sanctioned the exploitation of the weak, the superstitious, and the unenlightened.

The deceivers were about to discover that they had lost their right to belong to the German nation. Sneeringly, Pelz referred "to the time of 'freedom'" as one in which men of foreign nationalities and races had played havoc with the German people. All these "so-called miracle-makers and charlatans" were nothing more than "freeloaders and parasites" on the German national organism [Volkskörper]. In typical Nazi fashion, the book ended with a bellicose flourish announcing all-out war on the "exploiters of superstition" and promising the annihilation of "the false teachings of superstition."[191]

Eradicating the occult proved more difficult than Pelz anticipated.[192] Its roots had grown deeply into the fertile soil of superstition, anxiety, and disorientation that had been the seedbed for National Socialism too. Corinna Treitel has analyzed the Nazi government's campaign against occultism, using such sources as the SS weekly Das Schwarze Korps.[193] In 1937, the journal published a series of articles called Gefahrenzone Aberglaube ("Danger Zone Superstition"). Repeating many of the connections Pelz made between vile money-making, fraud, Jewry, and the occult, the SS weekly widened the attack by accusing Catholicism of also purposely mystifying the Volk.[194] The series scoffed at the occultists' inability to understand fundamental forces at work in history. For Nazis, Treitel explains, "Astrologers who took no note of racial differences clearly had no business calling themselves scientific."[195]

The commencement of hostilities in 1939 gave a renewed impetus to fortune tellers and prophets. Unlike 1914, the German population did not welcome this war: worry prevailed over a desire for revenge. According to an anonymously published article in the SPD's exile newspaper Der neue Vorwärts on April 28, 1940, an increase of astrological activity in Germany reflected widespread uneasiness and pessimism.[196] The SPD writer commented that Germans knew better than to talk openly about a setback like the recent English sinking of a German navy vessel. An alternative way to vent anxious feelings was to whisper veiled information about how Hitler's horoscope resembled Wallenstein's. Those in the know would understand this to mean a military disaster was imminent. Secret occult allusions minimized personal risk, but reckless public forecasting about the war exposed soothsayers to reprisal and persecution.

In Munich astrologer Margarete Luft's war prognostications resulted in her arrest and a sentence of six weeks imprisonment, followed by time in a women's labor camp. Luft's harsh punishment served to warn other prospective visionaries. The Munich police report, quoted in Der neue Vorwärts article, announced further reprisals against any fortune tellers, declaring that there was no room in the national community for "crooks and charlatans." (The SPD writer commented acerbically that while "crooks and charlatans" would not be tolerated among the German people, they were allowed to run the government.)

The anonymous SPD writer then recalled how astrological newspapers had multiplied like mushrooms in Weimar's end stage and, according to him, had enthusiastically supported Hitler. Among their followers, astrologers had promoted the ideas of "a strong hand" and the hope in a national savior. At this point in the article, the SPD writer made a curious turn away from a typical socialist ridiculing of the astrologers. Instead he accepted an occultist premise and admitted that "among us" there are some who are equipped with "especially finely tuned receivers" who can detect oncoming "historical earthquakes" before they happen: "Geniuses belong to this species, as do hysterical and insane people – and clairvoyants. Most of these miracle men take themselves and their craft very seriously. They believe in their mission with the same steadfastness as the – spiritually related – Führer Adolf Hitler believes in his."[197]

The SPD writer, having observed what Bry and Olden noticed fifteen years earlier, continued by twisting the current precarious situation around and interpreted the alleged subterranean occultist challenge with a renewed optimism. If astrologers in Germany risked making dark prophecies, then the journalist reasoned, there truly were impending disasters about to take place in the Third Reich. The journalist's references to Germany's first military setbacks revealed wishful delusions as German forces routed the Anglo-French armies. This writer probably joined the refugee exodus from Paris only two weeks later when victorious German troops approached the French capital (where the exile edition of Der neue Vorwärts was published until France's defeat).

The occultists were not a serious menace to the Nazis. Some were even allowed to continue their activities and publications, especially if the Nazis deemed them scientific rather than commercial. The underlying affinities between occultism and Nazism help explain why Nazi policies were ambivalent. Occultists too, oscillated between criticism and adulation of Hitler. Elsbeth Ebertin criticized the Führer for ignoring her astrological advice on the eve of the Beerhall Putsch. But in April, 1935, she sent him a birthday gift: a dedicated copy of her anthology of German poems about flowers.[198] In the Third Reich, she was allowed to continue publishing her popular annual "view into the future."

Endnotes

1. Siegfried Kracauer, "Zirkus Sarrasani," Frankfurter Zeitung, Nov. 13, 1929, in ed. Andreas Volk, Frankfurter Turmhäuser (Zürich: Edition Epoca, 1997), 126.
2. Kracauer, "Zirkus Sarrasani," 126.
3. Kracauer, "Zirkus Hagenbeck," Frankfurter Zeitung, June 19, 1926, in ed. Volk, Frankfurter Turmhäuser, 108.
4. Kracauer, "Zirkus Sarrasani," 127.
5. Kracauer, "Gespräch mit Grock," Frankfurter Zeitung, February 9, 1929, in ed. Volk, Frankfurter Turmhäuser, 125.
6. Kracauer, "Akrobat – schöön," Frankfurter Zeitung, October 25, 1932, in Siegfried Kracauer, Schriften 5.3 (Frankfurt: Suhrkamp, 1990), 127.
7. Ibid., 128.
8. Ibid.
9. Ibid., 130-131.
10. Ibid., 131.
11. Kracauer, "Berliner Nebeneinander," Frankfurter Zeitung, Feb. 17, 1933, in ed. Andreas Volk, Berliner Nebeneinander (Zürich: Edition Epoca, 1996), 29.
12. Ibid., 30.
13. Ibid.
14. Kracauer, "Der Hellseher im Varieté," Frankfurter Zeitung, May 28, 1932, reprinted in ed. Volk, Berliner Nebeneinander, 82.
15. Otto Seeling, Der Bernburger Hellseher-Prozess und das Problem der Kriminaltelepathie (Berlin: Linser, 1925), 41.
16. Ibid., 41.
17. Walther Gaudlitz, Okkultismus und Strafgesetz. Dissertation (Leipzig, 1932), 11.
18. Albert Hellwig, Okkultismus und Verbrechen (Berlin: Hanseatischer Rechts-und Wirtschaftsverlag, 1929), 42-44.
19. Sling [Paul Schlesinger], "Der Hellseher von Bernburg – Hypnotiseur oder Betrüger?" in Vossische Zeitung, Oct, 13, 1925.
20. Sling, Vossische Zeitung, Oct. 15, 1925.
21. Hellwig, 219.
22. Erich Gottgetreu, "Hellseher und Dunkelmänner," in Vorwärts, Oct. 30, 1925.
23. Sling, Vossische Zeitung, Oct. 15, 1925.
24. Hellwig, 218.
25. Sling, Vossische Zeitung, Oct. 15, 1925.
26. Ibid.
27. Sling, "Das Unerklärliche vor Gericht," Vossische Zeitung, Oct. 16, 1925.
28. Ibid.
29. Sling, "Wie ich Berichterstatter Wurde," in Richter und Gerichtete (München: Rogner und Bernhard, 1969), 14.
30. Sling, "Ein Hexenprozess," Vossische Zeitung, Oct. 18, 1925.
31. Ibid.

32 Ibid.
33 Albert Hellwig, letter to the editor of the Vossische Zeitung, published in "Sling und der Okkultismus," in Vossische Zeitung, Nov. 6, 1925.
34 Ibid.
35 Sling's rebuttal to Hellwig in "Sling und der Okkultismus," Vossische Zeitung, Nov. 6, 1925.
36 Ibid.
37 Ibid.
38 Kracauer, "Berliner Nebeneinander," in ed. Volk, Berliner Nebeneinander, 29-30.
39 Sling, rebuttal to Hellwig in "Sling und der Okkultismus," Vossische Zeitung, Nov. 6, 1925.
40 Hellwig, Okkultismus und Verbrechen, 12.
41 Ibid., 82.
42 Ibid., 12.
43 Ibid., 208.
44 Ibid., 106.
45 Ibid., 229.
46 Ibid., 232.
47 Ibid., 88.
48 Ibid., 89.
49 Lachen Links, Jan.1, 1926.
50 Ibid., 4.
51 Hellwig, 89.
52 August Drost, "Wie ich zum Hellsehen kam," Uhu, January, 1926 (Heft 4), 26.
53 Ibid., 92-93.
54 Ibid., 26.
55 Ibid., 97.
56 Ibid., 26
57 Ibid., 92.
58 Reinhold Zenz, Ist Hellsehen möglich? (Königsberg: Verlag der Königsberger Allgemeinen Zeitung, 1928), 30.
59 Ibid., 30.
60 Ibid., 13.
61 Ibid., 30.
62 Ibid., 31.
63 Ibid., 31.
64 Ibid., 137.
65 Ibid., 84.
66 Ibid., 52.
67 Rudolf Lambert, "Der Insterburger Prozess gegen die Hellseherin Frau Günther-Geffers," Zeitschrift für Parapsychologie, April, 1929 (Heft 4), 278.
68 Ibid., 278-279.
69 Ibid., 279.
70 Zenz, 117-122.

71 Ibid., 115.
72 Ibid., 138.
73 Lambert, 348.
74 Ibid., 237.
75 Ibid., 343.
76 Ibid., 344.
77 Zenz, 115.
78 Ibid.,115.
79 Carl Pelz, Die Hellseherin: Betrachtungen eines ihrer 'geistigen Führer' zum Insterburger Hellseherprozess (Stolp: Pfeiffer, 1928), 83.
80 Ibid., 89.
81 Lambert, 233.
82 Pelz, 73.
83 Ibid., 83-85.
84 Zenz, 205.
85 Max Dessoir, Vom Jenseits der Seele (Stuttgart: Ferdinand Enke, 1931), 185.
86 Ibid., 185.
87 Ibid.,180.
88 Zenz, 180.
89 Ibid., 180.
90 Ibid.
91 Ibid.,181.
92 Ibid.
93 Dessoir, 185.
94 See the discussion of the concept of subaltern groups in Kate Crehan, Gramsci, Culture and Anthropology (Berkeley: University of California Press, 2002), 146.
95 Lambert, 232.
96 Dessoir, 135.
97 Ibid., 288.
98 Seeling, 10.
99 Pelz, 19.
100 Corinna Treitel, A Science for the Soul (Baltimore: The Johns Hopkins University Press, 2004), 178-179.
101 See Ulrich Linse, Barfüssige Propheten (Berlin: Siedler Verlag, 1983).
102 Ulrich Linse, Geisterseher und Wunderwirker (Frankfurt: Fischer Verlag, 1996), 138-139.
103 Michael E. O'Sullivan, Disruptive Power: Catholic Women, Miracles, and Politics in Modern Germany, 1918-1965 (Toronto: University of Tronto Press, 2018), p.74.
104 Ibid., p.67.
105 Paramhansa Yogananda, Autobiography of a Yogi (New York: The Philosophical Library, 1946), 352.
106 Ibid., 354
107 Ibid. 358.
108 O'Sullivan, p. 140.

109 Anonymous, Das Rätsel von Konnersreuth (Düsseldorf: Gesellschaft für Buchdrückerei und Verlag, 1927), 9.
110 Fritz Gerlich, Die stigmatisierte Therese Neumann von Konnersreuth (München: Kösel und Pustet, 1929). For Gerlich's conversion, see O'Sullivan, pages 69-70.
111 Josef Deutsch, Konnersreuth in Ärztlicher Betrachtung (Paderborn: Bonifacius-Druckerei, 1932).
112 Ibid., 6.
113 Ibid., 47.
114 Ibid., 12, 44.
115 Ibid., 14.
116 Ibid., 65.
117 Ibid., 60.
118 Ibid., 63.
119 Ibid., 61.
120 Ibid., 65.
121 Georg Wunderle, Die Stigmatisierte von Konnersreuth (Eichstätt: Geschäftsstelle des Klerusblattes, 1927), 34.
122 Ibid.
123 Fritz Gerlich, Der Kampf um die Glaubwürdigkeit der Therese Neumann (München: Naturverlag, 1931).
124 Ibid., 68.
125 Ibid., 60.
126 Ibid., 55.
127 Ibid., 63.
128 Ibid., 63, 70.
129 AST, "Das 'Wunder' von Konnersreuth," (Wien: Freidenkerbund, 1928), Hefte 1-3.
130 AST, Heft 1, 1.
131 Ibid., 2.
132 Ibid., 5.
133 Ibid., 8-9.
134 Rudolf Olden, "Das 'Wunder' von Konnersreuth," (Frankfurt: Fravo-Bücherei, 1927).
135 Ibid., 6.
136 Ibid., 7.
137 Ibid.
138 Ibid.
139 William Christian, Visionaries: The Spanish Republic and the Reign of Christ (Berkeley: The University of California Press, 1996), 366.
140 Ibid., 162.
141 Ibid., 252.
142 Ibid. 162.
143 Ed. Rudolf Olden, Propheten in deutscher Krise: Das Wunderbare oder die Verzauberten (Berlin Rowohlt, 1932).
144 Ibid., 37.

145 Ibid., 37.
146 Ibid.
147 For Neumann's role regarding this publication see O'Sullivan, pages 107-108.
148 Olden, 16.
149 Carl Christian Bry, Verkappte Religionen (Gotha: Perthes, 1925), 15.
150 Ibid., 43.
151 Ibid.
152 Ibid., 44.
153 Ibid., 19.
154 Ibid., 99.
155 Ibid., 178.
156 Ibid., 26.
157 Kracauer, "Kampf gegen die Badehose," Frankfurter Zeitung Mar. 31, 1931, in Volk, Berliner Nebeneinander, 76.
158 Bry, 209-210.
159 Ibid., 226.
160 Ibid., 227.
161 Ibid., 36.
162 Ibid., 19.
163 Ibid., 26.
164 Elsbeth Ebertin, "Sterndeuter Hellseher Wahrsager und Zunftgenossen," (Hamburg: Dreizack Verlag, 1931), 8-9.
165 Ibid., 22.
166 Ibid., 21.
167 Ibid., 24.
168 Ibid., 24.
169 Ibid., 26-27.
170 Ibid., 27.
171 Zenz, 112-113.
172 Ibid., 112.
173 For the complicated ties between Nazism and occultism, see Eric Kurlander, Hitler's Monsters: A Supernatural History of the Third Reich (New Haven: Yale University Press, 2017).
174 Harald Keun von Hoogerwoerd, "Blick in das Jahr 1933," Der Querschnitt, December, 1932 (Heft 12), 888.
175 Ibid.
176 Artur Schumacher, "Blick in das Jahr 1933," Der Querschnitt, December, 1932 (Heft 12), 887.
177 Erich Carl Kühr, "Physiognomische Beurteilung des Bildes," Die Zukunft, June, 1932, Nr.6, 244-245.
178 Maria Hepner, "Beschreibung des wesentlichsten Eindrucks des Schriftbildes," Die Zukunft, June 1932, Nr.6, 242-243.
179 Rudolf Schneider, "Horoskop des nationalsozialistischen Führers Gregor Strasser," Die Zukunft, June 1932, Nr.6, 239-242.
180 Fred Karsten, Vampyre des Aberglaubens (Berlin: Verlag Deutsche Kultur-Wacht, 1935), 69.

181 Ibid., 7.
182 Ibid., 9.
183 Ibid., 10.
184 Ibid., 16.
185 Ibid., 28.
186 Ibid., 33.
187 Ibid., 33-34.
188 Ibid., 51.
189 Ibid., 53.
190 Ibid., 63.
191 Ibid., 65-66.
192 For Pelz's career as a debunker of occultism see Eric Kurlander, "The Nazi Magicians' Controversy: Enlightenment, 'Border Science,' and Occultism in the Third Reich," Central European History 48 (2015), 498-522.
193 Treitel, 238-239.
194 Ibid., 239.
195 Ibid.
196 Anonymous, "Hitler und die Sterndeuter: Ein Symptom der Unruhe und der Furcht," Neuer Vorwärts, Apr. 28, 1940.
197 Ibid.
198 Philipp Gassert and Daniel S. Mattern, The Hitler Library (Westport: Greenwood Press, 2001), 80.

Chapter Two. Colportage: Harmless Pleasure or Dangerous Diversion?

Siegfried Kracauer spied the soul of modern mass society in circus and variety hall audiences, but the most common destination for his expeditions into modernity was the cinema. Movie theaters in the 1920s had a magnetic power over people hungry for entertainment and escape. In the decade between 1919 and 1929, the number of cinemas in Germany increased from 2,836 to 5,267.[1] In the early 1920s, Berlin alone accounted for more than three hundred, including fabulous movie palaces like the Capitol on Auguste-Viktoria-Platz, the Titanic-Palast in Steglitz, or the Alhambra on the Kurfürstendamm.

Kracauer became one of Weimar's most prominent film critics, reviewing more than seven hundred films for the Frankfurter Zeitung between 1921 and 1933. Like his contemporaries, Kracauer was fascinated by the movies. For a while he even thought that film might illuminate spectators and make them more aware of social realities, but these hopes faded by 1932. Too many of the movies he reviewed were mediocre products espousing a defensive, conservative ideology that shielded the viewer from social reality rather than revealing it. Over and over again, Kracauer bemoaned the irrelevance of Weimar films. Instead of exploring a pressing contemporary problem filled with cinematic and educational possibilities, movie producers preferred to offer a tepid mix of happy-end romances, operettas adapted for the cinema, exotic adventure stories, superficial expedition documentaries, and patriotic fanfare. A typical film that met with Kracauer's disapproval was <u>Jennys Bummel durch die Männer</u> (<u>Jenny's Stroll Through the Men</u>, 1930), a comedy about a flirtatious model who eventually succeeds in baiting an American millionaire for marriage. "Fine, the audience deserves light amusement," Kracauer commented and declared "that we certainly don't favor offering the viewer only heavy fare." The film producers, Kracauer lamented, held a preconceived notion of the female office workers' naïveté and their films delivered an execrable message: "Are the female office workers supposed to think that paradise opens up to them simply because they have nice legs? That they can live like princesses in fashionable hotels always populated by rich Americans? The attitude [<u>Gesinnung</u>] of such films that exploit wishful daydreams [<u>Wunschträume</u>] is utterly reprehensible.

They don't only withhold reality from the public, a reality that beckons for change, but also falsify it so that nothing at all will be changed."[2]

2.1 Secretaries dream of liaisons with the wealthy in Weimar film

2.1 Siegfried Kracauer deplored films like Jennys Bummel durch die Männer (1929), which portrayed female white-collar workers as naïve and empty-headed. They dream of marrying their bosses or American millionaires. Kracauer felt such stories obfuscated reality and impeded the development of consciousness. *Illustrierter Film- Kurier* 1254 (1929).

A year later, Kracauer's tone became more aggressive as he condemned the glamour world evolving around film stars. The dreams of innumerable typists, sales clerks, and apprentices were projected on these stars, whose stories were publicized for the mass audience in fan magazines like Filmwelt.[3] With amazement the fans gazed at this false, ethereal world, Kracauer complained: "It is populated with princes and princesses, and the unknowing mix up reality with illusion [Sein und Schein] and stare, as if anaesthetized, at the higher spheres. So they are made useless and are sidetracked from a conflict that might actually help them achieve a better form of existence. Film's assignment or duty ought not to keep them spellbound in sleep but to awaken the beguiled."[4] In addition to transporting viewers into vicarious dream worlds of stardom and impossible fairy stories, the cinema industry followed the lead of popular illustrated magazines and took the public to irrelevant exotic lands by way of all sorts of expedition documentaries. Commenting on <u>Hunting Tigers in India</u> (1929), Kracauer asked, "If one equips film expeditions, must they always visit the domain of primitive people or animals? Why not, instead, follow up on the few documentaries that have attempted to inform people over their own conditions, as humane or inhumane as they may be. There is still a lot to be filmed in Germany."[5]

In a 1932 article "About the Task of Being a Film Critic," Kracauer dryly conceded that "film is a product in the capitalist economy like other products too."[6] In a detached marxist vein, he admitted that the vast majority of movies were not made in the interest of art or to enlighten the public but simply for their use value or profitability. What then was the film critic's task when he reviewed the average, run-of-the-mill movie? Kracauer insisted that simply making judgments of taste would not entitle one to be called a critic. His real job was to analyze and reveal the social purposes that lay hidden in the average films, "to expose them to daylight, which they not seldom shy away from."[7] Kracauer believed it was his job to reveal what a given film tried "to convey to the public masses and in what sense does it influence them."[8]

Furthermore, he would contrast the dream world with social reality and show how the former falsified the latter. Kracauer recommended a special approach for the few films of substance and artistic merit. They deserved an aesthetic interpretation in addition to sociological analysis. Two German films that Kracauer found exceptional were <u>Mutter Krausens Fahrt ins Glück</u> (<u>Mother Krausen's Journey to Happiness</u>, (1929) and <u>Mädchen in Uniform</u> (<u>Girls in Uniform</u>, 1931). The first gave a sober look at the atrocious housing conditions of many working class families, while the latter sensitively explored Junker educational methods in a private boarding school for the daughters of Prussian officers.[9] Such uncommon films fulfilled Kracauer's requirement of providing the spectators with an eye-opening experience that they personally could profit from and which might make them engage with society's problems in a more productive manner. These films were artistically refined and socially significant. Kracauer praised them in the hope that his accolades would help spur the production of additional noteworthy films.

By no means was Kracauer only interested in issuing seals of approval for superior films, while condemning the moviegoers' regular fare. Kracauer endorsed pure entertainment movies. For example, he enjoyed the action-packed thrillers of Harry Piel. Whether taming tigers, climbing smokestacks, chasing bandits on a motorcycle, or rescuing damsels in distress, Piel delivered suspense and excitement in the tradition of print colportage [<u>Kolportage</u>], the cheap, serial adventure stories that had gained a mass market by the latter part of the nineteenth century. Unlike most German intellectuals, Kracauer did not frown on colportage. He knew that the preposterous pulp stories were favorites for youthful readers. In reviewing Piel's <u>Die Mitternachtstaxe</u> (<u>The Midnight Taxi</u>, 1928), Kracauer agreed that if one judged the story from an adult standpoint, it was pretty dumb. But he accepted the fact that there were different ways to read a story or watch a film. From the perspective of boyhood logic [Knabenlogik] the sequence of events made plenty of sense.[10] Kracauer considered Die Mitternachtstaxe delightful entertainment. Piel's Seine Stärkste Waffe (His Strongest Weapon, 1928) was another crowd pleaser. Kracauer commented, "Harry tastes like candy [Lutschbonbon], a true colportage hero."[11] The film reviewer placed Die Mitternachtstaxe in a similar context by imagining "a boy reading a thriller, sucking on candy, and dreaming. Only Harry Piel can spring forth from these dreams."[12]

2.2 *Popular actor Harry Piel*

2.2 Kracauer admired the sensational action films of Harry Piel. The pulp industry exploited his popularity by marketing the print series *Harry Piel, der tollkühne Detektiv*. Anonymous, *Ein Abenteuer im Hotel "Astoria,"* (Leipzig: Speka-Verlag, c.1920-1923) vol.64. Postcard "Harry Piel," (Berlin: Verlag "Ross," c.1923).

Kracauer appreciated Piel's films because they were straightforward, skillfully crafted entertainment, without any allures of being high art or drama. "Once again Harry has cooked up a stimulating film," Kracauer wrote about Mann gegen Mann (Man against Man, 1928), "where he celebrates triumph after triumph as gentleman-adventurer… In short, the film is suspenseful and amusing, and every unassuming person will enjoy it more than any of the conceited art productions."[13] Kracauer despised the many ostentatious films that used all too clever plots and overly elaborate sets and costumes in an attempt to impress the viewers that they were more than mere entertainment. Colportage made no lofty claims, but it delivered what everyone could enjoy. Thus, for Kracauer, colportage was not a dirty word. In taking this position he occupied an unusual place among Weimar's intellectuals, most of whom automatically considered colportage to be worthless. To highbrow critics, colportage seduced ignorant, uneducated spectators in the form of sensational films or tantalized low-class and youthful readers as trashy pulp literature. Kracauer detected cynicism in German film producers who thought they could transform appealing colportage plots into artistic endeavors. The film critic scoffed, "As if colportage had to be saved like a fallen maiden!"[14] The outcome of such a mistaken approach was a string of "horror products" like Fritz Lang's spy films. Kracauer thought that colportage stories touched serious topics with more honesty than presumptuous mainstream cinema. He credited colportage with "the projection of great subjects on the level of the trivial. The conflict between good and evil, the miraculous, the reconciliation – many important themes are always presented by it in a rather distorted manner. That is why the expertly crafted sensation films of Harry Piel have their good right to be made."[15]

Piel developed his screenplays, directed, and acted in them himself. As a master of his craft, he understood how to create light entertainment, a gift most Weimar film producers lacked. "It characterizes the insensitivity of the film producers," Kracauer explained, "that they seek to transform into quality ware what by its very nature cannot be quality ware. What can breathe in the form of pamphlets, becomes suffocated in luxurious satin covers."[16] Here Kracauer made something crystal clear that was normally shrouded in fog in the Weimar years. He granted pure entertainment in film and literature a right to exist. One could applaud and recommend Harry Piel, despite the fact that his films were not works of art. In the same way, one could let youths enjoy reading adventure stories without admonishing them to read only the classics, and one ought to criticize Weimar's film makers when they pretend that clumsy, pretentious productions were works of art.

Film's origins were humble. Kracauer credited Max Skladanowsky for presenting the first primitive moving pictures in amusement parks around 1895. The story lines followed those of the cautionary street ballad [Morität] and the pictures were accompanied by simple ballad verses. Just as early film technology developed in the milieu of the amusement park, Kracauer found it no coincidence that its subject matter was derived from motifs that "subsisted below recognized literature. It is the world of popular entertainment [Volksbegeisterung] into which they probe, the primitively concocted and enjoyed adventure stories, the ten Pfennig pamphlets, that are available to the masses in stationery stores and backstreet courtyards."[17] Kracauer felt that Chaplin's wonderful films were direct descendents of this genre of popular culture.

The German word <u>Kolportage</u> stems from the French colporteur or peddler of Bibles and cheap books. In the late eighteenth century, the first reading revolution began as the market for reading materials rapidly expanded. By this period, about one fifth of the German population could read.[18] The growing appetite for literature and the publishers' desire and capacity to feed this appetite raised concerns by authorities who nervously observed what they called a growing reading addiction [<u>Lesesucht</u>], fever [<u>Lesefieber</u>], or craze [<u>Lesewut</u>].[19] Rudolf Schenda, in his studies of popular literature, has pointed to the sense of alarm that the turn to reading evoked among public officials: "A populace that reads too much could come up with false thoughts that might find fault with the authorities, might become disillusioned with its difficult lot in life, and might even start a revolution on the French model! So one wanted to put a damper on the reading craze, to submit popular literature to the test of the censor, to control the publishers, and keep a watchful eye on the peddlers."[20]

A cat and mouse game ensued throughout Europe when governments tried to exert some sort of control over the increasing mass of printed matter. At the same time, publishers and writers tested the limits of the permissible. A favorite strategy in satisfying the reading public's growing demand for stories of crime and violence was to couch these in the form of cautionary tales. Shocking ballads [<u>Moritäten</u>] and chapbooks successfully used this tactic. As literacy levels increased in quantity and quality, such simple fare was no longer enough.

Readers wanted book length stories seething with suspense, crime, and melodrama. The publication of Eugène Sue's <u>Les Mystères des Paris</u> in serial form in a French newspaper in 1842-1843 had a powerful influence on the development of popular literature all over the continent. Already in 1842 a German translation was published in Leipzig.[21] Many imitations followed about "the mysteries" of world cities such as Berlin, Hamburg, and Stuttgart. These serial novels offered the reader a voyeuristic journey through the underworld of the growing nineteenth century urban landscape. Installment plots exposed evil and crime in the urban milieu, depicting the metropolis as the new stage for the eternal battle between good and evil.

The German production of serial novels in pamphlet form exploded in the second half of the nineteenth century. As literacy rates soared to 90% by 1900, a second reading revolution spawned a desire for easily readable, exciting, entertaining literature.[22] Specialized publishers sought to satisfy this new, lucrative market. Between 1871 and 1880, 380 colportage novels were published, between 1881 and 1890, 300 more.[23] Purchased by subscription and delivered home by a colporteur, each installment was usually twenty-four pages long and part of a series of between 80 to 110 issues.[24] An issue cost ten <u>Pfennig</u>, making it affordable even for a worker, a domestic servant, or a farmhand. From its inception, the colportage novel [<u>Kolportageroman</u>] alarmed German authorities. The high publication figures, the targeted readership of workers, women, and youth, the skillfully commercialized methods of advertising and sales, raised the eyebrows of government officials as well as many self-proclaimed guardians of culture and education. An alliance of chaplains, teachers, writers, professors, lawyers, and politicians started the Schundkampf or "battle against trashy literature." The struggle against Schund intensified after 1900 when American dime novels, such as Buffalo Bill and the Nick Carter detective series, began flooding the German markets, gaining a huge following especially among youths and sparking the production of similar German mass series.

This pulp literature was different from the older colportage novel in that each issue was a self-contained story not necessarily connected sequentially with the previous issue. These new series had no definite endpoint since the number of a hero's or heroine's adventures was potentially unlimited.

Despite a good deal of public attention and an aggressive style of criticism that put colportage publishers on the defensive, the cultural warriors of the Wilhelmine Schundkampf would have to wait for World War I to score a major victory.[25] With Germany legally under a state of siege, regional army commands could bolster public security by issuing orders that by-passed Wilhelmine press laws. The various headquarters responded to conservative pressure groups and issued lists prohibiting specific Schund titles but how effective these proscriptions were is unclear. Many of the listed books' stocks had already been sold and therefore were not retrievable. On-going series could be banned, but several popular ones like Buffalo Bill, Nick Carter, Texas Jack, and Wanda von Brannburg had ended publication in the years preceding the war. Furthermore, a conflict erupted within the ranks of the Schundkämpfer [warriors against trashy literature] about how extensive the reading ban ought to be and what criteria ought to be used to eliminate individual titles.

During the Weimar Republic, about one hundred colportage novels were published. The genre had clearly passed its heyday, yet it still occupied a sizeable portion of the popular literature market. The various Schundkampf associations persisted in their relentless attacks on colportage. Their efforts finally bore fruit when the parliament passed the "Law for the Protection of Young People from Trashy and Filthy Writings" in December, 1926. The law was partly the achievement of Wilhelm Külz, DDP Minister of the Interior, who had warned: "Never has German literature, never have art and science been more hindered by filth, trash, and kitsch as now."[26]

The fact that this law was sponsored by a minister from a moderate party that upheld the Republic indicated that it had broad support and was not just a pet project of a cranky conservative fringe of cultural pessimists. Only the KPD and SPD voted against it, but even these two parties viewed Schund with critical eyes and considered it a deplorable by-product of capitalist publishing endeavors. The left's failure to support the law hinged on a fear that the law could be easily expanded and misused to threaten freedom of the press. The new law forbade openly displaying, selling, or advertising any book or journal which had been indexed by either of two review boards [Prüfstellen] in Berlin and Munich. Appeals about review board decisions could be made to a superior board [Oberprüfstelle] in Leipzig which had a final, irrevocable say.

Included among the first ten titles placed on the Liste der Schund und Schmutzschriften (List of Trashy and Filthy Writings) between December, 1927, and April, 1928, were six colportage installment novels, showing that this genre was the favorite target for the new law. What specifically did the review boards find reprehensible about these stories printed on cheap paper and bound together as twenty-four or thirty-two page pamphlets with a crudely illustrated cover? What did an unusually broad band of politicians and professional spokesmen view as dangerous in this genre of popular literature? By studying the decisions of the review boards and by examining the contents of some of these melodramatic thrillers, one can get a better idea of the stakes involved in this conflict between a highly visible and vocal alliance of Schundkämpfer and de facto censors on one side, and an unorganized interest coalition of readers, writers, and publishers on the other.

A new edition of a colportage novel originally published before the war became the law's first victim. Die schöne Krankenschwester (The Pretty Nurse, 1911, 1925) was placed on the list by decision of the Berlin Review Board of November 22, 1927. The novel's publisher hired lawyers and brought the respected, albeit controversial Schund expert Professor Karl Brunner to the Leipzig Superior Review Board to argue their case against censure. Brunner generally opposed Schund but did not have as sweeping a definition for it as most Schundkämpfer. For the sake of lower class readers, he felt that some of it ought to be tolerated. The publisher of Die schöne Krankenschwester noted that 10,000 copies had been printed and more could be produced. Sales were running successfully at 2,000 subscriptions per year.

The book order form carried notification that the order was being placed by an adult at least eighteen years old. In this way the publisher hoped it could circumvent the Schund law since it was only designed to proscribe literature for youths. Spokesmen for the company explained that subscription forms were included in newspapers or brought directly home to clients by colporteurs.[27] To advertise the novels, the first issue was free and placed randomly in many mailboxes in the hopes that recipients would take the bait and subscribe. The Superior Review Board determined that simply labeling the order form with "I guarantee I am eighteen years old" did not prevent underage subscribers from ordering or gaining access to the book. On the contrary, such a label might whet the appetite for youths seeking forbidden literature. The board explained to the publishers of Die schöne Krankenschwester that it was its duty to protect youths from any installment novels that they deemed "objective trash or filth."[28] The appeal was rejected in Leipzig on January 4, 1928.

Few colportage novels would be stigmatized as Schmutz or filth, a term referring to publications with luridly sensual or pornographic contents. It was the review boards' conceptualization and definition of Schund or trash that would be crucial to the fate of these works. The law itself had not provided a definition, but the law-makers anticipated that one would be worked out over time by the review boards.

The decision regarding Die schöne Krankenschwester established an important precedent, but formulating a definition as to what constituted trashy literature endangering youth proved to be a slippery task. This can be seen by examining the reasons given by the Weimar review boards, many of which were highly subjective and unconvincing. Long before the law even came into effect, Germany's Schundkämpfer were fighting opponents and arguing about the definition of Schund.

The Leipzig Superior Review Board decided that Die schöne Krankenschwester was Schund "in the sense of the law."[29] To be considered Schund, the board reasoned that a book had to fulfill a number of negative criteria. Flimsily, they reasoned it had to be "worthless in any case." Second, it had to display a certain contempt for the reader in that, in contrast to serious literature, there was nothing significant or noteworthy in it. "He who has nothing serious to communicate but prints it anyway is simply a businessman," the board pontificated, revealing a typical Bildungsbürgertum prejudice against commercial literature.[30] True literature, from their lofty perch, was supposed to aspire to be a work of art, not a mere commodity.

Yet the board recognized the public's desire for easy, entertaining literature and it magnanimously refrained from labeling all popular literature as Schund. A final, crucial attribute for literature to be considered Schund was its potential danger. The board maintained that a novel endangered the reader when it exploited the reader's "low instincts" or his "naïve lack of awareness or sense of reality." Applying these extremely subjective criteria would somehow, the review boards felt, separate "clean" popular literature from "trashy or filthy writings."

In specific reference to Die schöne Krankenschwester, the board found that the amount of nonsense spooned out to the reader was astonishing. The novel's characters behaved in an utterly exaggerated fashion. The board petulantly counted forty-eight cases of fainting spells in the story. They noted with consternation that the author mistakenly depicted slave plantations and a slave rebellion in Canada.[31] Furthermore, they argued that an uncritical reader "must assume that there is neither a police force nor a state prosecutor in Germany, England, Canada, or New York," the story's chief locations. Crimes are never investigated or resolved.[32] The board worried that the book could influence an immature person "to believe that if he tried to commit a crime like extortion, he ran little risk of getting caught."[33] In addition to modeling criminal behavior, the story could cause a young reader to lose his sense of reality or get so hooked on this type of spicy literature that he would not want to read anything else.

Any neutral observer could see that these arguments and this line of reasoning, contrary to the board's claim of objectivity, was highly subjective and open to question. The problem for the colportage publishers was that the superior board's decisions were final. Indexing on the Schund list was considered an administrative procedure and did not fall into the realm of civil law or normal court procedures. Thus there was no further recourse after the Leipzig Superior Board pronounced its verdict. The paternalistic frame-of-mind which characterized the Leipzig Review Board and its lack of objectivity in indexing Die schöne Krankenschwester was revealed in the board's concluding and seemingly self-evident judgment: "A test case is that no sensible father would place this book in his child's hands."[34]

Two weeks after the indexing of Die schöne Krankenschwester, another reprinted pre-war colportage novel would be added to the Schund list by the Berlin Review Board. This time the board attacked the plot of Die Bettelgräfin (The Beggar Countess, 1895, second edition 1925) as an endless chain of nefarious, roguish crimes to which the "good characters" were subjected. The story included murder attempts of all kinds, physical abuse, burglary, fraud, arson, and counterfeiting. The Berlin Review Board felt that the book endangered the moral development of youths:

> This is especially true for impressionable youths whose moral value judgments are clouded and whose moral powers of resistance must be shattered when they read books in which demonic criminals play a leading, proud role, while the noble people, in their goodness, have the unenviable role of being eternally jinxed.[35]

The review board was also appalled by the novel's extremely poor style: "All artistic value is missing and the composition is arbitrary and not organic. All these characteristics of the book can be traced back to the fact that it is not the product of a thoughtfully creative process of even the most modest kind but is rather constructed by factory means."[36] Like the Leipzig Superior Board's decision against Die schöne Krankenschwester, the Berlin Review Board revealed a Bildungsbürgertum distaste for writing that did not aspire to art but was simply meant to satisfy mass market demands. The review board members, who were nominated by professional associations of writers, publishers, youth welfare officials, teachers, and clergymen together formed a powerful coalition, truly a hegemony against the reading desires of disenfranchised lower class adults, as well as youths of all social classes.

Fedor von Zobeltitz was an author and member of the Berlin Review Board which indexed Die Bettelgräfin. He had written a novel, Die papierne Macht (The Paper Power, 1902) which had fiercely criticized the production of colportage during its heyday at the turn of the century. One of this story's characters, a colportage promoter, realistically explained the genre's role: "It is not our intention to educate the people – that we leave to others – we want to oblige their desires."³⁷ Zobeltitz described the colportage publishers as "people without a conscience" and as "rogues."³⁸ The colportage publishing house in Die papierne Macht is not located in an impressive publishing establishment but in a shabby old factory. Two large rotation printing machines occupy the bottom floor and consume huge masses of paper. A cutting and folding machine prepares the pamphlets for stapling.

Typesetting is done on the second and third floor by scores of employees. The whole grimy building seems to rumble and shake under the impact of indefatigable machines. Zobeltitz's descriptions of colportage production, although factually accurate and revealing his first-hand knowledge of the pulp industry, were filled with upper class prejudices against this literature: "The printed masses of paper that left this house did not carry the spirit of free science or noble poetry into the world, but of stupefaction [Verdummung]. No illuminating genius [came from here], rather a smirking demon who steals his way into the population by way of dirty back stairs to unleash the people's worst instincts...."³⁹

Over time, however, this impassioned anti-colportage writer would lose his fervor in what seemed to him an increasingly senseless endeavor. Twenty-seven years after publishing Die Papierne Macht, the wearied Schundkämpfer complained of his tedious work on a review board. "I am really getting tired of the whole business," he remarked in a newspaper article in 1929, "we board members are showered with thick volumes that need to be read conscientiously and that usually reveal themselves to contain absolutely no danger to youths. The board members need to attend meetings that take hours. They receive not a single penny for their lost time."⁴⁰ Zobeltitz's dismay indicated that the inordinate amount of time required to wade through volumes of installment novels was a factor favoring colportage publishers in their struggle with anti-colportage crusaders.

Another colportage novel submitted for review was Ernst Friedrich Pinkert's Trude, die Tochter des Milliardärs (Trude, the Daughter of the Billionaire, 1926). In contrast to Die schöne Krankenschwester and Die Bettelgräfin, this novel was not recycled Wilhelmine colportage, but freshly penned by one of the Weimar Republic's most prolific writers of popular literature and a specialist in serial novels. Ernst Friedrich Pinkert published six colportage novels between 1926 and 1932, a staggering quantitative output when one considers each installment novel was 2,400 pages long. A mature man in his fifties, Pinkert had reached the peak of his productive capacities as a writer, but his name never appeared in Kürschners, the thick Who's Who of German literature.

Pinkert was born July 20, 1876 in Erfurt. He attended school for eight years and then became an apprentice in the printing and publishing business. He learned typesetting, printing, and proofreading in various cities including Kassel and Frankfurt. In the decade before World War I, he managed a small publishing company and a journal for youths, Jugendwoche, but both endeavors failed. He then turned to writing his first adventure, crime, and romance stories for popular magazines. In 1915 he was drafted and served as an infantryman until the war's end.

Afterwards, he picked up his contacts to publishers and returned to the tough job of churning out fiction on demand. In a 1939 résumé for the Nazi Writers Guild, he described himself as non-political, formerly Catholic, and as a divorced father of four grown children. He noted with pride that, in the early 1920s, a manuscript he had submitted for a Harry Piel film production had won first place in a competition among four hundred entries.[41]

In 1927 he found himself in the unenviable role of defending his novel Trude, die Tochter des Milliardärs (written under the pseudonym Frank Robertson) in front of a review board. The Heilbronn publishing house Deutsches Roman Journal, like the publisher of Die schöne Krankenschwester, hired Schund expert Karl Brunner to help defend Pinkert's book. Part of Brunner's strategy was to argue on behalf of the lower class's right to have access to a literature that it enjoyed reading. Indiscriminately indexing all colportage, he said, would represent a gross imposition of one social class's values and tastes on those of another. "The measures [against Trude, die Tochter des Milliardärs]... amount to setting up a form of class justice acting against the tastes of intellectually primitive [geistig primitiver] people whose recreation and entertainment needs can only be satisfied by the colportage novel."[42]

Brunner's social description of Trude's readers was confirmed by a warning from the town of Offenburg's youth agency addressed to Baden's Ministry of the Interior. The agency had observed the sale of many Trude installments to young male and female factory workers in Offenburg.[43] Brunner advised the board to stop persecuting harmless colportage and instead turn to restricting truly dangerous works like the very popular Berlin crime story Klettermaxe (1927), which glorified a criminal character.[44] A Hamburg youth welfare officer, who had requested the examination of Trude, die Tochter des Milliardärs, countered Brunner's argument by affirming that through long experience schools and youth officers had come to the conclusion that all colportage was dangerous. The welfare agent claimed that the evidence accumulated by juvenile courts was overwhelming and showed that practically every young criminal was a victim of this fantastic literature.

In fact, youth agencies and courts had corroborated each other's findings about Schund since the battle began in Wilhelmine times. But the Munich Review Board rejected the youth agency's request to place Trude, die Tochter des

Milliardärs on the Schundliteratur list. They admitted that according to colloquial usage, the novel would be considered "trashy literature." The plot was a hodgepodge of events, the dialogue was rudimentary and tasteless, even unintentionally funny. The Munich Board noted that the gist of the law had nothing to do with educating popular literary tastes but with defending social virtues.[45] The review board showed understanding for the youth agency's concern that young readers could sympathize with the criminal characters described in Trude, die Tochter des Milliardärs, but they argued that the author had gone to great lengths to distinguish evil villains from noble heroes.

2.3 Cover of installment novel Grossstadtmädel

2.3 The cover of installment novel *Grossstadtmädel oder Das Vermächtnis des Dollarkönigs* (Leipzig: Marien-Verlag,1926) illustrates a secretary's melodramatic battle against lechery and in defense of female virtue.

According to the board, impressionable young readers were only in danger of becoming "confused in their moral concepts" when criminals were depicted as sympathetic or their crimes were viewed as pardonable.[46] The Munich reviewers gave

Pinkert credit for making sure the readers identified with the virtuous heroes, not the villains. They found the colportage writing technique crude and contrary to aesthetic norms and taste, but they could not impugn the novel's moral framework. Nor were they willing to accept the youth agency's grand claim that all popular, adventure writing was intrinsically damaging to youths. They felt that only in uncommon pathological cases could a youth be endangered by this genre.[47]

This early decision in favor of a colportage novel showed that the review boards were not going to act simply as a rubber stamp endorsing every agency's submission of an installment novel for censure. Although numerous decisions would seem arbitrary or even contradictory to prior ones, and despite their bourgeois prejudices and general distaste for colportage literature, the review boards generally made a conscientious effort to examine the individual works fairly. In contrast to submitting agencies, the review boards knew what it was like to face the pressures of publishers, authors, and a possibly critical press.

Pinkert could consider himself fortunate that the Munich Review Board had decided against censuring Trude, die Tochter des Milliardärs. A short while later, he was arguing his case again, this time in defense of Grossstadtmädel, oder das Vermächtnis des Dollarkönigs (Big City Girl or the Legacy of the Dollar King, 1926). The publisher appealed to the Leipzig Superior Review Board after the novel was indexed by the Berlin Board. He informed the board members that 5,000 copies of this installment novel had been printed and he lamented the low sales, which he suggested, was an indication that the story was just not spicy enough.[48] Pinkert also defended the content of his novel by comparing it to Trude, die Tochter des Milliardärs and reminding the Leipzig reviewers that their colleagues in Munich had decided against placing it on the Schund list. The author also claimed that Grossstadtmädel was written on a much higher literary level than older installment novels like Die schöne Krankenschwester and that it merited endorsement for its unimpeachable moral standpoint. Author and publisher sought to convince the Leipzig board that it was their intention to warn young women about the dangers of the white slave trade in Grossstadtmädel. Interspersed in the pamphlets were many warnings of real-life white slavery incidents, but all of these obviously self-serving efforts and arguments left the Superior Review Board cold.

The Leipzig reviewers doubted the book could effectively warn susceptible girls about the slave trade and instead thought that it might have the opposite effect on some female readers because of the portrayal of "the sensual delights" enjoyed by the story's prospective prostitutes.[49] Acknowledging that they were guided by their prior decision on Die schöne Krankenschwester, the Leipzig Superior Board detected similar shortcomings in this popular novel. Having denied the author's and publisher's argument that Grossstadtmädel had a socially redeeming value, the board categorized the book as "worthless" and as "exploiting the reader's low instincts or naïve lack of realism [Spekulationen auf niedere Triebe und ahnungslose Weltfremdheit]." Youths needed protection from such literature because it promoted "an entirely false world view, even in the realm of morality."⁵⁰ The reviewers frowned on the fact that the story's main villain escaped sentencing before the courts for an impossibly long time. They were perturbed by Pinkert's descriptions of the comforts and moral excesses savored by the story's crooks. The eventual victory of virtue over evil could not exculpate the book for its serious flaws and dangers.

All colportage writers and publishers would have to take into account the Superior Review Board's sweeping condemnation of Grossstadtmädel. How could they stay true to the vital, essential qualities of colportage, which made the genre so compelling for its poorly educated or youthful readers, without contravening the new canon? The Schund law forced Weimar's colportage industry to navigate a narrow channel bounded on one side by the desires for a literature of sensation and melodrama, and marked on the other, by the threatening demands and restrictions of the review boards. Out of necessity, publishers and authors would now have to exercise a preliminary self-censorship to avoid having their products restricted or banned from the market.

Pinkert had disingenuously compared Grossstadtmädel with Trude, die Tochter des Miliardärs, arguing that they were equivalent types. But Grossstadtmädel was actually a hard-boiled form of colportage containing episodes that transgressed the limits of the review boards' tolerance. Repeated imagery of desecrated corpses disgusted the reviewers. In one scene, an exhumed corpse gets tossed into the water to be ravaged by rats and fish, and in another, a corpse is thrown into a family tomb where one of the novel's characters has been imprisoned and left to die. The Leipzig Board also condemned repeated references to the rape of the colportage story's heroine.

Many of Pinkert's heroines are blonde, blue-eyed young women upholding high German standards of pious fidelity in a harsh, male-dominated world of seemingly endless adversity. These morally pure women are tormented by a parade of unscrupulous lechers. The main character in Grossstadtmädel, Else Marwitz, exclaims, "Great God, help me... What have I done to these men that makes them treat me as if I were fair game?"⁵¹ The heroines always fight for chastity. When an Arab sultan orders Else to undress, she defiantly replies, "Never... I would rather die."⁵² When her boss, Joseph Goldfaden, grabs her, she punches him in the eye, and in the same scene in a revised version of the story (marketed under the title Mädchenhändler), she threatens to cut her pulse with a broken vase if Goldfaden won't desist.⁵³

Richard Stites has traced the origins of European melodrama to the end of the French Revolution, and to "the storm and stress of early romanticism, and 'bourgeois sentimentalism.'"⁵⁴ He notes that in melodrama "a recurring conflict was that between a maiden ready to sacrifice her life to preserve her purity and the villain who falsely denounces her after his sexual advances are rebuffed. This surely resonates with Christian hagiography: Saints Agatha, Lucia, Margaret, and many others were martyrs not only to their faith but to the frustrated lust of men who brought about their deaths."⁵⁵ Pinkert's martyrs and despondent young heroines suffer so much abuse that they wonder if there is any moral design in the world at all. The colportage stories of these mistreated women are permeated by a sense of Hobbesian pessimism about human nature, or, more specifically, the enduring, rapacious nature of males.

2.4 *Cover of installment novel Schwarze Natascha*

2.4 Ernst Friedrich Pinkert's installment novel *Schwarze Natascha: Die Liebe des Wolgaschiffers* (Niedersedlitz: Wolga-Verlag, 1927) was prompted by Cecil B. DeMille's movie The Volga Boatman (1926). Pinkert repeatedly exploited popular American movie productions for his own colportage themes.

Pinkert's novel Schwarze Natascha (Black Natascha, 1927) is set in the Russian revolution and the author makes it abundantly clear from the beginning that nothing good can come of this upheaval. Although there are a few genuinely idealistic revolutionaries, the majority of people exhibit a kind of mob behavior that Pinkert construed as "the unleashing of the beast in man."⁵⁶ The novel's hero is the blue-eyed Volga boatman Boris Werrodin. Throughout the story, he struggles with the dilemma of either dedicating himself to the cause of the revolution or listening to the call of his heart. Pinkert and his colportage readers were convinced that love was a force more powerful and compelling than any social movement or political revolution. "Love conquers all" was the underlying message of colportage melodrama. In Schwarze Natascha, when Boris first meets refugee princess Natascha, he is instantly lovestruck: "A transformation was taking place in him. He had thought he could only live for his ideals, for the liberation of his poor... comrades. And now? He loved the wonderful girl, he worshipped her. All his resistance was useless, he could now see the light."⁵⁷ One hundred and fifty pages later, a troubled Boris needs to choose between love or revolution. "Oh, Natascha... why did destiny place you on my path? ...I am no longer in charge of my senses and my will... Because of you I have become a renegade, a traitor to the holy cause of freedom."⁵⁸

2.5 *Cover of installment novel Mein Sonny-Boy*

2.5 Another American movie, Archie Mayo's Sonny Boy (1929) inspired Pinkert's installment novel *Mein Sonny-Boy* (Niedersedlitz: Münchmeyer Verlag, 1930).

When Boris blames destiny for his dilemma, he touches the crux of the colportage universe. Despite seemingly endless, impossible coincidences (which particularly exasperated and irritated review board readers), nothing in this universe happens by accident. All the couples in Pinkert's novels undergo the same up-and-down cycles of fate. Boris and Natascha in Schwarze Natascha, Else and Thiele in Grossstadtmädel, Rotraut and Armand in Trude, die Tochter des Milliardärs, Eveline and Roger in Mein Sonny-Boy (My Sonny Boy, 1930), and Eva and Phil in Ihr Junge (Her Boy, 1932) are predestined to fall in love, to be separated again and again, and to be tossed about in a terrifying world before they can be brought together for a final apotheosis of romantic marriage and family happiness. The countless dramatic and painful separations serve as a kind of Calvary that makes the main characters worthier of each other and of love's ultimate reward.

Just as destiny mysteriously moves individuals apart and brings them together, it shapes the paths of peoples and the history of nations. In Schwarze Natascha, Pinkert told his readers that Russia's bloody civil war was a fate reserved for nations that had lost the war, grimly raising the specter of similar developments at home.[59] Russian settings in Weimar's popular literature were not uncommon: they titillated the reader, but also worked out scenarios that were scarily relevant. One year after the publication of Schwarze Natascha, Pinkert published another colportage novel set in tsarist Russia: Knute und Fessel (Whips and Chains, 1928). Other Weimar colportage novels set in Russia were Heinz Hart's Der rote Kosak (The Red Cossack, 1926) and Eugen von Blank-Eisenman's Rasputin (1932). The grand spectacle of Russian history and turmoil had assumed a place in European drama and literature long before the revolution. In her article "Melodramatizing Russia," Julie Buckler describes a genre of nineteenth century European plays wherein "fictional, melodramatic Russias served as a site for playing out western cultural fears and fantasies."[60]

Destiny in Pinkert's novels is not spasmodically autonomous, but a force framed within a strict Calvinist universe. When a nobleman's servant in Schwarze Natascha tells why an enraged mob killed his lord, he explains that "God's ways are predetermined."[61] Tiny man cannot be expected to understand His ways: man's job is to accept what happens; to resign himself even to the worst fate; to know that, in the end, God has a redeeming purpose for everyone and everything. Natascha acknowledges the terrible fate of the Russian aristocracy (despite her warm personal feelings for the Tsar's family) at the hands of workers and peasants was probably deserved.[62] In a typical colportage contrast, Boris dreams of liberating the Russian people, while Natascha believes God has chosen her to help free the Tsar.[63] Neither goal will be realized, but Pinkert credited his two central characters with having a good heart full of pure feelings. Idealism, not politics, is what counts. Their eventual union of opposites represents a synthesis of what is most valuable in the Russian people. Achieving political aims is a questionable, ephemeral endeavor, while romance uplifts and hints of something eternal. In this sense, Pinkert's primitive colportage ideology espoused a type of anti-political politics that permeated wide sections of Weimar's popular culture. In Fritz Lang's film

Metropolis (the screenplay was written by Lang's wife Thea von Harbou), a similarly melodramatic and anti-political reconciliation of opposites takes place. Here, though, it is the young capitalist Freder who unites with the Madonna-like Maria (leader of the enslaved workers) in a crude overcoming of class antagonisms.

In Schwarze Natascha, left and right, reds and whites, Bolsheviks and tsarists, were equally bad. White soldiers massacre entire villages, but bloodthirsty Bolsheviks kill and loot indiscriminately too. In one episode, an alcoholic shoemaker turned radical revolutionary, leads a crowd to ransack and destroy the stores in a village. A victimized storekeeper stands in front of his empty shop and burning home musing that "it had all been for nought. In a few minutes he had been ruined."[64] Boris scolds the crowd, but while he fights for ideals, the shoemaker firebrand "revels in cruelty and malice."[65] Pinkert acknowledged the skills of revolutionary agitators who "ably whipped up the temper of the poor and oppressed, and taught them despair and wild hatred."[66]

"In the countryside," Pinkert wrote, "the agitators wandered from village to village preaching the new religion, a religion of hatred and annihilation. They spiced up the teaching with enticing concepts like freedom and brotherhood."[67] Pinkert admitted that among the leadership there actually were a few men who sincerely believed in their new faith and substitute gospel. He praised Lenin's and Trotsky's efforts to restrain and bring order to the masses.[68] But all the efforts and idealism of real revolutionaries (as well as fictional ones like Boris in Schwarze Natascha) could not change or modify the sinful evil at the core of human nature. When political systems collapse, pulp writers warn that uncontrolled, enraged, revolutionary crowds sowing destruction are the inevitable outcome.

A sage (later revealed to be Boris's long-lost father) tells Boris that he will end up despairing in his ideals because "mankind has too many weaknesses and passions to be able to truly appreciate this revolution."[69] Pinkert foresaw a grim future for Russia: "It was a cruel, ugly system, but had the tsars done it differently? One merely copied the methods. The music was the same, only the tune was different."[70] In the end, Boris regretfully admits that he has become disillusioned and uncertain. Lenin makes a futile effort to convince the young revolutionary to remain in Russia, but instead he chooses to unite with his true love, Natascha, and departs for a new life in exile in England. The novel ends with a typically stretched colportage denouement: Boris, the humble Volga boatman and red revolutionary, accidentally discovers his long-lost aristocratic parents and in fairytale manner is transformed into the Duke of Worchester. Boris's miraculous change in status closes the colportage's story by outwardly confirming his inner nobility, proven in over two thousand pages of text. Moral purity evolves into deserved distinction and status. Appearance and substance unite in a synthesis satisfying the reader's desire for a sense of wholeness, completion, and transcendental reward.

A major theme in all of Pinkert's installment novels is that true nobility is not acquired by heredity but is achieved through hard work and moral action day by day. Characters who suffer and sacrifice, who practice chastity and show loyalty to friends and family, deserve their colportage rewards. To underline the point, the most despicable figures in Pinkert's stories are decadent aristocrats. These compulsive gamblers and debauchers populate his novels as dark forces of fathomless evil. In Grossstadtmädel, nobleman Harry von Plessenstein gets out of bed late in the morning, smokes a cigarette, and calls his brother to ask for 30,000 marks to pay his latest gambling debts. When his brother scolds him for his profligate lifestyle, Harry angrily reacts: "You only live according to your damned, so-called sense of duty…"[71] In another Pinkert novel, Mein Sonny-Boy, a hedonist Count Giovanni Solandra reveals similar behavior. He uses all powers at his disposal, including hypnotism, to steal his way through life, making others instruments for his selfish, wicked goals. Pinkert's degenerate nobles, like their precursors in nineteenth century literature, represent the spent force of feudalism, a system not based on merit but purely exploitative and self-serving. Pinkert's humble readers could relish the inevitable fall of the many doomed nobles who inhabit his novels. And the poorer ones could appreciate his message that true nobility could be found at all levels of society and most notably there where the going was toughest.

Yet, as shown in Schwarze Natascha, Pinkert refused to endorse any specific political force. In his autobiographical résumé, he affirmed that he never joined a political party. Like many of his contemporaries, he ambiguously regretted the passing of the old order, while complaining about its unfair class biases. His writings express a nostalgia for Wilhelmine paternalism, but this is mixed with a sense that the monarchy and the aristocratic elite had let the nation down. These contradictions are reflected in Pinkert's confused, smoky plots of collective aristocratic downfall and heroic individual regeneration. Colportage ideology included a murky idea that godly destiny manifests itself in a process of natural selection where virtue and inner nobility overcome decadence and degeneration.

In Pinkert's fiction, minor figures contrast themselves with characters of superior stature. When Eva, the heroine of Ihr Junge, replaces an injured singer in the opera Carmen, a member of the choir comments, "I saw immediately that she is something better than the rest of us. You can only be that classy if you come from a distinguished family."[72] In Mein Sonny-Boy, a smuggler tells his partners that blonde, blue-eyed Sonny "is carved out of a different wood than you and the rest of us."[73] Sonny's estranged mother Eveline, at one point, has to defend her chastity against a lascivious prison director who has summoned her to his office. He is amazed by her eyes, "these wonderful blue stars," and when she manages to push him away, he is consternated by the way she looks at him with "this pure gaze that repudiates any filth, any immorality."[74] While the old system of inherited stature and titles was doomed to die, colportage's replacement sometimes confusedly mixed the new morality of merit with individual and collective behavior based on biological traits.

In Ihr Junge, Eva's attractiveness and her astonishing opera voice are signs of her moral purity and beauty. When she inherits a Brazilian fortune, she asks, "Shouldn't it be spent for those who live in greatest need? All rich people should do so...then there would be no more misery in this world."[75] Just as some physical attributes like blonde hair and blue eyes suggest superior personal qualities and high standards of morality, there are other physical qualities, in the colportage universe, that indicate negative characteristics. In Mein Sonny-Boy, a freckle-faced, red-headed farmhand turns out to be a malicious, deceitful character.[76] Little Joachim, the child hero in Ihr Junge, encounters a redhead whose freckled face is a warning to the boy: "Without a doubt, he was a good-for-nothing. Joachim had enough savvy that he thought he could, with reasonable certainty, read it from his face."[77]

When Sonny ends up in an orphanage, he meets Tom, whose appearance forebodes trouble: "The boy was extremely ugly.. He had a broad nose... and slanted eyes."[78] Tom is the offspring of a Chinese coolie and an American maid. "This child had a low, dissolute soul," Pinkert wrote.[79] This inclination to size people up by physical characteristics and outward appearance was part of the colportage system of ethnic stereotyping. Lord Phil, a protagonist of Ihr Junge, comments with colonialist contempt about the Arabs: "They are big children. They are greedy, false, and underhanded... The more they swear and the louder they insist on something, the less you can trust them."[80] An oriental man in Grossstadtmädel has "a dirty yellow face that could be read as a large map of base instincts and passions."[81] In the same novel, the Jewish moneylender Isidor Rosenstock's head tilts to the side of his crooked neck, while pince-nez glasses are perched on an enormous, hooked nose that "looks like a vulture's beak. His eyes also struck one as being like those of a vulture."[82] Pinkert described Rosenstock as looking like "the embodiment of miserliness [der verkörperte Geiz]."[83] In Mein Sonny-Boy, the villain Solandra sells a necklace to the Jewish pawnbroker Ignaz Goldbaum, who runs the jewels "through his stumpy, filthy fingers."[84] Lecherous Joseph Goldfaden seeks to kiss Else Marwitz with "his thick, protruding lips."[85] Racial stereotyping typified Pinkert's novels. There was little room for fine shades of difference in colportage literature.

For readers living in a rapidly changing and confusing world, the fixed colportage types helped mark out features of a mental universe and system of meaning. Continually filtering into the stories was a crude Christian ideology of forbearance, promising eventual reward for those who persevered and for those who proved morally worthy. Lower class readers could identify with the suffering and eventual triumph of colportage heroines and heroes and draw comfort from their stories. They were taught that justice would eventually be awarded to all who deserved it, but this act would be divinely ordained and it was not their right to make demands, to organize politically, or to fight for it.

A challenge to this closed colportage doctrine of paternalism, ethnocentrism, and pietist endurance and rebirth, came from the increasingly visible phenomenon of Weimar's independent, modern "New Women" who wanted personal fulfillment in careers as well as romance. Pinkert's stories, heavily populated with female characters and largely conceived for female readers, raised the issue within the static moral gridwork of colportage. In each one of his installment novels, Pinkert drew a stark contrast between "the good woman" and "the evil woman." In Mein Sonny-Boy, Roger Worley, the famed American opera singer, is married to Eveline Steinberg, a blue-eyed blonde from Baden. Sonny is their darling boy. Eveline's rival is Ria Sintwell, a brunette vamp who is crazy about Roger. She has her chance when Eveline, following the mysterious calls of a stranger, abandons her family.

Roger falls into despair and eventually gives in to Ria's overtures. He soon discovers that she has a character diametrically opposed to that of his absconded, angelic wife. While Eveline always thinks of others first, Ria is selfish, conniving, and sensual excitement is her chief pursuit. She has worked in variety halls and cheap night clubs in Paris, aspiring to become an opera singer.[86] Through Roger she gets her chance to perform by his side in New York's Metropolitan Opera. She plays the role of an Indian and chooses a very revealing outfit that immediately draws the audience's attention. Male spectators' adjust their opera glasses. Part of the audience reacts angrily and someone shouts, "Indecent!" Ria is hissed and booed, while Roger receives enthusiastic applause. The performance is a fiasco for her. "Ria wanted to triumph through the beauty of her body," Pinkert wrote and later contrasted her with Eveline, who has a superb voice that, further on in the novel, draws an opera audience's furious applause.[87] Eveline's fine voice is an outward expression of her inner purity and "moral beauty." Ria can only exploit her good looks; her sensuality is the outward sign of a scheming, egotistical inner self. Pinkert described her as snakelike, demonic, and like "a wild tiger."[88] The hallowed, established world of the opera is not the appropriate venue for a grasping woman like Ria; she will have to turn to the glittering, corrupt world of modern cinema to score her successes.

Kracauer had criticized Weimar movies for offering cheap, seductive fantasy worlds to the growing number of young female stenographers and typists. Pinkert, in his contrasting portrayal of Ria and Eveline wanted to show his female readers the difference between art and moral purity on the one hand, and superficial titillation and moral decay on the other. Whereas Kracauer hoped that the office workers would reject the nonsense spooned out to them and instead attend films that truthfully dealt with their lives and their problems, Pinkert addressed them paternally with cautionary tales to avoid the alluring, dangerous influences of metropolitan culture manifested in films.

2.6 Two illustrations from Mein Sonny-Boy

2.6 Eveline is the blonde, blue-eyed protagonist in Mein Sonny-Boy (1930). She is German, beautiful, and good. Her antagonist is swarthy, self-absorbed Ria. Her androgynous haircut signals a challenge to traditional gender norms. Illustrations 43, 67.

This rejection of modern urban culture and its innumerable enticements echoed the condemnations of Germany's army of cultural pessimists. For them, the metropolis and its favorite medium, film, were evil by their very nature. In Pinkert's world, Ria is a woman of the city, she smokes and likes to frequent the sultry ambiance of Berlin's Imperial Bar.[89] She wants to enjoy herself, she has ambitions and sexual desires. In the world of colportage such a character is inevitably branded as evil and eventually crushed. Pinkert made Ria a warning to female readers. Ria's cousins in the real world were the "New Women" who were testing roles and possibilities in a society that had only recently opened new opportunities. One of Ria's most dastardly, selfish acts is the forging of Eveline's farewell letter to Roger which convinces him to give up all hope in ever seeing his wife again. Pinkert commented acerbically, "She was a woman who knew how to turn wishes into reality."[90] Eventually Roger recognizes his mistake in substituting Ria for Eveline. Ria is "a degenerate creature [ein entartetes Geschöpf]."[91] Pinkert elaborated, "Never would she be capable of giving such a pure, sublime love as Eveline's." Ria is "a typical representative of a certain sick passion and sensuality."[92] Pinkert wrote that even when she was in love with one man, she was already thinking of becoming involved with another.

2.7 Cover of Ihr Junge on Illustrierter Film-Kurier 1556

2.7 Kracauer called the film Ihr Junge "a sob story" of the worst sort. Illustrierter Film-Kurier 1556, (1931).

Ria knows she is the opposite of her adversary. Eveline's "cool disposition" contrasts with Ria's impulsiveness and fiery character.[93] Roger eventually is convinced that Eveline is not at fault in their separation: "She had loved only him, and he could have sworn that she would never have considered another man."[94] In fact, Eveline suffers innumerable torments in her separation from her beloved husband and child. Eveline is described as a hunted deer, as having the face of an angel, and as resembling "an atoning Magdalene."[95] Along the ocean shore, Eveline contemplates suicide as the waves beckon an escape to a peaceful and quiet sepulcher.[96] Her fall from grace is dramatic and fulfills a typical colportage function, letting the female reader reflect that her own personal problems were by comparison not so bad.

Eveline's fate suggested that all mankind, even the rich, were born to suffer: "Only a year ago, she was the happy wife of a famous singer envied by all for her lot in life. Now she wandered about homeless and abandoned...."[97] Only temporarily reunited with Roger about half way through the novel's one hundred installments, Eveline accepts her dismal fate: "...I cannot stay with him – destiny is stronger than us humans."[98] Finally in the last installment, Pinkert resolves the puzzling question as to why Eveline flees from her happy marriage. Like other colportage writers, he was influenced by the physiognomical theories of Johann Caspar Lavater. Lavater maintained that both moral qualities and physical characteristics were inherited and inextricably linked.[99] This idea became an axiom of colportage. Eveline, at an early age, pledged to her mother that she would watch over her twin sister Daisy and protect her from what her mother foresaw as a terrible, predestined fate. Eveline described the predicament: "When we were born, they discovered a tiny mole on my twin sister's arm. [My mother] was frightened to death. My father had had the same mole... She told me the mole was an indisputable sign of the family's physical as well as mental degeneration. All members of my father's family who were born with this mole tended to degeneration. As proof she named my father who was a completely immoral man...."[100] Eveline at first enjoyed the constant companionship of her sister, but then began noticing her sleepwalking, an early sign of the predicted degeneration.

While on a visit to Venice, Daisy fell under the control of the criminal nobleman Solandra who used her as an instrument in his illicit activities. Eveline tried all she could to help her twin, and, at one point, substituted herself and went to serve a jail sentence for her. Only after the evil hypnotist Solandra had been killed could Daisy be freed. At this point, Eveline could finally return to her beloved husband and son. This peculiar ending with its strange physiognomic overtones may explain why Mein Sonny-Boy was eventually censored by the Nazis.[101] For them, "serious topics" of this kind were a matter for racial science and not appropriate to frivolous colportage novels. In actuality, Nazi ideology and colportage narration bore striking and (for the Nazis) embarrassing affinities.

The Nazis could hardly have faulted Mein Sonny-Boy or Pinkert's other novels for his patriotic, nationalist views. The German countryside and its quaint little towns are always bathed in a romantic, idyllic light. When the American Roger Worley travels to the town of Bachweiler in Baden, he learns why "the Germans were such sentimental people."[102] Picturesque Bachweiler is surrounded by wooded hills, the red roof tiles of the houses poke out above the trees, and a river winds its way through the town. Roger is taken to a cozy inn that "lies like a swallow's nest on a hillside."¹⁰³ In the town, he visits the market square with its lovely baroque town hall. Children play near the fountain in the center of the square. In Ihr Junge it is the Englishman Lord Phil who has to admit that "Germany is beautiful, much more beautiful than my own country."¹⁰⁴ He visits the fairytale town of Remsheim located in the Odenwald. He realizes that racing about in a car is the wrong way to travel, so he takes a cue from the Wandervogel and discovers that "one can only really enjoy the beauty of nature by hiking."¹⁰⁵

Germany's natural and historical beauty, from the colportage perspective, reflects and expresses the nation's high cultural and moral stature. Outer appearance is a clue to inner virtue and a sign of being "chosen." Blonde, blue-eyed colportage heroines also embody this heritage of moral superiority. Since the heroines of Pinkert's novels are usually German women and since they are often taken advantage of and abused by foreigners, the reader could feel a connection between their mistreatment and the nation's lamentable exploitation at the hands of the Versailles powers. This theme of national disgrace met with a powerful sense of indignation from Weimar's hack writers and worked its way into the colportage narratives.

Pinkert's stories take place more often in exotic, foreign locales than in Germany. When he does shift the meandering plots to Germany, the hometowns present the essence of Germanness. In contrast to these timeless architectural wardens of German culture and ethics, stands the exciting but morally undermined, multicultural metropolis Berlin. In Schwarze Natascha, the visiting American detective Jonny Walker is delighted by what he discovers in postwar Berlin. He is impressed by how quickly Germany has recovered from a war it fought virtually alone against the whole world.¹⁰⁶ He tells his Russian companion that Germany will not go under by following Russia's path into self-destructive revolution. Walker also notices Berlin's many exiled Russians of "dubious origins."¹⁰⁷ His Russian friend admits that they take advantage of the land's generous asylum laws. Pinkert may have rubbed shoulders with this sizeable, economically shaky, émigré community since he himself scraped by in Berlin on his meager grub street writing income. Such contact may have stimulated the many Russian themes in his stories.

In Mädchenhändler, Pinkert described how the metropolis lured unsuspecting young women like flies into a spider's web. Gitta Falk lives with her parents in a Berlin slum. Her father is a war veteran holding a poorly paid job as a doorman and her mother makes a little money by washing laundry. When Gitta comes home from work with her pay, her father takes it away. He beats her when she is disobedient. On a rainy night, Gitta contemplates escaping her miserable life by jumping off a bridge into the "silence and peace" of a river. She decides against suicide and walks home: "The streets looked infinitely sad, they lacked the glamour and life of the streets in the city center."¹⁰⁸ Downtown, Gitta had seen "the doormen wearing purple, laced uniforms, holding a herald's staff, and majestically guarding the entrance to a place where... the delicate tones of sighing violins and the sadly comic whispering of the saxophone could be heard."[109] She had noticed and admired the flashy, flirtatious, cosmopolitan women. Overcoming her strict conscience and sense of family obedience, she decides to visit the heart of the city. When she arrives by train at Friedrichstrasse in Berlin's bustling center, her sorrows and fears disappear: "With astonishment she peered into this fairytale splendor which seemed to her as if it was another world."[110] Within a short time, Gitta is invited by a strolling gentleman to dinner and a glass of wine. It is the beginning of a fateful fall into the white slave trade and prostitution. In this first installment of <u>Mädchenhändler</u>, Pinkert rewrote portions of the indexed novel <u>Grossstadtmädel</u>, perhaps as a strategy for circumventing the latter's ban. Many of the installments of <u>Mädchenhändler</u> are identical to those of <u>Grossstadtmädel</u> and some of the pamphlet covers of <u>Grossstadtmädel</u> are simply stamped in ink with the new title <u>Mädchenhändler</u>. It seems that the publisher, Leipzig's Marien Verlag, in this way defiantly succeeded in marketing a portion of the indexed installments under a poorly disguised new title.

In <u>Mein Sonny-Boy</u>, Berlin is the scene of another type of crime. Protagonist Roger Worley is kidnapped and imprisoned, but an American detective and the Berlin police manage to rescue him.[111] The unemployed worker who agreed to kidnap Roger later explains to the police that the mastermind behind the plan had first shown him a good time in Berlin's amusement centers and then offered him a considerable sum of money to do this wicked deed.[112] Crime and corruption are the hallmarks of the city. In Pinkert's Berlin, the immorality of the urban population is exhibited in its thirst for lurid entertainment in the variety halls, the amusement parks, and movie theaters. For Pinkert, opera expressed true art and lasting cultural values, while film pandered to cheap sensuality and ephemeral pleasures. Opera is artistically and ethically uplifting, cinema is morally corrosive. The opera audience had rejected Ria because she lacked talent and tried to seduce them by wearing a revealing costume. Such impropriety offended the opera audience, but drew approval in the lowly world of cinema.

Pinkert, on the one hand, adopted the anti-film views of Weimar's cultural conservatives, but, on the other, tried to exploit the new medium's immense popularity for his own needs. Kracauer had discussed in his 1932 article "<u>An den Grenzen des Gestern</u>" ("On the Border of Yesterday") how early movies had thrived by copying stories from dime novels; now Pinkert and the colportage industry sought to inject new life and success into their antiquated form of entertainment by copying the movies.[113] Most of his colportage novels carried titles and story lines plagiarized from popular, current movies. <u>Schwarze Natascha</u> (1927) was subtitled "the Love of a Volga Boatman" and tried to exploit the success of Cecil B. DeMille's <u>The Volga Boatman</u> (1926). <u>Mein Sonny-Boy</u> (1930) drew inspiration from and copied Archie Mayo's film <u>Sonny Boy</u> (1929). <u>Ihr Junge</u> (1932) plagiarized story and title of Friedrich Feher's 1931 popular film starring his son Hans. The publisher of Pinkert's novel brazenly copied the photographic portrait of the adorable little Hans on the film's program booklets and used it to illustrate the pamphlet covers of their colportage version of Ihr Junge.

2.8 Cover of Pinkert's installment novel Ihr Junge

2.8 The publishers of Pinkert's Ihr Junge (Niedersedlitz: Münchmeyer Verlag, 1932) pirated the film portrait of boy actor Hans Feher for their installment novel cover.

Kracauer criticized this film: "An unequalled tear-jerker concocted of motherly love, tears, and wild Prague metropolitan life for the sole purpose of presenting little Hans Feher to the public. That the little boy is charming and perhaps even talented does not excuse the improper use of his childish innocence to create murky technical effects."[114] Kracauer's growing despondence with Weimar's maudlin movie fare suggests that he would have disapproved of the mushy sentimentalism dished out to the reading audience by writers like Pinkert.

While Kracauer defended straightforward entertainment and excitement in film or literature, he condemned sentimentalism and escapism in mass culture. By the 1930s, the age of installment novels was passing. For a time, Pinkert continued to scrape by writing maudlin stories for old-fashioned family papers like Das Vaterhaus. When the war started, paper shortages forced publishers to drop many of these popular journals. Cheated by a publisher who had commissioned a novel from him and used wartime paper scarcity as an excuse to cancel its contract, Pinkert appealed to the Nazi Writers Guild for legal and financial assistance. After lengthy litigation, the Guild managed to force the publisher to make a partial payment to Pinkert. Impoverished and suffering from diabetes, the aging colportage writer repeated his requests for financial help from the Writers Guild.[115] Pinkert's biographical trail vanishes at the end of World War II.

Endnotes

1   Paul Monaco, Cinema and Society (New York: Elsevier, 1976), 20.
2   Siegfried Kracauer, "Phantasien aus einem Modehaus," (Feb.8, 1930) in Kleine Schriften zum Film 1928-1931 (6.2), 334.
3   Kracauer, "Rund um die Filmstars," (May 10, 1931) in Kleine Schriften zum Film 1928-1931 (6.2), 504-505.
4   Ibid., 507.
5   Kracauer, "Über den Umgang mit Tieren," (Sept. 28, 1930) in Kleine Schriften zum Film 1928-1931, (6.2), 401.
6   Kracauer, "Über die Aufgabe des Filmkritikers," (May 21, 1932) in Kleine Schriften zum Film 1932-1961 (6.3), 61.
7   Ibid., 62-63.
8   Ibid., 62.
9   Kracauer, "Wedding im Film," (Jan.28, 1930) in Kleine Schriften zum Film 6.2, 329-330 and "Revolte im Mädchenstift," (Dec.1, 1931) in Kleine Schriften zum Film 1928-1931 (6.2), 562-565.
10 Kracauer, "Harry Piel: Die Mitternachtstaxe," (Mar.18, 1929) in Kleine Schriften zum Film 6.2, 229-230.
11 Kracauer, "Ein neuer Harry Piel," (Jan.1, 1929) in Kleine Schriften zum Film 1928-1931 (6.2), 190.
12 Kracauer, "Harry Piel: Die Mitternachtstaxe," 229.
13 Kracauer, "Harry Piel: Mann gegen Mann," (May 25, 1928) in Kleine Schriften zum Film 1928-1931 (6.2), 81-82.
14 Kracauer, "Der heutige Film und sein Publikum," (Nov. 30 and Dec. 1, 1928) in Kleine Schriften zum Film 1928-1931 (6.2), 160.

15 Ibid., 160.
16 Ibid.
17 Kracauer, "An der Grenze des Gestern," (July 12, 1932) in Kleine Schriften zum Film 1932-1961 (6.3), 78.
18 Gideon Reuveni, Reading Germany (New York: Berghahn, 2006), 152.
19 Ibid., 151.
20 Rudolf Schenda, Die Lesestoffe der kleinen Leute (Munich: Beck, 1976), 13.
21 Günther Kosch, Manfred Nagl, Der Kolportageroman (Stuttgart: Metzler, 1993), 12.
22 Reuveni, 6.
23 Kosch, Nagl, 25.
24 Ibid., 28.
25 Kasper Maase, "'Schundliteratur' und Jugendschutz im Ersten Weltkrieg," http://www.uni-frankfurt.de/fb03/K.G/B3_2002_Maase.pdf, 5.
26 Cited by Adelheid von Saldern, "Massenfreizeitkultur im Visier," Archiv für Sozialgeschichte 33 (1993), 23.
27 Oberprüfstelle Leipzig [OPS] (January 4, 1928), "Die schöne Krankenschwester," 4, (BArch) R 181.
28 Ibid.
29 Ibid., 6.
30 Ibid.
31 Ibid., 8.
32 Ibid.,9.
33 Ibid.
34 Ibid.
35 Prüfstelle Berlin [PS Berlin], (Dec.6, 1927), "Die Bettelgräfin,"2 (BArch) R 181.
36 Ibid.,1.
37 Fedor von Zobeltitz, Die Papierne Macht (Bielefeld: Velhagen und Klasings, 1902), 30.
38 Ibid., 24.
39 Ibid., 22.
40 Cited in Klaus Petersen, Zensur in der Weimarer Republik (Stuttgart: Metzler, 1995), 167.
41 Reichskulturkammerakte, (BArch) Pinkert, Ernst F. 20.7.1876.
42 Prüfstelle München (Dec,20, 1927), "Trude, die Tochter des Milliardärs".
43 Letter from Offenburg Youth Agency to Baden's Ministry of the Interior, (HStA Stuttgart), E151/09 277, Minister des Innern, No.51191 (May 10, 1928).
44 Klettermaxe was placed on the index by OPS Leipzig on May 11, 1928.
45 PS München (Oct.18, 1927), "Trude, die Tochter des Milliardärs", 1.
46 Ibid., 3.
47 Ibid., 4.
48 OPS Leipzig (Feb.22, 1928), "Grossstadtmädel," 2, (BArch) R 181.
49 Ibid., 4.
50 Ibid.
51 Ernst Friedrich Pinkert [written under pseudonym Leonore von Stetten], Grossstadtmädel (Leipzig: Marien, 1926), 9.

52 Ibid., 970.
53 Ernst Friedrich Pinkert, Mädchenhändler (Leipzig: Marien, no date), 125.
54 Richard Stites, "The Misanthrope, the Orphan, and the Magpie," in eds. Louise McReynolds and Joan Neuberger, Imitations of Life (Durham: University of North Carolina Press, 2002), 25.
55 Ibid., 27.
56 Ernst Friedrich Pinkert, Schwarze Natascha (Niedersedlitz: Wolga, 1927), 730.
57 Ibid., 54-55.
58 Ibid., 233-234.
59 Ibid., 68.
60 Julie A. Buckler, "Melodramatizing Russia," in eds. Louise McReynolds and Joan Neuberger, Imitations of Life (Durham: University of North Carolina Press, 2002), 55-78.
61 Pinkert, Schwarze Natascha, 209.
62 Ibid., 442.
63 Ibid., 498.
64 Ibid., 226.
65 Ibid., 197.
66 Ibid., 503.
67 Ibid., 153-154.
68 Ibid., 849, 991, 997.
69 Ibid., 564.
70 Ibid., 1621.
71 Pinkert, Grossstadtmädel, 17.
72 Ernst Friedrich Pinkert, Ihr Junge (Niedersedlitz: Münchmeyer, 1932), 343.
73 Ernst Friedrich Pinkert, Mein Sonny-Boy (Niedersedlitz: Münchmeyer, 1930), 2056.
74 Ibid., 365-366.
75 Pinkert, Ihr Junge, 1712.
76 Pinkert, Mein Sonny-Boy, 847-856.
77 Pinkert, Ihr Junge, 862.
78 Pinkert, Mein Sonny-Boy, 801.
79 Ibid.
80 Pinkert, Ihr Junge, 2113.
81 Pinkert, Grossstadtmädel, 114.
82 Ibid., 349.
83 Ibid.
84 Pinkert, Mein Sonny-Boy, 249.
85 Pinkert, Grossstadtmädel, 9.
86 Pinkert, Mein Sonny-Boy, 89.
87 Ibid., 105.
88 Ibid., 586, 591.
89 Ibid., 142, 703.
90 Ibid., 233.
91 Ibid., 411.

92 Ibid.
93 Ibid., 1927.
94 Ibid., 411.
95 Ibid., 430.
96 Ibid., 903.
97 Ibid.
98 Ibid., 1622.
99 Graeme Tytler, Physiognomy in the European Novel (Princeton: Princeton University Press, 1982), 70.
100 Pinkert, Mein Sonny-Boy, 2390.
101 Liste 1 des schädlichen und unerwünschten Schrifttums (Berlin: Reichsdruckerei, 1935), 93.
102 Pinkert, Mein Sonny-Boy, 954.
103 Ibid., 955.
104 Pinkert, Ihr Junge, 575.
105 Ibid.
106 Pinkert, Schwarze Natascha, 1949.
107 Ibid.
108 Pinkert, Mädchenhändler, 4.
109 Ibid., 5.
110 Ibid.
111 Pinkert, Mein Sonny-Boy, 2094-2101.
112 Ibid., 2101.
113 Kracauer, "An den Grenzen des Gestern," 76-82.
114 Kracauer, "Film-Notizen," (March 5, 1931), in Kleine Schriften zum Film 1928-1931 (6.2), 468.
115 A lengthy, repetitive correspondence is filed under Pinkert in the Nazi Party Archive of the Bundesarchiv. Although not a member of the NSDAP, Pinkert, as a writer, was required to be a member of the Reichsschrifttumskammer. He joined the guild on December 13, 1933 and was member 6664. His final plea for aid was dated September 9, 1944. The guild granted him one hundred marks on October 9, 1944. Reichskulturkammerakte, (BArch), Pinkert, Ernst F., 20.7.1876.

Chapter Three. The Schund Law: Defending Morality or Undermining Freedom?

The issue of Schund or "trashy literature" was unique because all Weimar political parties agreed that its execrable influence needed to be contained or eliminated. Yet the attempt to formulate a law to combat Schund would reveal how deeply divided and unable the parties were in finding a solution. The Weimar Constitution explicitly forbade censorship but left a door open for public control in the domains of film and Schundliteratur.

The proper means for carrying out these endeavors became the subject of heated parliamentary debate. Already in the summer of 1919, as delegates to the National Convention in Weimar discussed the writing of a new constitution, the different political perspectives on how to deal with "trashy literature" started manifesting themselves. For conservatives, the danger was dramatic. Dresden Pastor Franz Költzsch, member of the DNVP, warned against neglecting or underestimating the problem: "The filthy and trashy literature pollutes the air and contaminates our people."[1] Such hyperbole had long typified attacks on "trashy literature" from various political quarters. What distinguished the conservative position was a deep distrust in the people's own ability to defend itself from harmful Schund influences. Költzsch disagreed with much of the Weimar convention's talk about the populace's capacity to make good decisions for itself and for German society as a whole in a new, open democracy:

> Despite all that has been said so often in recent days, wide sections of this Volk are still rather immature [unmündig]. It is immature in its taste, immature also in its great respect for all printed matter. It thinks that everything that printed matter recommends is allowable. Bad literature stimulates its passions and cravings. In prisons one can see how many have been shown the way and pushed into a life of crime by Schundliteratur. In the insane asylums it is also confirmed and proven how many have lost their understanding, their senses and nerves over it. And one needs to know how the bad literature, in particular, effects youth. Devastating! We must be responsible for the Volk. We must show the right path and educate it. It needs to be able to count on us. We do not allow poisonous medications on the market. Nor can we allow spiritual poisons to be freely offered to the Volk.[2]

Költzsch also claimed that the purchase of pulp literature robbed the people of a large quantity of its modest income:

> It is like a bloodsucker on the body of our people... As soon as a single sensation is available – the unfortunate death of King Ludwig, the death of the Austrian Crown prince – the subjects are handled in a mass of horror novels. It is primarily the ordinary people [die kleinen Leute] who first reach out for it. The stories are simplified and made palatable for them in pamphlets, at ten Pfennig a piece... In one hundred or more installments, on whose every page a murder or some other horrible crime takes place, these novels that are not worth a cent, take ten, fifteen, or twenty marks away from each servant girl or young working lad.[3]

Költzsch made a final appeal to incorporate effective measures against Schund in the constitution by emphasizing that these were particularly confusing times in which the people desperately needed protection.

From the opposite spectrum of the national convention, the Independent Social Democrat Wilhelm Koenen picked up Költzsch's image of the bloodsucker and placed it into a marxist context. Koenen explained that "trashy literature" was a typical product of a capitalist system that reveled in money and profits.[4] Koenen pictured Költzsch and his conservative friends in the same boat with the Schund publishers because they all had irresponsibly glorified war and violence. Once the Volk learned to reject war and bloodshed, Koenen argued, the phenomenon of "trashy literature" would come to an end. Koenen's spiteful criticism of Költzsch foreshadowed the difficulties in finding a consensus on how to treat "trashy literature," despite the fundamental agreement that it was a source of great harm to society. The confrontation between left and right over what Schund actually was and how it could be opposed would continue in the years leading up to the passage of Schund und Schmutz ["trashy and filthy literature"] legislation in December, 1926.

Many parliamentary representatives called Reinhard Mumm, a DNVP delegate who served in the Reichstag for more than twenty years, the "father of the Schund und Schmutz law." Politically skilled and stubbornly determined to pass an anti-Schund law, Mumm persevered until his pet project was approved. Mumm had joined Adolf Stöcker's Christian Social movement as a student of theology at the turn of the century. His political home base was the Siegerland, a hilly region fifty miles east of Bonn, characterized by sleepy, rustic villages and rapidly growing iron-mining towns. In this region of social-economic contrasts, Mumm helped organize Christian unions and was elected to parliament in 1912. A strong nationalist, he combined a pro-worker position within the framework of a new, conservative Protestant politics.

He envied German Catholics for being far ahead of Protestants in their political organizations and experience. Mumm knew that many Protestants tradition-

Chapter Three. The Schund Law: Defending Morality or Undermining Freedom?

ally shunned politics as pointless scheming and bickering. He warned his fellow Protestants about the consequences of their mixture of aloofness and political apathy. In his memoirs, written in 1932, he reflected on this problem and found it unbearable that Christian organizations still tried to keep a safe distance from political life. "Politics has become unavoidable destiny for all of us," he wrote, "including our church. And where leaders are missing, seducers rule."[5] He argued that politics signified "a manly seriousness that no great society could do without."[6] Politics was the "taking of clearly aimed actions within the context of possibility" and "the art of leading the national soul."[7] He reiterated a barely disguised worry about Hitler's ascendancy by writing that "if leaders are missing in politics, so the seducers will take over."[8]

Throughout his life, Mumm had sought a happy fusion of politics and religion, of socially responsible conservatism joined with Protestantism. Mumm's political promotion of Christian values was linked to his concern that Germany's estranged workers were drifting into the dangerous orbit of atheistic socialists. At the end of his career, Mumm broke away from the DNVP because he disagreed with the party's leadership for steering the conservatives on an anti-union, pro-capitalist path. Mumm was also perturbed by party leader Alfred Hugenberg's media empire, which, he felt, did not uphold the high moral standards expected of conservatism. Too many of Hugenberg's Ufa films offended Mumm and the powerful entrepreneur's press carried articles and stories incompatible with Christian politics. In an angry exchange with the editor of Hugenberg's daily Nachtausgabe, Mumm had condemned risqué columns in the advertisement sections and the corrupting content of stories it published such as the offensively titled "Urlaub von der Ehe" ("Vacation from Matrimony").[9]

He commented on the fact that specific Ufa films that he attacked had also raised the ire of the Nazis. Although he himself was politically savvy enough to recognize the dangers of Hitler's program, Mumm's conservative cultural positions often coincided with Nazi opinions. While Mumm claimed to detest radicalism, he espoused antisemitic views. His greatest worry was that too many uneducated Germans were ready to follow the pied pipers of left and right. Political apathy and inexperience specifically among German Protestants, Mumm warned, opened the door to dangerous figures like Mannheim's radical socialist pastor Erwin Eckert or to the National Socialists.[10] Like many conservatives and particularly followers of Adolf Stöcker's Christian Socialism, Mumm blamed an array of social problems on what he labeled "Jewish capital." This kind of conservative antisemitism had earlier manifested itself in his anti-Schund campaign. In an article defending the Schund law and published on July 6, 1926, in the Süddeutsche Zeitung, Mumm lambasted the profit-seeking publishers of Schund who, he claimed, were supported by the culturally corrupting forces of Jewry:

> Artistic freedom is not in danger today. We are dealing with completely different processes. Publishers of the worst sort want to make money, lots of money, by sparking the lowest instincts. They contract a semi-educated scribe who today processes the murderer Haarmann, or, tomorrow, "the executioner of Berlin," into one hundred installments, each sixteen pages long. The last two pages of each installment must be "breathtakingly exciting." Who thinks that this widespread mass literature has anything to do with art? Certain gentlemen, the well-paid lawyers of lust may use the finest-sounding arguments. Certain sections of Jewry want to see the freeing of every form of lasciviousness but have no understanding for Christian-German sensibilities. They may all get upset, but the German Volk, not least German youth, demand protection for the national soul from these lowly forms of profiteering.[11]

When a respected leader like Reinhard Mumm made these kinds of stinging comments, he helped proliferate antisemitism and failed to realize that he provided a stamp of social approval that would ultimately benefit the Nazis. In a parliamentary debate on Schund on November 27, 1926, the Nazi delegate Wilhelm Kube wondered aloud if the intense arguments about Schund were a new form of Kulturkampf in Germany. His party strongly endorsed a tougher stand against Schund, adding that all youth movements, even the Jewish ones, opposed this low literature. Kube assessed colportage pamphlets as extremely dangerous and warned that they were undermining the middle class social order. He then berated Weimar's literary establishment for attacking what he called "a little harmless law."

In particular, he condemned the leftist writer Bernard von Brentano for provocatively labeling nationalist literature and cinema as the real Schund. He maintained that Brentano's categorizing of the memoirs of retired generals and popular movies about Frederick the Great as Schund was a demonstration of leftist intellectual disrespect for the nation and its great patriots. When leftist delegates jeered, Kube responded with a typically crude Nazi polemic, uttering, "One ought to photograph the gentlemen who are the worst hecklers, Dr. Levi, Rosenbaum, Dr. Löwenstein, Dr. Rosenfeld, and a few others. Then one could show the Volk why it ought to stand up for German literature."[12] While the Nazi delegates cheered Kube, a female delegate of the DDP, Toni Pfülf, called out, "These are cheap shots!"[13]

Kube's racist visualization of the Schund law opponents as a block of Jews elaborated Nazi imagery of a flaccid literary establishment in close allegiance with racially non-German or anti-German parliamentarians. The majority of Germany's leading writers had denounced the Schund law much to the chagrin of conservatives as well as Nazis. Kube let it be known that a large part of the German population had turned its back on such prestigious but patriotically unworthy writers like the members of the Prussian Academy.

Kube admonished the SPD for suspiciously asking why the churches were so interested in the passage of this law. By defending the churches' anti-<u>Schund</u> engagement, he cleverly reached out to the conservative and Catholic delegates, implying that they together with the Nazis formed a patriotic, moral force truly representing the national interest. The other side of this new <u>Kulturkampf</u> included effete literary snobs who had lost touch with the Volk, unpatriotic socialists, communists, Jews, and <u>Schund</u> capitalists. Kube said the SPD's position made no sense. They proposed to be against "trashy literature" but opposed the law to defend the population from it. Kube ridiculed the SPD concerns that the law might be abused and become an instrument for censoring literature that offended conservative political or religious forces. The Nazi delegate argued that these views were hypocritical and he complained that SPD policies, in various German states, had led to the harassment of nationalist causes and activities, like fraternity dueling.[14]

Kube concluded by stating the law simply sought to keep "the most base filth" away from German youth.[15] Hoping to build a political bridge to the churches and influential conservative delegates like Reinhard Mumm, the Nazi concluded: "We völkisch representatives say: thank God the majority of our Volk is Christian and opposes the undermining Jewish criticism which once again comes from the left side of the House."[16] The Nazis' uncompromising position against "trashy literature" must have impressed and drawn appreciation from "the father of the <u>Schund</u> law." This shared stand between Nazis and political exponents of Church views revealed an area of coinciding interests that presaged later Church and conservative cooperation and collusion with the Nazi regime. The new Kulturkampf of the 1920s and early 1930s was a three-way struggle between left, center, and right, with the Catholic and Protestant churches finding themselves on the same side with conservatives and Nazis, ostensibly defending morality in German society. Significantly, in this cultural conflict, the SPD showed its deep distrust for its erstwhile Catholic allies.

Communist delegate Edwin Hoernle adamantly opposed the <u>Schund</u> law and called it "a weapon of bourgeois class domination over the proletariat."[17] Hoernle declared that the proletariat would not accept that class's endeavor to choose "what was good or bad for proletarian youth." Even more so than Social Democrats, Communists were convinced the law would be used to stifle leftist publications. Hoernle explained that it was impossible to define <u>Schund</u> "in absolute and abstract" terms because it always depended on the class standpoint of the viewer.[18] He found the whole battle against "trashy literature" misconceived and misdirected: "The true source... of the brutalization [<u>Verrohung</u>] of youth, the reason why thousands go to ruin in today's society, is not the pair of little pamphlets that lie down there on the House table [sample copies of "trashy literature" were displayed during the debate]. To a much greater extent, the cause lies with those stylish magazines and their alluring pictures that only the dandies and members of high classes can afford to buy. No, the true source of the brutalization of thousands of youths lies in plight and poverty... in the terrible living conditions and unemployment."[19] Hoernle concluded his speech by saying that the new, rising class would not let the old ruling class impose its self-serving values and morality on them.

SPD delegate Rudolf Breitscheid reminded the parliament that a far more important cause for the brutalization of Germany's youth than "trashy literature" was the war. Breitscheid described the Schund law as doctoring around with symptoms "while failing to attack the root of the problem."[20] The law was misguided and full of contradictions. To prove his point, he asked how one could identify "trashy literature." He then quoted a number of passages from egregiously violent, sadistic stories that he had found in a newspaper. Everyone would agree that these were examples of "trashy literature." Yet the Schund law would not be able to index them because they appeared in a political daily, the Berliner Lokal-Anzeiger—a form of media not normally subject to censorship. His example was not only intended to show the weakness of the law, but also the hypocrisy of the conservatives. The sample newspaper happened to be part of conservative leader Alfred Hugenberg's media empire; its editorials had all been in favor of the Schund law. Kurt Löwenstein of the SPD declared that one could be against "trashy literature," but also against the Schund law. The SPD was very concerned about the inability to agree on a precise definition as to what constituted "trashy literature." Löwenstein's SPD colleague Max Seydewitz thought that the lack of a definition opened the law's application to an overly wide interpretation and to subjective decisions.[21] While the law painstakingly avoided a definition, the government had provided a possible one that Löwenstein believed would be followed by "a number of judges."[22] According to it, Schund was "writing of no artistic or scientific value produced for mass distribution, whose form and contents worked to coarsen and undermine morality. Writings that harmfully influenced the moral, spiritual, or physical development of youths or overstimulated their imagination." Löwenstein worried that "this definition was very flexible."[23]

As an example of how the law might be applied in an arbitrary fashion, Löwenstein referred to Carl Zuckmayer's popular 1925 play Der Fröhliche Weinberg (The Jolly Vineyard). While the play had received good reviews from the critics, its ridiculing of a small town, conservative milieu had drawn a harsh response from offended churches and nationalist parties. Löwenstein noted Reinhard Mumm's terrible indignation over this work and suggested that he and Mumm would disagree as to whether or not it should be put on a Schund index. Löwenstein also believed that the changing membership of the review boards could lead to capricious and contradictory decisions as to what ought to be indexed and what not. The determining factor would not be the law, but the momentary political composition of the board. Rudolf Breitscheid sarcastically commented that Artur Dinter's racist novel Die Sünde wider das Blut (The Sin Against the Blood, 1917) was "trashy literature" for the SPD, but the finest "blossom of literature" for the Nazis.²⁴ The unforeseeable consequences of the law made it impossible for the SPD to grant support, despite their disapproval of Schund.

Löwenstein also argued against the powerful endorsement given to the law by the young DDP delegate Theodor Heuss. His anti-Schund entreaty had received wide approval in the media. Heuss had insisted that the law was necessary and tried to win SPD support by reminding Social Democrats that among the earliest and most respected opponents of popular literature was Hamburg's SPD Schund expert Hermann Popert. Löwenstein insisted that the whole endeavor was misguided and he rejected Heuss's view (loudly cheered by the right) that a hypothetical welfare officer in working class Berlin was a greater authority on "trashy literature" than the entire Prussian Academy. Loewenstein said, "...we notice that people who work a lot with these things are infected by a kind of mania to guard against filthy publications and thus lose sight of all sorts of other dangers."²⁵ Löwenstein also pointed out how impractical and ineffective a law would be when review boards needed months to determine the Schund status of an installment novel. The novel's stock would have been sold out long before a decision was made.²⁶

Heuss had forcefully presented his case before the parliament and claimed to have read Schundliteratur: "I had the dubious pleasure... of reading through a pile of this literature... The nasty taste of it remained on my tongue for a week."²⁷ Heuss did not specify what he had read, nor (unfortunately) did any of the parliamentarians specify what titles actually lay among the samples on the Reichstag table in front of them. As Heuss continued his attack, he worked himself into a typical anti-Schund frenzy.

> The law is meant to hit a literature of the underworld. It is the widespread, cheap and poorly printed pamphlets circulating among school-age youth. It is not at all "immoral" in the ordinary sense of the term. It works immorally through its mendacious imagination, its inferior linguistic quality, its false heroism, and its contrived adventures. It encloses an unhealthy blurring of world realities and a confusion of ethical as well as taste values. If it does not sound too sentimental or full of pathos: there is not just a social politics of wage contracts, but there is also a social politics of the soul (Here Heuss's speech was cheered by delegates of the right and center). There is not only a physical, but also a spiritual exploitation.²⁸

Inadvertently, the democrat Heuss was pouring fuel into the right-wing fire. He was shifting the political focus to the right's favorite topic of the nation's moral crisis. Heuss's DDP colleague, Gertrud Bäumer, a few days later would try to incorporate socialist criticisms of the law by saying that "trashy literature" and social conditions together ruined youth's nerves and had a mind-numbing effect on how they perceived the world.[29] Heuss, stubbornly optimistic, envisioned a broad consensus gaining momentum in favor of the law: "A great many of my political friends view the whole procedure of drawing up of this law with considerable skepticism. They fear, after the embarrassing experiences of the past, that in this Volk torn by differences, it will be difficult to find an objective and calm way of reaching a verdict. They are worried about the meddling of the government in this sphere. I myself am not skeptical because all the different groups have already worked together on this matter."[30] Heuss was convinced that a consensus could be reached. Reinhard Mumm, in one of his first requests for the realization of a Schund law in 1919, had placed faith in a great cross-party coalition "of decent human beings."[31] Six years later, Mumm was still hoping for broad endorsement and quoted SPD Schundkämpfer Hermann Popert as preaching "it is absolutely necessary to pass a law that will oppose Schund capital."[32] Mumm, however, dropped his conciliatory overtures to the left when he got jeered by communist delegates. These he reflexively identified as representatives of "Jewish libertinism."[33] Mumm was convinced that the overwhelming majority of the German people were on his side and wanted the law passed.[34]

Helene Weber of the Center Party echoed the hopes and frustrations of the conservatives, and some moderates like Heuss and Bäumer, who could not understand why any party would dispute a law that only sought to protect society's most vulnerable age group. The worst experience for her in the Schund law conflict was "the mutual distrust" it revealed.[35] She discounted all the criticism focusing on the law's lack of a concise definition of "trashy literature." She trusted the good intentions of prospective review board members who would represent the will of the people in working out a concept that defined Schund. German youth alone, she warned, could not withstand the power of cheap media capitalism. Weber was dismayed by the appeal of many leading German writers and intellectuals to reject a law which, she felt, was so badly needed to fight "trashy literature."

The issue of artistic freedom, she argued, had to be placed in the larger framework of values dear to nation and society. Artistic freedom was neither unlimited nor did it signify the arbitrary acceptance of everything: "The Center Party does not pray to the idol of false artistic freedom."[36] She scolded intellectuals who failed to understand that art could only flourish if "it grew out of the roots of German Volkstum." Like the völkisch delegate Kube, she insisted that the intellectuals had alienated themselves from the people. They stood for "hyper-individualistic opinions severed from all ties of community [Gemeinschaftsverbindung]. How sad that they are loudly acclaimed in the circles of artists, thinkers, and academics! We reject an individualism that carries no communal sense of responsibility for the Volk or for our youth."³⁷ Weber felt that the leftist parties were not truly representing the interests of the population at large or their working class clientele and instead had become the spokesmen for egocentric intellectuals. She appealed to the left to stop blocking the law and join those in favor of what she called a new alliance of Christianity and humanism. The Center delegate said the moment had arrived to transcend party bickering and to do something together in the national interest. Instead of tearing the nation apart, the law should bring a new sense of common purpose. Finally, Weber expressed her desire to offer an olive branch to her opponents, proposing that as a woman and delegate from the political center, she viewed it as her role to be a peace-maker. The Schund law debate, in her eyes, had revealed a problem deeper than that of a struggle against bad literature. She wanted the parliamentary factions to overcome the seemingly unbridgeable gap between world views.

Weber's hopes were not fulfilled. Instead of a unifying consensus, she discerned political acrimony and entrenched positions, jeering and catcalls, a refusal to listen to the other side and an only limited effort to seek constructive compromises. She herself, however, showed little regard for the many serious and sensible objections to the law's possible abuses. Weber's interventions revealed the strains of debate and political conflict in the Reichstag. The "harmless, little law" had become a lightning rod attracting thunder bolts from all parties and the debate indicated vastly different ways of perceiving society's problems. On the surface it had first seemed that all parties wanted to fight "trashy literature." In the attempt to write a law, the deep fissures within Weimar politics and society made themselves more and more apparent. No unity or national consensus could be reached; suspicion and mistrust prevailed; perplexed moderate delegates like Weber and Heuss grew increasingly disheartened by the escalating conflict.

On November 26, 1926, the official sponsor of the law, DDP Minister of the Interior Wilhelm Külz (who, in friendly competition with Reinhard Mumm, also liked to be called the father of the Schund law) presented the government's position. Külz recapitulated the development of the law, noting wide-ranging political support from many sectors of society: welfare agencies, teacher associations, and youth organizations of all stripes. He bolstered his argument by referring to local state measures already taken by SPD governments in Saxony and Thuringia against Schund.³⁸ Külz argued it was everyone's moral duty to help stop the waves of "trashy literature" inundating Germany. He refuted leftist intellectual concerns about artistic freedom by using statistics from the film board's censorship work. 11,600 film reviews had led to the forbidding of a mere three hundred films. Külz admitted to the left that the banning of the famous Soviet film Battleship Potemkin (1925) had been a mistake.³⁹ Communists and Social Democrats had repeatedly used this case as an example of what could go wrong with the Schund law too.

But Külz argued that the low percentage of indexed films ought to assuage fears that the review boards would become bastions of "cultural reactionaries." The review boards, as well as the institutions proposing material for review were subject to parliamentary control and oversight, making it impossible for them to abuse the law. Külz sought to reassure writers and intellectuals by stressing that artistic works were not to be submitted for review, but only "the most repugnant manifestation of capitalism." These works were of no artistic value and "machine-produced by the ton and tossed into the population." Külz hoped his ingratiating, anti-capitalist rhetoric would move the left to support the law: "Not only politically, socially, and economically do we live in a time of great ferment. In this area of print media that pushes its way to youth, we live in a particularly chaotic situation. The mature man can find his path. The mature man can find his way around on his own, but there is no question that youth needs protection and guidance and this is what the law will give."[40]

The law finally passed on December 3, 1926. It pleased few. For the left, it meant another reversal, a step back into Germany's authoritarian past with dangers of creeping censorship. For the right, the law carried too many restrictions to combat "trashy literature" effectively and failed to include protective measures for adult readers. 248 delegates voted to pass the law and 158 opposed it. Supporting parties were the DNVP, DVP, the Wirtschaftsvereinigung, BVP, and the Völkisch Party. The 28 delegates of Külz's own party, the DDP, split into twelve votes for the law, fifteen against, and one abstention. Rudolf Breitscheid pointedly asked how could a minister sponsor a law that his own party did not unanimously back? He considered it inevitable that Külz would have to resign, for a parliamentary democracy's decisions had to be based on the will of the elected parties and not idiosyncratic policies made by individuals without a mandate.[41] The question remained hypothetical in this case as the coalition government led by Chancellor Wilhelm Marx collapsed (over a foreign policy matter) on December 17, 1926, a few days after the law was passed.

For fifteen years, Potsdam judge Albert Hellwig had closely followed the public debate about "trashy literature." He considered the law a step in the right direction, arguing that although problems like youth crime were part of larger social-economic challenges, it would be remiss if the government failed to take any measures against a morally corrosive force like Schund. The indefatigable and seemingly omnipresent Hellwig had supported legal action against psychic detectives and occultism because he felt government had an obligation to intervene against the forces of darkness. From his perspective, a largely ignorant public was being hoodwinked by sly and fraudulent occultist entrepreneurs. Hellwig viewed the battle against "trashy literature" from a similarly paternal position. It was the government's duty to shield the public from exploitative Schund publishers who

Chapter Three. The Schund Law: Defending Morality or Undermining Freedom? 109

capitalized on the lower class's and youth's need for distraction by enticing them to empty their pockets for lurid, discombobulating stories.

As in the debate about the validity of occultism, Hellwig took an unusually empirical approach to the problem. He carefully examined conjectures about an inevitable connection between reading "trashy literature" and committing crimes. Most conservatives repeated the claims linking Schund to youth crime over and over again, accepting and echoing the views of their Schundkampf allies and predecessors from the Wilhelmine age. Hellwig did not. As in his highly skeptical investigations of parapsychology's effectiveness in solving crime cases, Hellwig carefully checked the data. Court proceedings and newspaper articles claimed a causal link between youth reading habits and juvenile crime, but the Potsdam judge admitted that in fifteen years he had been unable to find a single case that convincingly showed a direct link.[42] Hellwig's intellectual honesty stood out in an age when excited, inflated opinions shaped public discourse, while hard facts were often overlooked or ignored.

He himself was dismayed by the facile acceptance of repetitive, unproven anecdotes by supporters of the Schund law, including his own judicial colleagues.[43] Still, despite the general overeagerness to accept hearsay rather than fact, Hellwig believed the opponents of "trashy literature" were fighting an elusive, yet real threat to society. Hellwig took a strongly conservative position complaining that the law should not only have been designed to protect youth but should have been extended to include the adult reading public too. In a legal commentary on the Schund law (Jugendschutz gegen Schundliteratur, 1927) published shortly after the law's passage, he reluctantly accepted the parameters established by the lawmakers. Hellwig's influential book argued for an interpretation focusing on what he called "ethical Schund" which he distinguished from "aesthetic Schund." He maintained that the actual intent of the law was to restrict writings that could harm the moral development of youth[44]. The law was not meant to set standards of literary taste. Hellwig realized that the law's omission of a definition of Schund was a serious flaw. It would be a source of difficulties and tempt some review boards to overextend themselves into imposing standards of literary taste. Decisions based on aesthetic, rather than ethical views would place the review boards in a quandary and open them up to harsh attacks from the media and anti-Schund law political forces that had predicted review board abuses. Hellwig cautioned the boards to restrict their index only to such literature that profited from "exploiting the most base mass instincts."[45] He tried to give historical force to his argument by stating that the popular movement against Schund was generated by a desire to fight morally corrosive literature, but not by an attempt to set aesthetic reading standards. Mixing these two elements, Hellwig feared, would only weaken the whole effort and make it vulnerable to attack from its detractors. Despite his caution, Hellwig also seemed to think there was a body of literature that could incontestably be labeled "trashy literature." The literature to be singled out was "the typical, unmistakeable Schundliteratur that was recognized by every reasonable person and that every ordinary citizen would condemn."⁴⁶

Hellwig vaguely described typical Schund as stories about Indians, highwaymen, criminals, detectives, soldiers, and also lascivious erotic tales [lascive Sittengeschichten]. Publishers were in tune with the changing taste of their readers and were quick to react to it. According to Hellwig, war stories, bloodthirsty Indian tales, brigand novels, and even Nick Carter thrillers were losing ground to romances.⁴⁷ He advised review boards not to make the mistake of simply concentrating on the genre most in fashion at the time, for the publishers were extremely supple in shifting to the latest popular topics. Hellwig used crime stories to illustrate the fact that any subject in itself could be handled either appropriately or inappropriately. How the writer processed the material would determine whether or not it deserved to be classified as "trashy literature:" "For the manufacturer of Schund crime stories, the crime is an end in itself. He details all the gory horror of it. There is no interest in the psychological motivation for the deed or in any higher artistic idea."⁴⁸ Agreeing with Schund opponents, Hellwig felt that the continual reading of pulp literature could lead to a worsening of a reader's moral sensibilities because it "whipped up the senses" while blurring concepts of right and wrong.⁴⁹

Hellwig admired and was influenced by the scholarly work of his Leipzig colleague Walter Hoffmann, juvenile court judge and author of Die Reifezeit [Adolescence, 1922]. In Hoffmann, Hellwig found a fellow mandarin seeking to protect what he perceived as weak, uneducated social groups. Foremost were youths whose emotional immaturity or mental vulnerability made them easy victims of Schund, as well as potential threats to the bourgeois social order. Referring to Hoffmann's work, Hellwig suggested that "the printed word serves to convey a collective rhythm to a larger circle of readers. While that literature whose line of thought is in harmony with the dominant culture seeks to have a positive social effect, Schundliteratur leads into a world of ideas ruled by a completely contrary rhythm. In accordance with the law of psychological resonance [seelische Resonanz], the child's life rhythm will thus be negatively influenced. The degree of this influence will vary according to how powerfully his imagination is excited."⁵⁰

Hellwig pointed out that there were other types of dangerous literature besides Schund. Pseudoscientific publications in the realms of popular medicine and superstition were mentioned. He bemoaned the fact that large segments of the population were superstitious and prone to exploitation by clever occultist writers. This type of "trashy literature" deserved special attention and countermeasures, but Hellwig thought it should not be subsumed under the new law. The writings of quacks and charlatans had dangerous effects "not in the moral realm, but in the intellectual one," and, he added, they were of no interest to youth.⁵¹ What Hellwig did not realize (and this showed that he did not bother to read "trashy literature") was that occultist themes and questions had already been incorporated into the mainstream of many colportage novels, as well as the detective dime series. Pinkert, who had briefly managed an occultist publishing house, was one colportage writer who liked to spice up his stories with occultist episodes.

Hellwig warned the Schund law's supporters not to expect too much from the application of the law. Following Hoffmann's multi-causal paradigm for explaining juvenile crime, he maintained that "trashy literature" was only one of many factors influencing youth crime and certainly not primary.⁵² In the past, Hellwig admitted, "trashy literature" had become a scapegoat blamed too easily for being the cause behind an unsettling rise in youth crime.⁵³ More significant was the role of the family and the fact that some parents failed to live up to their "educational duties."⁵⁴

Agreeing with leftist politicians, Hellwig believed problems of the urban environment like overcrowding, unemployment, and exposure to criminal milieus, were far more important in provoking youth crime. For youths who grew up in good surroundings and benefitted from normal social and educational development, Hellwig thought the risks from "trashy literature" were minimal.⁵⁵ This sober view was rejected by the majority of fervid Schundkämpfer for whom the battle had become a national crusade.

Thus, the objective, reasonable Prussian judge and opponent of "trashy literature" found himself in the unsettling company of many fanatics whose repetitive appeals and exaggerated claims disturbed him. Yet his concept of himself as a guardian of culture and as a protector of young or poorly educated and exploited readers made him embrace a law that at least showed government concern and willingness to take action. Hellwig had also been involved in the early creation of laws aimed to eliminate the excesses of uncensored movies.

Bevormundung [tutelage] was not a dirty word for Hellwig. To him it was guardianship and tutelage, a civic duty of the state on behalf of the weak, uneducated, and poor. Hellwig's paternal views on "trashy literature" fit smoothly with his mandarin role as an upholder of the accepted code of morality and as defender of a cultural hegemony embodied by the Bildungsbürgertum. Not all of Weimar's educated class was part of this conservative block. Weimar society also included liberal journalists at the Frankfurter Zeitung like Wolfgang Petzet and Siegfried Kracauer. These had a view of Bevormundung very different from Hellwig's. For them, it was a residue from Wilhelmine times, an anachronism in a modern democracy. Bevormundung was not responsible, paternal oversight but patronizing interference in the rights of adults and citizens. They did not want to be told by the state what books they could read or what movies they could watch. In a 1931 article, Kracauer objected to the film review board's capricious censoring of films.⁵⁶ He scoffed at recent decisions like the censorship of the innocuous film D-Zug 13 hat

Verspätung (Express Train 13 is Delayed) which, according to the review board, endangered public safety and could induce someone to seek to assassinate the German President. "Instead of intervening only in extreme cases," Kracauer complained, "the [board] determines to take it upon itself to tell a mature nation what it can and cannot see." [Statt nur in den äussersten Fällen einzuschreiten, nimmt sie sich faktisch das Recht heraus, ein reifes Volk zu bevormunden.][57] Where the conservative Hellwig saw a gullible, easily manipulated population requiring governmental supervision and guidance, the liberal Kracauer imagined responsible adults and a competent citizenry whose freedom was threatened by government interference.

Discussing the validity of censorship in his Verbotene Filme: Eine Streitschrift (Forbidden Films: a Polemic, 1931), Wolfgang Petzet thought that the terrible influence of colportage on youths was vastly exaggerated, especially when compared to factors like social milieu and personality. Petzet wondered if "crude, but rather harmless things" were being forbidden, while more truly dangerous influences were allowed to pass: "Especially, one could argue about the review boards conduct towards hidden nationalist propaganda."[58] As an example, he referred to the early sound film Die Melodie des Herzens (The Melody of the Heart, 1929). In it, a young officer is shocked when he finds his girlfriend working in a brothel. Having been disowned from her parents for coming home late, she had ended up in the brothel as a place of last resort. Deeply ashamed when her suitor discovers where she lives, she decides to drown herself. Petzet found the melodramatic film full of double standards, false military conventions, and outworn ideas of honor. He believed the nationalist content of such films was far more nefarious than the censored movies of the immediate postwar period, which closely resembled the colportage stories printed in "the ten penny pamphlets with their gory covers and poor quality paper."[59]

Reform-minded educators were another group who rejected the establishment of review boards. One of the founders of the Bund entschiedener Schulreformer (Federation of Determined School Reformers), Paul Oestreich questioned their purpose and accomplishments in his 1931 article "Schutz der Jugend vor Schund und Schmutz?" ("Protection of Youth from Trashy and Filthy Literature?"). Oestreich thought that the application of the Schund law had, after four years, led to a sense of resignation among its proponents. The boards had failed to establish clear boundaries defining "trashy literature" and were spinning their wheels in a senseless endeavor.[60]

Oestreich believed that it was impossible to determine objectively the influence of "trashy literature." At most, he felt, it could have deleterious effects on youths who were exposed to various deeper troubles: unemployment, a sense of meaninglessness, or a radical political indoctrination. Far more deleterious than Schund, was the Nazi influence on youth: "The murderous plague among political youth leagues, particularly the followers of the National Socialist Party, is certainly not a consequence of reading Schund literature, despite the fact that the 'perpetrators" have read Schund! But which reading material would deserve to be labeled and persecuted as Schund and Schmutzliteratur in this case? The Völkischer Beobachter with its irresponsible reports or the book of Ernst von Salomon [a reference to Salomon's autobiographical Die Geächteten, 1930, in which he glorifies his Freikorps exploits]? The inspirational writings of the nationalists or the Fridericius films?"[61]

Oestreich raised an important question. How relevant was it to monitor the contents of popular literature when a major political party openly encouraged youths to defy the law and engage in daily violence against its political opponents and the Republic? "The inflammatory daily newspaper reports, the incessant coverage of horrific events, the plague of uniformed youth demonstrations is definitely more trashy and filthy than the literature (justifiably condemned for its tastelessness) of a certain type," he wrote.[62] Considering the tension and conflicts taking place all over Germany in 1931, often involving radicalized youth, it seemed ludicrous to Oestreich that a government agency should persist in pursuing pulp literature as a source of youth misbehavior. Oestreich's article appeared in the liberal journal Die Stimme der Freiheit (The Voice of Freedom) which adopted a highly critical view of the Schund law and saw itself as a watchdog guarding the freedom of the press.

A supporter of the Bund entschiedener Schulreformer, child psychoanalyst Siegfried Bernfeld was another opponent of the Schund law. He argued that the battle against "trashy literature" was an entirely misconceived enterprise conducted by adults who failed to understand the connection between maturation and imagination. Bernfeld believed the Schundkämpfer mistakenly exchanged cause and effect. Youths did not first read "trashy literature" and then act on these fantasies. Instead, they had fantasies and urges that Schund provided an outlet for. According to Bernfeld, the reading of such literature marked a normal stage in the child's development from play with toys to imaginary "play," an advance in which the individual learned to distinguish between fantasy and reality. In a 1926 article, "Das Kind braucht keinen Schutz vor Schund! Es schützt sich selbst!" ("The Child Does Not Need Protection from Trashy Writings! It Protects Itself!"), Bernfeld explained: "Oh horror, what does the child choose to read with fervor? Crime and the victory of virtue, adventure and murder, wild and sentimental, sweet kitsch and warm tears, in short: trashy and filthy writings! The child reads what we call bad books (and like to read ourselves). The child reads what we call good books (and we sometimes find boring). However the adult judges the book, whether he values it as art, or condemns it as Schund, has nothing to do with its suitability for fostering the development of the child's psyche. Sometimes this happens through books that we do not like to see in the child's hands. Sometimes it fails to happen through books that we force him to read. Our taste is not the point here."⁶³

Normally, Bernfeld continued, the child eventually outgrows its taste for "trashy literature" and moves on to more sophisticated reading. But, in numerous cases, psychological development and literary taste remain stuck at this rudimentary level. There is no danger that such individuals develop into criminals, Bernfeld concluded: "Reading does not even minimally lead astray into action. Rather it is the substitute for the already overcome impulses of infantile aggression. It is the means to prevent the actualization of repressed offensive impulses in that these, pale and distorted enough, are given satisfaction in the realm of the imagination."⁶⁴ This psychoanalytic view presented a radically contrary position to that of the Schundkämpfer, who had argued for three decades that "trashy literature" was pure poison for youth and society, eliciting dangerous forms of juvenile deviance.

In an article in the Berliner Tageblatt of December 11, 1926, journalist Stefan Grossmann discussed the psychoanalytic view that Schund offered a type of safety valve releasing the pent-up aggressions of its readers. This new, unorthodox view of Schund immediately drew an angry, typically crude response from the Nazi press, which labeled it a Jewish provocation. The Völkische Wacht signaled Grossmann out as a Jew and sarcastically commented that filthy literature might be a necessity for Jewish youth, but certainly not for Germans: "It almost leaves one speechless, when one reads the views of this Jewish swine [Judensau]. In other words, it means: because I, the Jew, feel great when I roll around in the mud, so this must be the case too for the German."⁶⁵ Instead of engaging the Schund defenders in dialogue, the Nazis resorted to racial slander and their own defamatory brand of trashy writing.

In two cases Nazi or völkisch publications came up for review by the boards. Düsseldorf's youth agency submitted an article about a supposed case of child molestation published in the Westdeutscher Beobachter on September 9, 1928. The article followed a formulaic pattern established by Julius Streicher's notoriously racist Nürnberg paper Der Stürmer which, throughout the 1920s and 1930s, crudely portrayed Jews as innately perverse and sexually dangerous. The Westdeutscher Beobachter article describes a Jewish employee of the Tietz Department Store who lures a nine year-old girl to come visit the toy display. On the back stairs, he molests the child. She runs home and tells her father. He notifies the police, the perpetrator is arrested, and Director Tietz (himself a Jew) conspires to hush up the affair by offering the father a bribe to remain silent.⁶⁶ The article concludes by recommending Artur Dinter's Die Sünde wider das Blut as enlightening reading on the issue of racial blood pollution. It also applauds Der Stürmer's success in framing other supposed Jewish child molesters and opening the populations eyes to Jewish depredation. Accompanying the story was an illustration that particularly irritated the Berlin Review Board because it showed the man reaching under the girl's skirt while she cries out.

The board recognized the fact that the Weimar Constitution explicitly protected the political press but rejected the Nazi publisher's position that, on this account alone, all of the paper's contents were off-limits to the board's purview. It determined that the article and the picture together did indeed merit the label of <u>Schmutz</u> [filth]. They did not, however, deem the article a danger to youth because the specific edition had long since disappeared from the market. Thus, they voted not to index it because it was no longer in circulation.

Düsseldorf's youth agency appealed the decision to Leipzig, arguing that the law intended to index any published material endangering youth. Berlin's decision, the agency maintained, made no sense because it gave a green light to all newspapers to publish whatever they wanted, knowing full well that they would not be cited on account of the time lapse between publication and a possible board review. The agency pointed out that "a change in tone and presentation of a periodical could only be reached if past, out-of-print issues were placed on the <u>Schundliste</u>."[67] While Leipzig agreed that the article's contents were filthy, they accepted Berlin's reasoning and rejected the appeal. <u>Schund</u> expert Hans Wingender asked, "Is this really the intent of the law? I think the decision is legally incorrect."[68] The case, he felt, established a deleterious precedent, making it virtually impossible for the review boards to censure youth-endangering filth and trash in the daily press.

The publisher of Ellegaard Ellerbek's <u>Der Herr des Lebens</u> (Die Sünde wider den Samen) (The Master of Life [The Sin Against Semen], 1923), like the Nazi publisher of the <u>Westdeutscher Beobachter</u>, argued that its book could not be censured because it represented a political viewpoint. The Munich Review Board agreed that the Weimar Constitution protected freedom of expression, but they explained that the law "did not establish a privilege for world view authors to express themselves in a literary form that fit the case of trashy or filthy writing."[69] Citing various sadistic and sacrilegious passages from the book, the board was appalled and disgusted by Ellerbek's sustained attack on Protestantism, Catholicism, and Judaism. They labeled it as a type of particularly reprehensible filth that endangered youth by claiming to stand for the ideals of national resurgence. This was a rare instance of a review board taking a firm stand against radical right-wing literature. It is likely that the Munich Board acted decisively because Ellerbek's hostility to Christians equaled his hatred for Jews. If he had limited himself to writing an antisemitic diatribe, the work would probably have made it past the reviewers as a manifestation of an acceptable political perspective [<u>Tendenz</u>].

Liberal and leftist critics of the <u>Schund</u> law liked to point out how much heinous and deplorable writing appeared in Weimar's daily newspapers which usually escaped the scrutiny of the boards. <u>Die Stimme der Freiheit</u> compared the supposedly objectionable content of the colportage novel Giuseppe Musolino, der kühnste und verwegenster Jäger seiner Zeit (Giuseppe Musolino, the Boldest and most Wreckless Hunter of his Time, 1926) to crime stories in a Berlin daily. The anonymous reporter for the liberal journal noted, "We have the 'novel' before us. The usual kitsch. The usual source of pleasure [Freudenspender] for servant girls, washer women, farmhands, lumberjacks, and wagon drivers."[70] The Berlin Review Board complained that Giuseppe Musolino contained passages of "sadistic cruelty." The novel's cynicism, according to the board, could have a morally corrupting influence on youths. The reporter scoffed at this opinion and found far greater sadism and cynicism in a series of articles entitled "The Werewolf of Düsseldorf," published in a Berlin newspaper. Here a girl's futile struggle against a rapist is described at length. In another part of the series, a murder victim's injuries, the stab wounds and damaged organs, are graphically described. The reporter for Die Stimme der Freiheit called the articles "a guideline for Lustmord [sex murder]" and considered these uncensored reports, which normally did not fall under the scrutiny of the review boards, good examples of truly cynical, sadistic writing.[71] He contrasted them with the "overwrought, boring descriptions in the popular tomes" and recommended that the particularly zealous board member Franz Hecker take note.

That review board decisions made little sense was further proven, Die Stimme der Freiheit argued, by comparing the indexing of Giuseppe Musolino with the decision not to index Rinaldo Rinaldini, a similar colportage novel about an eighteenth century highwayman. The Berlin Review Board believed the time and setting of Rinaldo Rinaldini precluded a dangerous influence on youth: "It takes place in a setting other than that of reality, in a land completely removed and unreal for youth, and in a time period endlessly distant from the present. It seems impossible that the reading of these fantastic occurrences could have repercussions on the development of today's youth."[72] If this was the case, then how could a similar-narrative like Giuseppe Musolino present a threat to juvenile morals? Such glaring contradictions underlined the uselessness of the entire Schund law endeavor according to Die Stimme der Freiheit. The journal thus reiterated a viewpoint that had already been made by the law's fiercest critics in the parliamentary debates preceding the law's ratification. These two diametrically opposed colportage verdicts for the same type of novel seemed to prove that the decisions were indeed highly subjective and arbitrary.

While neither proponents nor opponents were pleased with the Schund law's results, colportage publishers and writers were forced to adapt to the exigencies of the new law. Their jobs depended on finding a modus vivendi with the review boards. The publishers of Giuseppe Musolino, the Mignon Publishing House of Dresden, had edited away the most provocative scenes in the vain hope that the Schund examiners would consider it acceptable. They tried the same strategy with

Sonja oder um Liebe willen unschuldig verbannt (Sonja, or Mistakenly Banned on Account of Love, 1926).
This was another colportage novel written by the same author as Musolino, Viktor von Falk (pen name for Heinrich Sochaczewsky). Von Falk was one of the most popular and prolific colportage authors around the turn of the century. The Berlin Review Board indexed this novel too on February 11, 1930. The reviewers criticized the book for being full of clichés. The significant historical figure Michael Bakunin was reduced to "a backstreet conspirator, meant to satisfy primitive sensational needs."[73] Although they recognized the fact that a pre-revolutionary Russian setting would, by necessity, include some descriptions of violence, the reviewers felt the author had gone overboard in depicting gory and sadistic scenes of torture and violence.

The board also found it necessary to index the novel because the multiple descriptions of cruelties could overexcite the youthful imagination in an unhealthy manner.[74] Günter Kosch and Manfred Nagl, in their introductory overview to the history of German colportage, show how Mignon's editors modified the text, removing the juicier parts. Kosch and Nagel note that what was tolerated in Wilhelmine times, fell to the censor's axe in the supposedly liberal Weimar Republic.[75] The Weimar review boards, in fact, expressed the accumulated hostility of four decades of anti-Schund struggle by teachers, clergymen, youth welfare officials, and numerous organizations founded to rid the reading market of "trashy literature." The Schundkämpfer dreamed of a print world freed from sensual titillation, melodramatic adventure, and egregious violence. Colportage had flourished in its golden age in the latter half of the nineteenth century. What had freely proliferated in a mass market in 1900, a quarter of a century later had to face cross-examination by the stern members of the review boards. Thus Viktor von Falk, trademark for exciting literature among underprivileged readers of Wilhelmine Germany, became an excoriated writer in the Weimar Republic. Von Falk's novels Giuseppe Musolino, Sonja, and Vertrieben am Hochzeitsabend (originally published in 1913 and re-issued in 1927), held a claim to notoriety as all three were placed among the first one hundred publications appearing on the official list of Schund und Schmutzschriften. Notwithstanding their failed efforts to clean up and get Viktor von Falk's Giuseppe Musolino and Sonja past the review boards' inspection, Mignon managed to keep most of its colportage production off the Schund list. They published eighteen of these giant volumes during the interwar period. Only four were placed on the index: the two new editions of Viktor von Falk's potboilers, and two Weimar works by Ellmar Pfeil (another prolific author who even outdid Pinkert by writing eight colportage novels for Mignon between 1924 and 1933).

The Berlin, Munich, and Leipzig review board decisions were made in secret meetings and were explained in brief one to three-page announcements. These decisions contained important information for colportage publishers and writers.

What were the red flags that surely led to indexing? Were there any redeeming qualities that would help make a colportage novel more acceptable to the arbiters of parliament's anti-<u>Schund</u> mandate? One key to understanding the review boards' behavior and pattern of response was their concept of "impressionable, easily influenced youth" [labile Jugend]. Whatever they found in a novel that could adversely affect this fabricated cohort would surely lead to a negative verdict. The indexing of the novel <u>Ohne Ring und Myrte</u> (<u>Without Ring or Myrtle</u>, 1910, republished c.1925) was a case in point. Another recycled Wilhelmine potboiler, the Berlin Review Board issued a damning opinion about this book: "The intellectual-moral development of youth is primarily endangered in this novel by the fact that evil people can do their deeds undisturbed in a seeming vacuum. The impressionable, less gifted part of youth must come to the conclusion through such reading that, in actuality, the common criminal, protected by magic powers, can succeed in fighting and ruining society. The foundation of public life can be destroyed by criminals blessed with extraordinary powers."[76] In addition, the reviewers discovered "a sadistic undertone" in the descriptions of endless crimes and cruelties.[77] Love themes were handled in a distorted, untruthful manner. The board concluded that reading material of this kind "acted like opium" and confused the feelings and consciousness of a defenseless youth.[78] The colportage novel <u>Heimlich getraut oder die Privatsekretärin des Eisenkönigs</u> (<u>Secretly Betrothed or the Private Secretary of the Iron King</u>, 1924) was another case in point. After a litany of complaints about the novel's style and impossible plot, the board condemned the book for endangering the moral development of an "impressionable youth."[79]

The Munich Review Board decided not to censure <u>Hanna die Prinzessin von der Landstrasse</u> (<u>Hanna, Princess of the country Road</u>, c. 1925) in what it considered a borderline case: "Purely by appearances the work would seem to be the same as other novels put on the list... the layout, paper, and print are bad: factory ware. The contents, however, differentiate it from indexed volumes."[80] The Munich reviewers, by closely examining and actually reading colportage novels, discovered that colportage did not automatically equate with "trashy literature," a position that probably puzzled politicians and public alike. In the case of Hanna, the board argued that the story actually warned "impressionable youth" to avoid committing crimes: "the reader sees with frightening clarity that no crime goes unpunished."[81] Was the Munich Board suggesting that colportage could have an educational value? Such a view contradicted all received knowledge and would rarely be mentioned in decisions favorable to colportage novels. Usually the board decisions in favor of a novel would stamp it as a borderline case just barely acceptable, and leave it at that.

A basic premise of the <u>Schund</u> law, according to the Munich Review Board was that the writing had to endanger the youthful reader to warrant its addition to the list. It would go against the lawmakers' intent to list a work only because it was

Chapter Three. The <u>Schund</u> Law: Defending Morality or Undermining Freedom?

judged "inferior" or "worthless." Over and over again, the parliamentarians had declared that legally defined <u>Schund</u> was an industrial product that for the purpose of profit caused a mass poisoning among German youth. "Its sole purpose was to appeal to the raw instincts of human nature. For <u>Hanna</u> this definitely was not the case," concluded the Munich reviewers.[82] Interestingly, the board sought to bolster its verdict by referring to Hellwig's position that it was not the job of the review boards to implement a "censorship of taste" and that it was wiser to err in favor of a book in borderline cases.[83] The Munich Board's decision was a conscientious effort to distinguish harmless from harmful colportage. By not placing all colportage in the same <u>Schund</u> basket, this review board was advancing into unknown territory. Unlike most <u>Schundkämpfer</u>, they actually read the books and were distinguishing contents between one book and another. For colportage's vociferous and prejudiced opponents, these novels were all the same and deserved the same fate. In allowing the majority of colportage novels to stay off the index list, the review boards were defying the alliance that had created them and which had gathered hegemonic force over a period of thirty years. The conflict was made apparent when review boards complained that they were being inundated by titles indiscriminately submitted by overly zealous youth agencies. Situated between disappointed conservative <u>Schundkämpfer</u> and vigilant liberal opponents of the <u>Schund</u> law, Weimar's review boards tried to fulfill their difficult mission. The trickiness of the task was revealed in stern advice to the Heilbronn publisher of <u>Hanna</u>. After determining, seemingly to its own surprise, that <u>Hanna</u> did not merit a place on the list, the Munich Board warned the publisher that its decision was based solely on review of the novel's first twenty-two installments. Should the author change direction by glorifying evil or allowing its triumph over virtue in coming installments, the board could reconsider its decision.[84]

The review boards liked to take this admonitory role. It was more than a mere gesture of power. They knew that publishers were eager to avoid censure; thus they sought to steer and influence the direction of colportage writing and they achieved some success. If publishers conformed to their guidelines, review boards would (usually somewhat grudgingly) tolerate their endeavors to satisfy the needs of what they condescendingly called the "primitive reading classes." The Berlin Review Board, for example, acknowledged the Mignon Publishing House's <u>Der Liebestraum des Maharadscha</u> (*The Maharaja's Love Dream*, 1925) for "integrating certain culturally interesting descriptions into the plot." The board found "that one could not fail to appreciate the fact that the novel could serve to entertain primitive readers."[85]

In early 1930, Württemberg's Ministry of Labor and Welfare submitted Ernst Friedrich Pinkert's <u>Knute und Fessel</u> for addition to the <u>Schund</u> list. The submission was rejected in Berlin on February 25, 1930, despite the board's many reservations about the book. The board did not like the "contrasting and primitive" portrayal of characters: "As usual, nothing but evildoers and paragons of virtue."[86] The style was criticized as "extremely simple" and the story contained the usual "cases of mistaken identity, assassinations, kidnappings, and robberies," but also included the descriptions of some historical events, like Bloody Sunday in Petersburg, that "reveal a certain skill of reportage."[87] The reviewers did not like the book's "crassness" but, on the other hand, were pleased that it did not linger on events in Siberia where some colportage writers liked to dwell on "describing selected cruelties."[88] The reviewers concluded that the book was not of "extreme inferior quality" [äusserster Minderwertigkeit] and was "suited to satisfy the entertainment needs of primitive readers."[89] Pinkert, after having his first colportage novel Grossstadtmädel indexed, had learned to tone down the lurid writing to the point where it became acceptable for the Schund reviewers.

Weimar's colportage writers had to avoid the garish sensationalism that characterized Wilhelmine colportage but also needed to be careful not to lose those elements of excitement and tension that made them so popular with their condescendingly labeled "primitive readers." Not all writers were as adroit as Pinkert in finding just the right ingredients to be successful and to avoid censure by the review boards. Some erred on the side of "trash" and were indexed, while others were not sensational enough to attract or hold the interest of the targeted readers.

Two examples serve to illustrate these different types of failure. Mignon Publishers told the Berlin Review Board that they considered their colportage novel Rasputin (1932) a failure. Only 3,000 copies were printed and few sold. The board, in its decision report, noted that the novel operated in the usual "black-and-white manner." It could not be evaluated by the same criteria as for books "designated for educated people."[90] After the board decided not to index Rasputin, the Berlin Youth Office appealed the decision to the Superior Board in Leipzig. The Leipzig reviewers characteristically took a harder line than Berlin, describing Rasputin as "a bloodless, purely industrial piece of junk" [ein blutleeres, rein industrielles Machwerk], whereby the publisher tried to hook customers into buying the installments by means of endless suspense and "cheap thrills" [Nervenkitzel].[91] Yet the installments failed to deliver what they promised or what was needed to keep readers interested from the first pamphlet all the way to the one hundredth. In the end, the Leipzig Superior Board agreed with Berlin against indexing because, over all, the book was "harmless" and could hardly influence or even attract youths on "account of its boring content."[92]

The second type of failure is illustrated by the Marien Publishing House's Der "Fetzer," Deutschlands grösster Räuberhauptmann (The "Fetzer," Germany's Greatest Highwayman, c. 1928). This publisher had managed to avoid censure by review boards for its colportage novels with the sole exception of Pinkert's Grossstadtmädel. In a 1926 advertisement for the colportage novel Madame du Barry in the magazine Buch und Zeitschriftenhandel, the Marien Publishing

House announced that the novel was produced with the utmost care regarding the proposed Schund law.⁹³ Yet such public obeisance apparently did not mean that the publisher would refrain from trying to slip some coarse, old-fashioned potboilers past the overworked Schund boards. It seems like Marien got away with renaming Grossstadtmädel and selling it, in a slightly modified form, as Mädchenhändler. Passing off an indexed publication under a new name was expressly forbidden by the new law, but, in this case, it appears that the ploy succeeded. This publisher was not so lucky with Der "Fetzer," Deutschlands grösster Räuberhauptmann.

Their colportage version of the highwayman Matthias Weber's (1778-1803) story was submitted for review by Berlin's youth agency. The board was irritated by the careless, anachronistic writing that placed telephones, smoke bombs, and hand grenades in an eighteenth century setting.⁹⁴ It described the narrative as utterly chaotic. When discussing the highwayman's antisemitic views (in actual history, many of Weber's robbery victims were Jewish merchants in the Rhineland), the Berlin Review Board took a typical position. It stipulated that it could not attack the book on account of antisemitism for this was a Tendenz, a perspective, or political viewpoint protected by law.⁹⁵ But it could reproach the book for expressing a Tendenz in an outspokenly trashy (schundig) manner. Brutal and sadistic cruelties could not be condoned, whether political or not. In one episode, a Jew is tied to a horse's tail and dragged away. In another disgusting, misogynistic episode, a noble woman is stripped, tied to a tree, and whipped. This scene smacked of "sexual lechery" [sexueller Lüsternheit], an ingredient common to Wilhelmine colportage, but a red flag for Weimar's review boards and a reason for labeling a book as filth rather than trash.⁹⁶ Finally, the ostensible noble-mindedness [Edelmut] of the highwayman starkly contrasted with his actions. This could cause "a confusion of feelings" in the reader. For the Berlin Review Board, Der "Fetzer" was an unquestionable case of "trashy literature" and almost qualified for the rarely given label of "filthy literature" [Schmutz].⁹⁷ Had the Marien Publishing House risked distribution of this novel and thrown caution to the winds in a gamble to regain readers demanding old-fashioned spice and disenchanted with the dull tomes approved by the review boards?

Between colportage that was unpalatable to the review boards, like Der "Fetzer," or unappealing to readers, like Rasputin, stood the novels that succeeded in finding that middle ground where censure was avoided, but the contents still managed somehow to appeal to enough of Weimar's readers of popular literature to make it a profitable publishing investment. The Berlin Review Board found that the crime scenes in Süsse kleine Friedel (Sweet Little Friedel, 1929) were not bloodthirsty or offensive. The story did not let romantic elements overstep the boundary of propriety into eroticism, nor did it present crimes in a manner that would elicit imitation. Although the reviewers could hardly recommend the book to young readers, they also could find no reason for indexing it, and they rather liked its restraint.⁹⁸

How difficult it was to predict review board reactions was made clear in the case of the colportage novel Regina (c.1928). After lambasting the novel for having a senseless plot based solely on suspense and the writer's shifting moods, the Berlin Review Board managed a rare and remarkable word of praise for a colportage publisher (Verlagshaus Freya): "It cannot be denied that the publisher has made an effort, not only in outward appearance, but also by avoiding provocative crassness or indecent scenes, in improving the genre of the installment novel."⁹⁹ The more conservative Leipzig Superior Board did not see this at all and rejected Berlin's seal of approval for Regina. It indexed the novel for "strongly endangering youth."¹⁰⁰ Such glaring reversals gave further credence to those who had argued all along that Schund board decisions would be purely subjective, inconsistent, and lacking in substance.

3.1 An antisemitic illustration in the installment novel Der Fetzer

3.1 Censorship boards forbade installment novels that depicted sadism. The Marien Verlag overstepped the limits with an unusual colportage scene of antisemitic violence. Highwaymen threaten to cut an orthodox Jew's beard in *Der Fetzer* (Leipzig: Marien Verlag, c.1928), Figure 31.

Alois Haspinger's Die Wildschützen der tiroler Grenze (The Poachers of the Tyrolean Border, 1922) suffered the same fate as Regina. The Berlin Review Board considered it a typical installment novel in which hero and heroine were exposed to innumerable crimes and misfortunes, and always saved in "the most unbelievable manner." A "trite factory product" deserving the stigma of "literary worthlessness" and condemned as <u>Schund</u> "in the sense of the law."[101] But the Berlin Board decided against indexing it because the novel avoided "crass, ugly scenes," "the glorification of crime," or "scenes of lechery."[102] The Leipzig Superior Board reversed the decision for the same reason that it gave for indexing <u>Regina</u>: tersely and bluntly it announced that it considered both novels serious dangers to youth.[103]

In the summer of 1929, on the initiative of the Prussian Welfare Ministry, the study <u>Was liest unsere Jugend? (What Does Our Youth Read?</u> 1930) was undertaken to determine if the review boards were examining literature that youths and children were actually reading. Hertha Siemering's contribution to the essay collection modestly noted that the official study amounted to little more than spot checks and random samplings because youth and welfare agencies, as well as schools, were not trained to collect data and unsure how to define "trashy literature." Further confusion was revealed in the discrepancy between schools that reported their pupils did not read "trashy literature," while local youth agencies claimed that they did.[104]

Siemering noted dryly that "a suitable method for ascertaining the spread of <u>Schund</u> has not yet been found."[105] Notwithstanding these caveats, she proceeded to discuss the results of the responses to the investigation. In the category of colportage, Siemering discovered that indexed and approved novels were all circulating among juvenile readers, as well as novels not yet submitted for review: "The restricting influence of the <u>Schund</u> list has had little effect so far."[106] Thus the indexed <u>Musolino</u> and <u>Die schöne Krankenschwester</u> were being read, along with tolerated colportage, like Pinkert's <u>Schwarze Natascha</u> and <u>Knute und Fessel</u>.[107] While Pinkert's romance fiction, and many of the other colportage works listed in Siemering's study, were mainly geared for a female audience, a number of texts belonged to the subgenre of "highwayman novels" which were slanted more to a mixed male and female audience.

These <u>Räuberromane</u> had a long pedigree going back to Friedrich Schiller's drama <u>Die Räuber</u> (1781), Heinrich Zschokke's <u>Abaellino, der grosse Bandit</u> (<u>Abaellino, the Great Bandit</u>, 1793), and Christian August Vulpius's early bestseller <u>Rinaldo Rinaldini, der Räuber Hauptmann (Rinaldo Rinaldini, Captain of the Highwaymen</u>, 1799). The real highwayman Schinderhannes, who was guillotined in 1803 by French authorities in Mainz, was the subject of revived interest in the Weimar Republic. Clara Viebig's popular novel <u>Unter dem Freiheitsbaum</u> (<u>Under the Liberty Tree</u>, 1922) was followed by the play <u>Schinderhannes</u> (1927), by Carl Zuckmayer, Weimar's most successful playwright. Zuckmayer said that he wrote his melodrama as an antithesis to the plays of <u>Neue Sachlichkeit</u>. The drama was transformed into a movie in 1928. In the summer of 1929, 40,000 spectators attended the open-air performances of dialect author Wilhelm Reuter's Schinderhannes, de rheinisch Räuwerschelm (Schinderhannes, the Rhineland Robber-rogue). The play was staged near Frankfurt, in Vockenhausen im Taunus, and performed by local inhabitants.[108] The highwayman's long lineage in German popular culture was manifested in these dialect performances. Accompanying the show, was a story-teller, who in the centuries-old tradition of the Bänkelsänger or balladeer, narrated story highlights as he pointed to pictured episodes on a large oil canvas

During the heyday of colportage literature, in the Wilhelmine period from 1870 to 1914, the colportage highwayman novels had numbered in the hundreds. In the period from 1919 to 1933 another dozen were published. That their appeal lasted into the final years of the Weimar Republic deserves examination. Like romance colportage, the highwayman novels firmly fixed gender roles for heroes and heroines. Masculinity meant daring bravado, decisive leadership, and steadfast loyalty [Treue] to followers, friends, and lovers, and an unbending will to reach private as well as appropriately altruistic public goals. As in romance colportage, heroines were staunchly faithful to their betrothed and had to defend themselves against persistent attacks from "demonic," rival women. The latter showered their overabundant desires on the highwayman. Their scheming attempts to wrest the heroes away from the gentle, passive heroines marked them as evil and as acting in a way unnatural and perverse for their gender.

Recalling anti-urban themes in romance colportage, heroines in these novels often fall victim to the evils emanating from the city. In Rigo Muratti (1924), the abducted Roswitha is put up for auction in the white slave trade which is centered in the Argentine capital. Roswitha's nemesis Mercedes takes sadistic pleasure in letting the highwayman Rigo know that his "white rose," who has been shipped to Brazil, now is subjected to "the kisses of Negroes." [109] Mercedes admits that only the "vampire metropolis" Buenos Aires can satisfy her appetites: "I want to live and enjoy, I want to get to know all forbidden pleasures."[110] In this world city she experiments with hashish, cocaine, and opium.[111] "If you men can search out your amusements always and everywhere," Mercedes asks, "then why shouldn't women do so too?"[112]

In Heinz Gronau's Der Hiesel (1933), Marie Antoinette, after being saved from woodland bandits by the hero, invites the highwayman Hiesel to serve her in Paris. Hiesel replies, "I don't belong in Paris... I belong in the Bavarian Forest. Here where the old oak leaves rustle, here where the stag cries out... this is my homeland [Heimat], and this is my heart. Take Hiesel away from this soil that bore him, and he is no longer anything."[113] Suspicion and aversion to the city is tied to misgivings about foreigners and their distant lands. Heimat is where true happiness can be experienced. The exiled noblewoman Inge von Waldenfels comes to realize in Rigo Muratti, that romantic love can only be fulfilled in Germany and not "in this land where the hunt for gold has become the main goal in life."¹¹⁴ Over and over again, in Rigo Muratti, German emigrants to Argentina are misled, cheated, and exploited. Sadly, they fled Germany in the hope of finding a new, better home, but instead experience nothing but setbacks amid foreign evils.

Roswitha, the heroine of Rigo Muratti, symbolizes the enduring strength of German virtues in the face of the alien, corrupting city: "She was so beautiful, this shy, female flower from the virgin forest. All temptations of the metropolis and of sinful pleasure had not been able to touch her."¹¹⁵ In Der Hiesel, an educated member of Hiesel's band of highwaymen propounds a characteristically anti-urban, colportage philosophy: "I prefer the freedom in these great forests to the tightness and limitations of your cities. The city people's hearts are as stone hard as the walls that surround them. All they have in mind is to exert evil on each other or to take away the last remnants of freedom belonging to the people who live in the forest and along the riverbank."¹¹⁶ In Die Wildschützen der tiroler Grenze (The Poachers of the Tyrolean Border, 1923), the heroine Gretchen and her Tyrolean friends view the New York skyline from their ship: "So far behind them lay their sweet homeland. And as they looked in astonishment at the bustling ships and the endless row of buildings, Gretchen's thoughts raced home to her beloved Kastelruth and to her loved one."¹¹⁷ An adoring audience in New York listens to Gretchen sing Tyrolean songs, pouring out her love for the faraway Heimat.¹¹⁸ For colportage characters, the New World often serves as a foil upon which they can express their homesick attachment to Germany. They long to return to the national repository of noble values and virtues. Other countries do not live up to this high standard. In Rigo Muratti, Argentina is revealed as a land of lawlessness and corruption. Similarly, in Die Wildschützen der tiroler Grenze, the reader discovers that there is no justice in the United States where the rich can literally get away with murder.¹¹⁹ An underlying message to any readers contemplating emigration was to think twice, for whatever hardships one faced in Germany, they were only magnified and worsened in the cold, materialistic lands of the New World.

Likewise, rural and small town inhabitants ought to stay put and forebear rather than allow themselves to be drawn into the world's tempting Babylons. In contrast to tough conditions faced abroad, the beautiful homeland evokes a moral vision and a romantic utopia. While foreign lands are harsh and the metropolis is alienating, mountains and forests bring a sense of well-being and patriotic identification. In Der Hiesel, the highwayman and his wife Monika are reunited in the sacred woods: "Forest – forest, the forest of home, this wonderful cathedral, this holiness, this sublime stillness."¹²⁰ In Die Wildschützen der tiroler Grenze, the persecuted hero Gamsbartel finds solace and freedom in his beloved Tyrolean Alps: "Oh what a beautiful, blessed land. How sublime and grand with its mountains, its fertile valleys! How the heart is moved, how happy and proud wanders the gaze of the lonesome man up there surrounded by the celestial blue. It is his homeland, his beloved Tyrol that spreads itself out beneath his feet."¹²¹ In Rigo Muratti, the expectant wife Roswitha "searches for the path to the Heimat... into the raw mountains... into the virgin forest... where she wanted to give birth to her child..."¹²²

3.2 Outdoor Schinderhannes performance in Vockenhausen

3.2 The ongoing popularity of highwaymen stories was manifested in an annual Schinderhannes outdoor play performance in the village of Vockenhausen (near Wiesbaden). The postcard shows a "shocking ballad" storyteller in the lower left. He points to a canvas of pictures of the brigand's feats. (1920s postcard)

This symbiotic union between Heimat and hero or heroine reveals what is best and most pure in the nation. The people of the mountains and forests recognize this and turn to the highwayman for leadership, even if officially they are considered renegades and outcasts of society. Paradoxically, the lone highwayman is the last source of true virtue and morality. Governments are corrupt and cities have become cauldrons of crime and sin. While some rulers may be well-meaning, they are distant and have lost oversight, and their appointed civil servants are self-serving tax collectors and exploiters of the people (often referred to in colportage as Blutsauger or blood-suckers).

Only the highwayman is left to defend the Volk. For his fearless service, the people reward him with solidarity and a respect that borders on adulation. In the beginning of Rigo Muratti, the highwayman asks, "Is there only injustice in this country?" When someone replies that no avenger has yet stepped forward, Rigo portentously announces, "The avenger may still come. With the force of a thunderstorm he will rush and destroy all injustice and guilt that he discovers."¹²³ In a later scene, Rigo comments ironically that in his country "justice has had to flee to the brigands."¹²⁴ One of Rigo's recruits ponders the role of the leader and his men: "Only the courage of a few, faithful men can save the country from the exploitation of greedy tyrants." Rigo alone embodies a force strong enough to take on the tyrants and it is the country's fortune that he has appeared "as if fallen from heaven" [wie vom Himmel gefallen].¹²⁵

3.3 Illustration of a popular highwayman in an installment novel

3.3 All hail the bandit leader Rigo Muratti from the installment novel of the same name. Bandits, according to these stories, truly represented the common folk and were legitimized by direct plebiscite of the crowd (not unlike a lynch mob). Karlheinz Berghoff, *Rigo Muratti* (Dresden: Mignon Verlag, 1924), illus.31.

In Der Hiesel, the heroine Monika declares, "I know that Bavarian Hiesel can only be what he is: a protector of the poor people, a fighter for justice, an avenger of the downtrodden."¹²⁶ The farmers "love him because he has often helped them in the struggle against the tax-collectors and because he poaches and shoots wildlife."[127] When the authorities come to expropriate indebted farmers, these victims appeal to Hiesel for help.[128] The poaching is appreciated by local farmers whose crops are devoured by proliferating wildlife.

At one point, Hiesel's band marches into the town of Friedberg and in a revolutionary act deposes the local judge: "The Volk has pronounced judgment over you long ago. Justice and humanity are the first qualities that one expects from a judge. You have never known them. If only the Elector in Munich knew what a disgraceful wretch you are, you would not be allowed to sit in the judge's seat for another hour. But the Elector is far away and heaven is high. So we judge you by the right of free men, like our fathers did before us."[129] Hiesel is not a crazed revolutionary but a just, visionary leader. His execution of justice represents the true will of the people, while that of the Bavarian state merely serves to enrich unscrupulous officials. The union and harmony between Hiesel and the Volk is further manifested at the highwayman's wedding in the town of Kissing. Armed peasants and farmers converge on the Bavarian town to protect "the man of the people" by "a wall of human flesh."[130] He is their beloved "woodland devil, the king of the forests."[131]

To what extent did colportage's social bandits have the right to exert justice? Could they execute their wicked opponents? Here colportage writers usually drew the line. Although some heroes, in climactic scenes, come very close to punishing their conquered, cruel adversaries with death, usually they draw back in the last instant, recognizing that only God has the right to administer capital punishment. In <u>Die Wildschützen der tiroler Grenze</u>, the poacher Gamsbartel is pursued by foresters who want him "dead or alive." When he traps the chief forester, who once had brutally beaten and imprisoned him, the hero's desire to avenge past wrongs almost causes him to pull the trigger. The captured villain pleads, "By Christ's blood – take pity! I have a wife and children, Gamsbartel!"[132] The hero relents and lets the forester go free after he swears never to pursue Gamsbartel again.

In <u>Rigo Muratti</u>, Rigo has taken an oath to avenge the death of his mother, who was killed by the nefarious governor Carlos Brambilla. The Argentine highwayman is repeatedly described as merciless in his struggle against the tyrant. But when he has a chance to kill Carlos' equally cruel sister Mercedes, he relents and confesses that his is not the role of the executioner.[133] In an early episode in the novel, two German emigrants discuss the famed highwayman. One of the Germans reflects, "It isn't good when people claim the role of avenger. God expressly declared: revenge is mine."[134] The themes of appropriate moral action and vengeance run through the novel. Eventually, Rigo realizes that it is indeed presumptuous for humans to assume the status of avenging angel. He even goes a step further when he admits, "Man has no right to try to be the shaper of destiny."[135]

In <u>Der Hiesel</u>, the highwayman's girlfriend Monika preaches the same view and tells Hiesel that vengeance "belongs to the Lord, not us."[136] But when Hiesel learns that Monika has been kidnapped, his emotions take over and he declares "blood will flow" and his enemies will be "wiped from the face of the earth."[137] Hiesel's endless struggles harden him and he loses sight of his initial mission to reestablish justice. When he captures an enemy leader, his face reveals "no sign of pity, no trace of mildness. In Hiesel's eyes was a steel-hard glare."[138] One of his followers has to remind him, "Do we have the right to pass sentence, Hiesel? Is it not the right of a higher power to pass a judgment?"[139] Thus colportage literature taught that while highwaymen might cleanse the system and restore justice in the name of the people, they ought not transform themselves into vindictive executioners or killers. They ought to exercise restraint even for the worst evil-doers and normally do so. Hiesel, unlike Rigo or Gamsbartel, does however eventually dispatch his two chief enemies. This dark, double execution is only adumbrated in a couple of sentences at the novel's end.[140] <u>Der Hiesel</u>, published in 1933, adorned with a cover depicting a fanatical glare in Hiesel's eyes reminiscent of Hitler's, thus deviates from earlier highwayman novels on this point.

To some extent, Weimar's colportage authors usually refrained from allowing their heroes to kill for fear of review board disapproval and censorship. Killing a villain could also blemish the idealized moral stature of the hero. A residue of Christian piety permeated most colportage literature. In an early monograph on highwayman novels, Carl Müller-Fraureth noticed that "in the early decades of the nineteenth century, strangely enough, many of the writers are evangelical country pastors from the province of Saxony."[141] Although the writers and publishers were no longer the same, it is worth noting that most major colportage publishers in the Weimar Republic were still located in Protestant Saxony: the Marien-Verlag in Leipzig; Mignon and Adolf Ander in Dresden; H.G. Münchmeyer and Verlagshaus Freya on the outskirts of Dresden in Niedersedlitz and Heidenau.

The question as to who has the right to eliminate evil from the world formed a part of an internal discourse taking place within colportage. Where, according to the writers, did this evil originate and why did it exist at all? Colportage heroines often cry out and ask why they are subject to endless ordeals. The relentless power of evil is, of course, a colportage literary device keeping the suspense and action alive so that the narrative can endure for one hundred installments and thousands of pages, much to the annoyance of review board readers. It would be a mistake, though, to view colportage as simply crude, endless stories of good battling evil: in its own peculiar way, it incorporated wider moral and social questions that troubled society. In trying to explain the source of evil, colportage writing reveals a befuddling mixture and synthesis of Christianity and Social Darwinism, including physiognomic ideas derived from J.C. Lavater and Cesare Lombroso.

3.4 Cover of installment novel Der Hiesel

3.4 The bandit Hiesel, dressed as an Alpine hunter, protects his girlfriend. His intense stare recalls the fanatic determination expressed in Hitler's eyes. One of the last colportage novels, *Der Hiesel: Ein Räuber und doch ein Volksheld* (Heidenau: Verlagshaus Freya, 1933) was published in the same year that Hitler became chancellor.

In its plot structure of clashing contrasts, colportage easily fit with a pseudoscientific ideology of racial struggle that fused moral and physical qualities onto specific ethnic, biological, and national types. The pigeonholing of individuals by physiognomic categories characterized colportage writing and seemed to make it perfectly suited for transporting racialist ideas to a wide audience. Yet Christian mores, to some extent, worked against such a system by proposing possible redemption for individuals who through action or insight overcome their sinful, evil ways. Good and evil were thus categories still applicable to individuals and their interactions, and this contradicted the rising notion that race and physical constitution irrevocably determined behavior. A universalist Christian notion of morality conflicted with a particularist code of national-racist ethics.

Even the worst sinners have a chance to atone for their wrongs in some colportage episodes. In <u>Die Wildschützen der tiroler Grenze</u>, the villainous poacher "red Michel" had succeeded in pinning the blame for two murders which he committed onto the hero Gamsbartel. At the story's conclusion, "red Michel" begs for absolution from his deathbed. The priest considers the unanticipated appearance of Gamsbartel to be miraculous and exclaims, "God has sent you in this hour! Forgive him, for he has admitted and regretted his guilt!" Gamsbartel obliges, "Yes Michel! I pardon you from my heart! I do not want to stand between your poor soul and the mercy of dear God!"[142]

In <u>Der Hiesel</u>, the chief villain is a red-haired hunchback named Rotkopf. Red hair, ruddy skin, or freckles in colportage almost invariably indicate an evil character. The literary and artistic convention of evil redheads has a long history going back to ancient and medieval times. In <u>Outcasts: Signs of Otherness in Northern European Art of the Late Middle Ages</u> (1993), Ruth Mellinkoff observed "Redheads and redbeards have been called liars, cheats, traitors, murderers, devils, witches, churls; they have been besmirched with such adjectives as false, dangerous, tricky, shameless, oversexed, deceitful, hot-tempered, unfaithful, foxy, foolish, warlike, crude, vulgar, low-class, and unlucky for those who meet them. These attributions reflect the pseudoscience of physiognomy ... the art of divining character from physical characteristics."[143] Mellinkoff also discusses how medieval paintings portraying Judas and Jews with red hair used the color red to signal the evil enemies of Christ. In the nineteenth century, the association was perpetuated in literature by popular novelists like Charles Dickens and Honore de Balzac.[144] The negative stigma of red hair shows up in colportage too and reveals a link between medieval Christian iconology and modern racialist thinking as a genetic trait becomes associated with and helps explain a type of behavior.

In <u>Der Hiesel</u>, the villain Rotkopf's adversarial nature is marked by both his red hair and his Gypsy background. At the story's beginning, he tells the doleful tale of his childhood to the heroine Monika. Ridiculed, bullied, and miserably treated even by his mother on account of his unappealing appearance, Rotkopf remembers that he was "lower than the courtyard dog... who was fine-looking [while I looked like] the devil they paint in the chapel."[145] For an instant, the heroine feels pity for him, but when he makes a shameless advance, he reveals his usual "raw and brutal" behavior.[146] Later, when Monika learns that Rotkopf is a Gypsy, this "explains" a lot for her: "That's why he is so different from everyone else in Kissing. That's where the wild blood pounding in him came from. That explained the concealed treachery and deceit in his nature. That's where the blazing eyes and impetuous passion came from."[147]

When Wolf Leixner, Hiesel's childhood friend and an officer in the Bavarian army, confronts Rotkopf and reminds him that his ugly exterior suits his terrible reputation, the redhead agrees and helps confirm a physiognomic truth: "I want to be the way nature made me, ugly on the outside and bad on the inside."[148] Just at the point where Lavater's and Lombroso's theories seem to prevail, Leixner calls them into question with contrary Christian speculation: "Listen Rotkopf, I once spoke to Klemens Wenzeslaus, the archbishop, about how the human soul appeared deep down inside. And His Merciful Highness told me: 'Remember one thing lieutenant, no man is completely bad and completely depraved. There is no one in whose soul all goodness has died. And the worst scoundrels are sometimes the ones who can be most easily saved by allowing them the chance to come around through a single great, good deed.'"[149] Rotkopf does not know how to react and uneasily replies that he is not interested in philosophizing. This encounter in Der Hiesel shows a discourse taking place within colportage, touching the sensitive and highly relevant question as to what extent racialist or physiognomic theories could explain human behavior. Was moral behavior a matter of individual choice, social conditioning, or genetic inheritance? The reader of Der Hiesel is confronted with all three as possible explanations for Rotkopf's actions.

That being a "Gypsy" did not necessarily mean one would have to follow a pre-established path is further manifested in the character of Gita, a girl who falls in love with the handsome Leixner. Greatly admiring blonde, blue-eyed Monika, Gita repeatedly helps the story's heroine despite her racial otherness. Gita struggles against her Gypsy destiny to serve as chattel to a husband who will send her to beg and steal. The young woman's efforts to free herself is one of the more interesting sub-narratives in Der Hiesel.[150] It, too, seems to be at crosscurrents with the more typical colportage synthesis of national or ethnic traits with an individual's moral behavior. On the one hand, Gita seems irrevocably tied to her race: "Duty called her to her tribe [Stamm]. Loyalty to her blood relatives, obedience... forced her to return to the Gypsy camp."[151] She has animal-like traits and is compared to a wildcat, a deer, and a snake.[152] Her people are described as godless rascals, thieves, and swindlers. During a pitched battle between the Gypsies and a Bavarian military contingent, Leixner's life is saved when Gita stabs a Gypsy assailant. Her love for the "blonde prince" has caused her to betray her people and overcome her seemingly predetermined destiny. This love is eventually returned by the Bavarian officer who charts out an uplifting, romantic future for them. He envisions "pulling her up to a nicer, clearer world free of restless, homeless wandering, without ostracism and scorn. He wants the little Gypsy to grow into a world that offers a better life worthy of true humanity."[153] After numerous setbacks, this unlikely multiracial couple finally has its way. Love trumps racial antagonism.

In Die Wildschützen der tiroler Grenze, a typically materialistic American villain is served by a "frightfully ugly" mulatto woman whose "mean features and stabbing black eyes remind one of a Gypsy."[154] In another episode that takes place in India, the reader is introduced to fanatical and violent Hindus thirsting for revenge against their English colonial rulers. But in this colportage novel too, other

Chapter Three. The Schund Law: Defending Morality or Undermining Freedom? 133

races are not automatically enemies of the story's white heroes. The black American Jonny, a literary descendent of Uncle Tom, becomes a valuable ally to the heroine Gretchen and her Tyrolean friends.[155]

In Rigo Muratti, a certain "Mother Israeli" runs a house of prostitution in Buenos Aires and is involved in the white slave trade.[156] Another minor Jewish character is the director of a circus that harbors someone a detective is looking for.[157] The detective offers the Jew a reward of two hundred pesos if he will bring him to the missing person, but the Jew haggles and tries to increase the reward to a five-fold sum. Such standard antisemitic literary fare contrasts with a lengthier episode in which an aging Jew named Lazar and his multiracial granddaughter provide a safe refuge for the wounded hero Rigo. Lazar Pascilla fled Russian pogroms to seek a better life in Argentina. In his new home he became a wealthy merchant. His son married into high society turning his back on Judaism and the elderly parents. His reckless desire to assimilate ended in disaster when he accumulated large gambling debts and then got killed in a duel.

Lazar recounts his personal loss stoically and laments the tragedy that has befallen his family. The man who killed his son happens to be Carlos Brambilla, the archenemy of Rigo Muratti. When Lazar took legal action against the affluent governor, he had to learn once more that he was a second-class citizen: "I forgot that I am a descendent of a Volk that is persecuted everywhere, from whom one takes money, but whom one curses when it is time to pay the debt."[158] Lazar's granddaughter Ria is described as a beauty with typical Jewish features and a dreamy quality that evokes her Germanic side.[159] She falls in love with Rigo and is saddened when she discovers that he already has a lover named Roswitha. Despite all the crude stereotypes, it is worth noting that Lazar and Ria are benevolent, not evil characters, who courageously risk their safety to assist the hunted, injured hero.

While the oft-criticized colportage contraposition of good and evil easily lent itself to incorporating racialist antinomies, the genre sometimes made room for unexpectedly positive portrayals of traditionally despised minorities. The fact that a majority of these improbable characters are women may be due to an affinity between the poorly paid colportage writers and their downtrodden, largely lower class female audience. Despite advances made by Weimar's highly publicized "New Woman," most women of the 1920s were still victims of male domination and economic exploitation regardless of their ethnicity. The highwayman novels are about freeing the oppressed and reestablishing justice. In being doubly oppressed as women and as members of persecuted minorities, Gypsy and Jewish women could radiate and project precisely those kinds of extreme conditions that characterized colportage writing and that made it appeal to its subaltern readers.

The good, virtuous female characters of colportage, whose love is pure, eternal, and incorruptible are related to similar figures in nineteenth century theater melodrama who, Peter Brooks observed, struggled "to preserve and impose moral vision."[160] Brooks found that plays of the early nineteenth century carried an important message to their audience that certain powers more profound than the merely physical ones continued to shape material reality: "The melodramatists refuse to allow that the world has been completely drained of transcendence and they locate that transcendence in the struggle of children of light with the children of darkness."[161] Precisely this battle between the forces of good and evil in colportage literature irritated the members of the Munich, Berlin, and Leipzig Review Boards. They despised the stark, overblown confrontation of opposites and viewed colportage's repetitiveness and predictability with contempt.

Michael Denning, in his study <u>Mechanic Accents</u>, has suggested that bourgeois readers read in a different manner than the less educated: while they read "novelistically," working class readers read "allegorically."[162] These different reading styles could help explain why the anti-<u>Schund</u> activists and the review board members entirely missed the point as to what colportage's core attractions were for its consumers. While board members were exasperated with the highly unlikely coincidences that often took place in colportage plots, for installment novel readers these coincidences presaged weighty events and transcendental intervention in the lives of the story's characters.[163] The subaltern reader appreciated colportage for something that the mandarins could not see in it or understand because its concerns and worries were not part of their lives or their mental universe. Anti-<u>Schund</u> activists viewed colportage as crude reading material for entertainment with potentially dangerous side effects, especially for youths, and could not conceive of it as fulfilling another social class's need for sense-making. What Peter Brooks discovered as a central source of meaning for the audience of melodrama was also central to the meaning of the closely related genre of colportage: "Melodrama starts from and expresses the anxiety brought by a frightening new world in which the traditional patterns of moral order no longer provide the necessary social glue. It plays out the force of that anxiety with the apparent triumph of villainy and it dissipates it with the eventual victory of virtue."[164] Weimar's colportage revealed but failed to resolve the contradictions between older universalist Christian notions of morality and rising particularistic nationalist or racialist systems of "morality."[165]

The non-political, theatrical connection between popular melodrama and colportage was illustrated by the prolific Wilhelmine colportage author Paul Walter who liked to act out scenes for his novels while he wrote them. In his Berlin home, he had a room filled with costumes and weapons, which he used to enact episodes for each installment.[166] Dressed as a highwayman and flailing away with his sword, he dictated the story to his secretary who tried to keep pace on her typewriter. Another room contained his huge collection of crime texts – old court records, broadsheets, and street ballads lamenting horrible murders and executions.¹⁶⁷ These had been purchased from antiquarian dealers and were sources of inspiration for Walter's more than forty novels that mainly featured sensational criminals and unjustly persecuted highwaymen. In colportage novels of highwaymen, the reward for those who fought on the side of virtue is to live "happily ever after" in a domestic <u>Biedermeier</u> utopia where time stands still and patriarchal figures benevolently preside over their families. Often there is a Cinderella ending whereby a tormented heroine discovers that, in reality, she is of noble birth and is reunited with a long-lost parent. This is the case in <u>Die Wildschützen der tiroler Grenze</u>: "Suddenly the stagecoach driver's daughter, little Gretchen of Kastelruth, has been transformed into the Duke's daughter, a princess!"¹⁶⁸ The aging Duke embraces and "kisses her with fatherly tenderness." The novel concludes with Gretchen's marriage to Prince Max, who, she had been warned at the story's beginning, was an impossible social match for her.¹⁶⁹ The novel's main hero, the poacher Gamsbartel, is cleared of charges of murder and receives a monetary reward for his daring mountain rescue of an Austrian archduke. This money he immediately donates to a peasant woman whose house had been destroyed in a fire.

In <u>Rigo Muratti</u>, justice is restored after the evil governor Carlos Brambilla falls to his death from a cliff.¹⁷⁰ The state is put into the hands of Juarez Messerbarba, whose nickname is "the incorruptible."¹⁷¹ The new governor is a great admirer of Germany. He tells the German immigrants that he expects their "fatherland" to rise once again to a position of international prominence.¹⁷² He also recognizes Rigo and his band of highwaymen for their legitimate struggle against "the tyrant and usurper Carlos Brambilla."¹⁷³ The former brigands deserve to be rewarded for their commitment to justice and the natural rights of the people. They receive uniforms from Messerbarba and are transformed from highwaymen into a mountain patrol in government service.¹⁷⁴

Rigo and Roswitha decide to leave Argentina and move to Germany where a large inheritance awaits them. Countess Waldenfels, in the novel's sixty-seventh installment, had brought the unforeseen news of Roswitha's noble lineage and inherited wealth, but only after overcoming a whole row of misadventures can Roswitha and Rigo enjoy destiny's bounteous reward. The couple and their child board a ship for Germany. They are welcomed at Castle Waldenfels by local youth who strew flowers before them.¹⁷⁵ Roswitha, from her carriage, gazes with awe at the unfolding marvel: "She could not believe that this was now all her property... the beautiful forest, that was so different from the one back there. The forest with sturdy oaks, mighty beech, and proud pines that reached on high, then the wide fields which were cultivated with winter seed. And then the old castle appeared."¹⁷⁶ Roswitha finds it hard to believe what a turn in fortune she enjoys. She has to touch Rigo's hand to assure herself that she is not dreaming.¹⁷⁷ The fruition of the couple's good fortune will have beneficial social repercussions on the local community. One of the new proprietor's first official acts is to establish a charitable home for the poor.[178] Colportage thus teaches what true nobility entails: not just the fulfillment of personal and family happiness for society's lucky few, but a social conscience and a desire to realize philanthropic endeavors.

Toward the end of <u>Der Hiesel</u>, when Marie Antoinette offers the highwayman a position in her royal bodyguard, he and his men decline the offer and instead decide to start a new life in the French territories of North America. They found the colony of Matthiastown "in the heart of the wilderness, in the virgin forest."[179] In contrast to Rigo Muratti, these heroes exchange a corrupted Old World for a fresh start in the New where "courage and a sense of adventure" are the highest male values and the highwayman's uncorrupted sense of justice is the basis of the law.[180] The colony cultivates peaceful relations with the Indians and sick natives are offered medical attention. Hiesel's men have become fur traders doing a brisk business with the French as well as the Indians. Their little colony prospers economically and socially: Hiesel and his men are all happily married, their children play in the streets of idyllic Matthiastown.

Endnotes

1   Reichstag Stenographic Reports [July 16, 1919], 1590.
2   Ibid.
3   Ibid.
4   Ibid., 1591
5   Reinhard Mumm, <u>Der Christlichsoziale Gedanke</u> (Berlin: Mittler und Sohn, 1933), 10.
6   Ibid., 143.
7   Ibid., 146.
8   Ibid., 143.
9   Ibid., 137.
10 Ibid., 47.
11 <u>Süddeutsche Zeitung</u>, July 6, 1926.
12 Reichstag Stenographic Report [Nov. 27, 1926], 8244.
13 Ibid.
14 RSR, 8247.
15 RSR, 8248.
16 RSR, 8246.
17 RSR [Nov. 29, 1926], 8271.
18 Ibid.
19 Ibid.
20 RSR [Dec. 3, 1926], 8362.
21 RSR, 8252.
22 RSR [Nov. 27, 1926], 8248.
23 Ibid.

24 RSR [Dec.3, 1926], 8362.
25 RSR [Nov.27, 1926], 8250.
26 Ibid.
27 RSR [Nov.27, 1926], 8234.
28 Ibid.
29 RSR [Dec.3, 1926], 8368.
30 RSR [Nov.27, 1926], 8235.
31 RSR [Oct.16, 1919], 3163.
32 RSR [Nov.26, 1926], 8217.
33 Ibid.
34 Ibid., 8219.
35 RSR [Nov.26, 1926], 8224.
36 Ibid.
37 Ibid.
38 RSR [Nov.26, 1926], 8210.
39 RSR 8212.
40 RSR, 8212-8213.
41 RSR [Dec.3, 1926], 8360.
42 Albert Hellwig, Jugendschutz gegen Schundliteratur (Berlin: Stilke, 1927), 54-56, 67-71.
43 Ibid., 145.
44 Ibid., 134.
45 Ibid., 43.
46 Ibid.
47 Ibid., 44.
48 Ibid., 47.
49 Ibid., 52.
50 Ibid., 73.
51 Ibid., 53.
52 Ibid., 72, 74.
53 Ibid., 69.
54 Ibid., 76.
55 Ibid.
56 Siegfried Kracauer, "Film-Notizen," [April 28, 1931] in Kleine Schriften zum Film 1928-1931 (6.2), 487.
57 Ibid., 487-488.
58 Wolfgang Petzet, Verbotene Filme (Frankfurt: Sociatäts-Verlag, 1931), 67.
59 Ibid., 118.
60 Paul Oestreich, "Schutz der Jugend vor Schund und Schmutz?" Die Stimme der Freiheit No.7/8 (1931), 121.
61 Ibid., 122.
62 Ibid., 123.

63 Siegfried Bernfeld, "Das Kind braucht keinen Schutz vor Schund! Es schützt sich selbst!" Die literarische Welt (Dec.3, 1926) No. 49 Sondernummer Kinderbücher und Jugendschriften, 1. http ://www.soziales.fh-dortmund.de/diederichs/funde/bernfeld.htm [Oct.19, 2010]
64 Ibid., 2.
65 Völkische-Wacht Leonberg (Dec.24, 1926).
66 Hans Wingender, Erfahrungen im Kampfe gegen Schund- und Schmutzschriften (Düsseldorf: Selbstverlag, 1930), 51.
67 Ibid., 53.
68 Ibid., 54.
69 PS Munich [May 28, 1929] "Der Herr des Lebens (Die Sünde wider den Samen)," (HStA Stuttgart) E 151/09 Bü 282
70 Anonymous, Die Stimme der Freiheit No.4 (1931, 56.
71 Ibid., 57.
72 Ibid., 56.
73 PS Berlin [Feb.11, 1930] "Sonja oder Um der Liebe willen unschuldig verbannt," 2, (BArch), R 181.
74 Ibid., 2.
75 Günter Kosch and Manfred Nagl, Der Kolportageroman (Stuttgart: Metzler, 1993), 59.
76 PS Berlin [Oct.23, 1928] "Ohne Ring und Myrte," 1, (BArch), R 181.
77 Ibid., 2.
78 Ibid.
79 PS Berlin (Oct.15, 1929), "Heimlich getraut oder die Privatsekretärin des Eisenkönigs," (BArch), R 181.
80 PS Munich (June 13, 1928), "Hanna die Prinzessin von der Landstrasse," (HStA Stuttgart) E 151/09 BU 290.
81 Ibid., 2.
82 Ibid., 3.
83 Ibid.
84 Ibid.
85 PS Berlin (Dec.17, 1929) "Der Liebestraum der Maharadscha," 2, (BArch), R 181.
86 Letter from Saxony's Welfare Ministry regarding the Berlin Review Board's decision not to place Knute und Fessel on the list of harmful books and citing the decision at length. [Mar. 14, 1930] (HStA Stuttgart) E 151/09 Bü 284.
87 Ibid.
88 Ibid.
89 Ibid.
90 PS Berlin [Aug.29, 1933] "Rasputin," 2, (BArch) R 181.
91 Ibid.
92 OPS Leipzig [Oct.20, 1933] "Rasputin," (BArch) R 181.
93 Kosch, Nagl, 58.
94 PS Berlin [June 28, 1932] "Der 'Fetzer'," 1, (BArch), R 181.
95 Ibid., 2.
96 Ibid., 2.
97 Ibid., 3.

Chapter Three. The Schund Law: Defending Morality or Undermining Freedom?   139

98   PS Berlin [Jan.27, 1931], "Süsse kleine Friedel," (BArch) R 181.
99   PS Berlin [Jan.14, 1930], "Regina," (BArch) R 181.
100 OPS Leipzig [July 25, 1930], "Summary of Decisions," (BArch) R 181.
101 PS Berlin [May 13, 1930], "Die Wildschützen der Tiroler Grenze," (BArch) R 181.
102 Ibid.
103 OPS Leipzig [July 25, 1930], "Summary of Decisions," (BArch), R 181.
104 Hertha Siemering et. al. Was liest unsere Jugend? (Berlin: R. von Decker's, 1930), 8-9.
105 Ibid., 9.
106 Ibid.
107 Ibid., 9-10.
108 http//www.eppsteiner-zeitung.de "Vockenhausen im Bann des Schinderhannes," Nov.5, 2003 [Feb.27, 2011].
109 Karlheinz Berghoff, Rigo Muratti (Dresden: Mignon, 1924), 859.
110 Ibid., 225.
111 Ibid., 226-227.
112 Ibid., 227.
113 Heinz Gronau, Der Hiesel (Heidenau: Verlagshaus Freya, 1933), 1289.
114 Berghoff, Rigo Muratti, 378.
115 Ibid., 771.
116 Gronau, Der Hiesel, 189.
117 Alois Haspinger, Die Wildschützen der Tiroler Grenze (Dresden: Adolf Ander, 1922), 576.
118 Ibid., 584-585.
119 Ibid., 856.
120 Gronau, Der Hiesel, 1519.
121 Haspinger, Die Wildschützen der Tiroler Grenze, 2821.
122 Berghoff, Rigo Muratti, 1020.
123 Ibid., 38.
124 Ibid., 306.
125 Ibid., 736.
126 Gronau, Der Hiesel, 1148.
127 Ibid., 1102.
128 Ibid., 1116.
129 Ibid., 1199.
130 Ibid., 1077.
131 Ibid., 1076.
132 Haspinger, Die Wildschützen der Tiroler Grenze, 479.
133 Berghoff, Rigo Muratti, 795.
134 Ibid., 443.
135 Ibid., 2235.
136 Gronau, Der Hiesel, 58.
137 Ibid., 139.
138 Ibid., 2977.

139 Ibid.
140 Ibid., 3358-3359.
141 Carl Müller-Fraureuth, Die Ritter- und Räuberromane (Hildesheim: Georg Olms Verlagsbuchhandlung, 1965) [reprint of 1894 edition], 104.
142 Haspinger, Die Wildschützen der Tiroler Grenze, 2896.
143 Ruth Mellinkoff, Outcasts: Signs of Otherness in Northern European Art of the Late Middle Ages (Berkeley: University of California Press, 1993), 148.
144 Ibid., 153-154, 158.
145 Gronau, Der Hiesel, 85-86.
146 Ibid., 87.
147 Ibid., 673.
148 Ibid., 793.
149 Ibid., 794.
150 Ibid., 797.
151 Ibid., 1210.
152 Ibid., 1211-1215.
153 Ibid., 2482.
154 Haspinger, Die Wildschützen der Tiroler Grenze, 655.
155 Ibid., 660-662.
156 Berghoff, Rigo Muratti, 157, 1229.
157 Ibid., 2243.
158 Ibid., 853.
159 Ibid., 845.
160 Peter Brooks, The Melodramatic Imagination (New Haven: Yale University Press, 1995), 87.
161 Ibid., 22.
162 Michael Denning, Mechanic Accents (New York: Verso, 1998), 72-73.
163 See Cornelia Strieder, Melodramatik und Sozialkritik in Werken Eugene Sues (Erlangen: Verlag Palm und Enke, 1986), 89-90, 226.
164 Brooks, 20.
165 On particularist versus universalist systems of morality see Raphael Gross, Anständig Geblieben: Nationalsozialistische Moral (Frankfurt: S. Fischer Verlag, 2012).
166 Adrian Mohr, Volkslesestoff (Frankfurt: Verlag für Sozialwissenschaften, 1954), 27.
167 Ibid., 26.
168 Haspinger, Die Wildschützen der Tiroler Grenze, 3189.
169 Ibid., 7.
170 Berghoff, Rigo Muratti, 2339.
171 Ibid., 1958.
172 Ibid., 1982.
173 Ibid., 2097.
174 Ibid., 2376.
175 Ibid., 2381.
176 Ibid., 2383.

177 Ibid., 2386.
178 Ibid.
179 Gronau, Der Hiesel, 3353.
180 Ibid., 3354.

Chapter Four. Detective Pulps: Modeling Justice or Glamorizing Crime?

Colportage authors often tried to pepper the family romance with themes and characters that would broaden its appeal: occultist or movie milieus; crime and "white slavery." The intervention of a detective, or even science fiction elements, could be mixed into the gigantic narratives. Despite all these attempts to adapt to new reader desires, colportage novels were like dinosaurs doomed to extinction. Their environment was under attack from two sides: the Schund law, and changing reader demography and taste. By drawing a line against sex, horror, and gore, the review boards hampered colportage writers from offering some of the essential ingredients that attracted a loyal adult readership. Young readers, on the other hand, although interested in some installment novels, were drifting more towards the self-contained dime novels with their flashy covers featuring an intrepid detective. This trend had already begun before the war. When Alwin Eichler returned to Germany from New York in 1903 with the copyrights for Buffalo Bill and Nick Carter, America's Greatest Detective, a major transformation began in the production and marketing of German popular literature.[1]

Mass-produced serials of this type soon reached weekly sales of 80,000 copies.[2] Each pamphlet cover pictured a dramatic scene from the story in vivid color. These eye-catchers were reproductions of the original American covers (with titles left in English). Anti-Schund activists immediately recognized the threat and campaigned hard against this new hydra. In 1909 they scored a first, small success when the sales of Buffalo Bill and Nick Carter were prohibited in Württemberg's railway stations.[3]

Alarmed Schundkämpfer called out the usual epithets of "plague" and "poison," dramatically warning that Germany's youth and future were at stake. Briefly successful in snuffing out many dime novels in the 1910s and during the war, the anti- Schund campaign witnessed setbacks with a new explosion of publications in the immediate postwar years.

4.1 SPD advertisement for a "trashy literature" bonfire

Kampf gegen Schund und Schmutz

Der Schund und Schmutz verschwinde,
Die Jugend will's!
Wir tun dies Werk am Kinde,
Auch ohne Külz!

EINTRITTSKARTE
für beide Veranstaltungen:
Erwachsene, Jugendliche 25 Pf.

Freitag, 24., und Sonntag, 26. Juni 1927

Große Kundgebung

der

Sozialistischen Arbeiter-Jugend Groß-Leipzig
SPD Groß-Leipzig
Gemeinschaft Kinderfreunde Groß-Leipzig
Elternratszentrale für die weltliche Schule Leipzig

LEIPZIGER BUCHDRUCKEREI AG., LEIPZIG

PROGRAMM

Freitag, den 24. Juni 1927:

GROSSE KUNDGEBUNG
im großen Saale des Volkshauses
Verlauf der Kundgebung:
JUGENDCHOR:
Weckruf . . . . Heinz Thiessen
Volkshymne . . . . Bach-Guttmann
VORSPRUCH:
MEINE BÜCHER. Ludwig Lessen
Referat:
BUCH UND GESELLSCHAFT
Spruch: WISSEN IST MACHT
JUGENDCHOR:
Warschawjanka . . . Russische Weise
ALLGEMEINES LIED:
Die Internationale

DER KUNDGEBUNG GEGEN SCHUND UND SCHMUTZ

Sonntag, 26. Juni 1927:

Früh stellen in den Bezirken
Marsch nach d. Reichsgerichtsplatz
Der Jugendchor singt:
Warschawjanka . . Russische Weise
Hebt unsre Fahnen in den Wind
von M. Engbert
Dann Abmarsch nach dem Festplatz
(Sportplatz des Arbeiter-Turn- und
-Sportvereins Leipzig-Schleußig)

Programm des Waldfestes

10–12 Uhr: SPORTLICHE SPIELE
12–15 Uhr: Mittagspause. Die einzelnen Gruppen spielen unterdessen
Beginn des eigentlichen Waldfestes
15–16.30 Uhr: MASSENSPIELE UND VOLKSTÄNZE
17–17.30 Uhr: LIEDERCHOR-KONZERT
18–19.30 Uhr:
BUNTES ALLERLEI
Hans-Sachs-Spiele
Kasperletheater
Tanzvorführungen · Singspiele
Kinderfreunde-Spiele
Musikvorträge
Bei eintretender Dunkelheit:

Am Marterpfahl der Siox

Ein Schmökerspiel mit Musik u. Tanz
von Franz Osterroth
Anschließend: Verbrennung von Schundliteratur

4.1 In the summer of 1927, the SPD organized a two-day youth protest against "trashy and filthy literature." At nightfall, the program culminated with a musical parody of a colportage novel, followed by a bonfire of "trashy literature." Advertising card: *Kampf gegen Schund und Schmutz: Grosse Kundgebung* (Leipzig: Leipziger Buchdruckerei, 1927).

Anglo-Saxon detectives seemed to appear everywhere and ruled the day in myriad series: James Robertson (1919-1922, 1924), Frank Allan (1920-1932), Fred Parker (1920-1923), Fred Pinkerton (1920-1922), Timm Fox (1921), Hannibal Blunt (1921), Nic Pratt (1922-1923), Sir Ralf Clifford (1922-1925), John Kling (1926-1939), Tom Shark (1928-1939), and John Baxter (1929-1931). Only two German detectives competed with this crowd: the short-lived Rolf Karsten (1930) and the very popular Berlin detective Harald Harst (1919-1934).

In 1930 the Prussian Welfare Ministry published a study about youth reading habits. In Was liest unsere Jugend? (What Does Our Youth Read?, 1930) the researchers presented facts that would send a chill up a Schundkämpfer's spine. A fourteen year-old male eighth grader, in a Thuringian town, listed over two hundred Frank Allan, one hundred Harald Harst, and fifty Tom Shark dime novels on his reading inventory.[4] He also mentioned colportage novels like Mary's Verhängnis (Mary's Downfall, 1926) and Erika, die Haideprinzess (Erika, Princess of the Heath, 1924). Although he read other adventure stories and a few classic novels like Uncle Tom's Cabin, the bulk of his pleasure reading was devoted to detective stories. Prussian researcher Willy Gensch went on to cite a Swiss newspaper which reported that youth were reading the detective stories not only in their spare time but also during school, particularly during religion and choir classes.[5] The Swiss report noted with alarm that neither teachers nor parents were aware of their children's bad habits. From mornings (on the toilet) until nightfall (under a blanket and by flashlight), young readers were gripped by the adventures of their favorite, intrepid detective. Without hesitation, one pupil could list forty-eight dime novel titles he had recently read. In the Thuringian school attended by the eighth grader, researchers discovered that girls too were reading sizeable quantities of detective pulps, particularly the girls of low academic ability.[6]

Teachers were perplexed when they were told how much "trashy literature" was consumed by their pupils.[7] Where did they purchase Frank Allan, Harald Harst, John Kling, or Tom Shark stories? Gensch praised those stationery stores which no longer displayed dime novels and applauded the association of stationery merchants for campaigning to market only good literature to its school-age customers. Yet one stationery vendor, quoted in the study, honestly admitted that she continued to sell dime novels because it was an important part of her income from her young customers.[8] Anti-Schund activists had been fighting local battles against stationery store distribution for a long time, as confirmed by a 1921 letter from a Tübingen trade school principal to his superiors in Stuttgart.[9] The principal complained of an adjacent stationery store, frequented by his pupils, that was selling a large quantity of "trashy literature." The owner at first refused to give in to school pressure to stop selling pulps, audaciously ignoring the institution's anger and a new school rule that punished pupils who brought dime novels to school. Only after the city applied new regulatory ordinances did the owner relent, but not before he advertised a large final sale on his remaining stock (which further incensed school officials).

While anti-<u>Schund</u> pressure on stationery stores catering to school youths seemed to have had some success, the distribution of dime novels simply changed venues. Gensch related how sales shifted to street vendors, barber shops, and tobacco stores.[10] A brisk trade was also taking place in the numerous private lending libraries. Pupils could return used stories, receive credit, and purchase other used or new issues. Why were youths so attracted to the dime novels? There was a tone of helpless resignation in the Prussian study's conclusions. Gensch did not simply attribute the problem of dime novels to the evil machinations of unscrupulous pulp producers. He thought it was a result of a general malaise in society. A lack of juvenile empowerment, he speculated, might be part of the reason why youths preferred action-packed "trashy literature" to the "high literature" promoted by schools and anti-<u>Schund</u> organizations. "Pulp intoxication," Gensch warned, "was not bound to any social class."[11] Feelings of alienation and uselessness permeated society.

"Although the mass has the right to exert its influence everywhere," Gensch observed, "the individual cannot thereby find satisfaction."[12] The dime novels offered compensation for a life that failed to offer experiences of fulfillment. So, Gensch concluded, no one ought to be surprised that <u>Frank Allan</u> and <u>Harald Harst</u> topped the reading list for a class of forty-one fourteen year-olds selected in a middling Prussian town of 30,000 inhabitants.[13] Clearly, Gensch conceded, the task of channeling these wayward readers towards good literature was daunting. "The highest form of reading is when the reader experiences art," he maintained with characteristic <u>Bildungsbürgertum</u> aplomb and pessimistically conjectured that many German readers would never learn to appreciate artistically significant literature.[14]

Siegfried Kracauer viewed the question of reading habits, literary tastes, and art versus trash, from a different vantage point. For him, the rigid contraposition of good literature which elevated the reader into the lofty realm of art and bad literature designed to tantalize inner demons was flawed and revealed nothing more than stuffy bourgeois prejudices. He rejected the notion that detective stories were low fare of no interest or value to the educated reader. In his perambulations around Berlin, Kracauer enjoyed visiting private lending libraries. His attraction to these urban oases was determined just as much by his own need for pleasure reading, as it was an additional way for him to observe, from an oblique angle, what was really transpiring in mass culture and society. In <u>"Eine kleine Leihbibliothek"</u> ("A Small Lending Library"), Kracauer took the side of pleasure-reading and teased the bourgeois readers for their highfalutin tastes and snobbery. Confessing that he had returned to his old, bad reading habits on account of a new lending library that had recently opened in his neighborhood, he described it as "a dark blue treasure chest that piques my appetite."[15] Its books beckoned through the display window like savory items in a delicatessen. Kracauer extended the epicurean imagery of fine food to emphasize that reading could satisfy a basic craving, including his own specific one for detective literature.

He playfully and satirically contrasted his reading habits with those of a more pretentiously sophisticated type of reader: "Often, ladies entered the store, whom I rather admired, because they only requested the most noble products of literary labor and could not be appeased with anything less than Thomas Mann. In their presence, it gave me special pleasure to request crime novels. I think the ladies were disappointed in my lowly sphere."[16] While, he speculated, they felt sorry for him since he failed to devote himself to "true literature," he poked fun at them for being unable to read for pleasure. These different and conflicting appraisals of literature pointed to a key aspect in the battle over Schund. To what extent should the state be involved in the persecution of one form of literature and the promotion of another? How and to what extent could the state take measures to foster ennobling, artistically stimulating reading? And how could it curtail the rising demand for the coarse reading that satisfied the appetite for sensation and melodrama? Revealingly, a clause in the Schund law actually prohibited the indexing of literature identified as harmful to youth if it was considered to have artistic value.

What drew Kracauer to a genre of fiction that most custodians of German culture frowned upon? He was not just intrigued by the detectives' step-by-step solving of a mystery. For Kracauer, the figure of the detective itself expressed a mystery in that he was a relentless force of ratio (in the sense of ratiocination) but not someone who could penetrate beyond the surface world of cause and effect.[17] The detective's modernity was manifested in his insubstantiality. Kracauer began a review of several detective novels by mentioning the start of a movie he had recently seen. The film's protagonist carried "the smooth, indeterminable features of most contemporaries."[18] His face, Kracauer noticed with consternation, could just as easily be that of a rogue as that of a decent human being. Later, Kracauer claimed this indistinguishable, substanceless quality to be an essence of modern man who precariously endures in a world shaped by ratio. The tragedy was that this modern man was incapable of breaking out of an imprisoning social-economic grid into a liberating, noumenal realm, which Kracauer enigmatically identified simply as "reality." Reality, for Kracauer, is the goal that ratio, and its product, modern man, unfortunately fail to reach: "The man who closes himself off to the break-through to truth is merely possible, not real. Basically, it cannot be written on his face who he is because he isn't at all. Perhaps he is a rogue, perhaps a favorite hero. He himself won't know it, the possibilities are endless [die Perspektiven sind ohne Abschluss]."[19] Contemporary man's peculiar intangibility in an existential no-man's land is the result of modernity: "Out of the structure of modern society follows the indeterminate quality of its people [Aus der Struktur der modernen Gesellschaft folgt die Unbestimmbarkeit ihrer Menschen.]"[20] This ambiguous condition is a central element of crime fiction and potentially opens everyone to suspicion. The shadow of crime attaches itself to all individuals, making "society the eternally green hunting ground for the detective."[21] The detective, like everyone else, is trapped in the surface world and, despite his uncanny rational powers, unable to penetrate into the highest sphere and thus ultimately incapable of explaining the deepest recesses of the human soul or the deviant behavior of the culprits whom he tracks in endless, Sisyphean labor.

Notwithstanding his limitations, for Kracauer the detective exercises an attraction in a refreshingly straightforward manner. His ongoing entanglement with surface phenomena reveals more about modern conditions than do the contents of much so-called "high literature." Yet, as soon as the figure of the detective was created, he was banished, according to Kracauer, into the realm of Schundliteratur and prohibited from "entering the higher regions of writing."[22] Kracauer's admiration reverberates with a sense of identification in the detective and his underlying mission: "[the figure of the detective] is not a cultural asset that has sunk downwards, but rather a plant of the lower regions that first had to proliferate to gain attention from the upper classes. Their blindness derives from self-preservation because [the detective] reveals society. [Selbsterhaltung hat ihnen die Blindheit auferlegt: denn jene Figur verrät die Gesellschaft.]"[23]

While left liberals like Siegfried Kracauer and Walter Benjamin praised much-maligned detective literature, the review boards were about to mount an increasingly forceful attack on the genre's most vulnerable specimens: the dime novel detectives. "Jack Nelson vom Tric Trac Tric: Der Bund der Drei" ("Jack Nelson of Tric Trac Tric: The Triple Federation"), by Stanley Hyne, was indexed by the Berlin Review Board on May 22, 1928.[24] A confused, abstruse explanation supported the decision. The review board found the story absurd and tagged it as "completely worthless." It was also dangerous to youth, but not because young readers might imitate the story's action. The problem lay in what the reviewers described as the intoxicating type of reading induced by such stories which "fogged up the minds and sense of immature readers."[25] Referring to Walter Hofmann's study of German youth, Die Reifezeit (which had also influenced Albert Hellwig's view of youth and Schund), the board maintained that the detective pulps led to the creation of a disturbed mindset characteristic of social outsiders and criminals. The board did not explain why they had chosen one isolated booklet to unleash their ire. Perhaps it was simply picked to serve as a warning to publishers, authors, and vendors.

One year later, five issues of Walther Kabel's detective series Harald Harst were examined in two separate meetings of the Berlin Review Board. The first decision on August 6, 1929, held that the stories "Der blaue Weiher" ("The blue Pond") and "Die Hölle der Verdammten" ("The Inferno of the Damned") ought not to be indexed, although the latter story came very close to warranting censorship.²⁶ Overall, the board viewed the stories as "primitive, childish-romantic variations of the detective theme."²⁷ It found the writing level "not high, but not thoroughly inferior" either. Such stories, concluded the Berlin reviewers, could not endanger youths. Only two weeks later, however, a differently staffed Berlin Review Board indexed three other Harald Harst stories. While the first decision report correctly attributed the stories to Walther Kabel, the second wrongly thought that the author was Max Schraut, the fictional detective character's assistant and pseudonymous "author" of the series. The reviewers seemed to be in a hurry as they made little effort to explain their decision, preferring to repeat shopworn generalities. The stories were "suited to endanger the ethical development of youth" and were based exclusively on "crass sensation and criminal cruelty."²⁸ Furthermore, "the immature imagination of youths could be whipped up in a pathological manner."²⁹

This sporadic indexing of a few detective pulps had no effect on their diffusion or popularity. The pervasiveness of these booklets and the widespread complaints from anti-Schund associations and youth agencies made an eventual showdown between the review boards and the detective pulps inevitable. The first draconian measures were taken against the most popular series, Frank Allan, der Rächer der Enterbten (Frank Allan, the Avenger of the Expropriated) in 1930. The Berlin Review Board's explanation for banning the entire series of 533 issues was both predictable and highly controversial. The reviewers made all the usual complaints. The stories lacked logical plots or psychological depth. The style was poor and they smacked of factory production.³⁰

While Schund activists celebrated, others criticized the sweeping decision. What validity could the board's standard and highly subjective objections have on more than five hundred separate stories written by numerous authors? What proof was there that Frank Allan stories actually "numbed the emotional life" or "overexcited the imagination of youths" as the board maintained? Critics laughed at the board's perfunctory explanation, including its claim that the described crimes were especially repulsive or sadistic. Defenders of Frank Allan pointed out that the stories followed a simple formula in which the detective and his black assistant, after some initial setbacks, always brought the instigators of crime to justice. The writing was competent and straightforward without pretensions to being literary art.

Herbert Lewandowski argued, in the liberal journal Die Stimme der Freiheit, that "the numbing of emotional life" could be linked to economic stresses, like high unemployment and a lack of adequate housing, but not to Frank Allan.³¹ This same argument had been made by leftist delegates during the parliamentary debates about the Schund law. Fedor von Zobeltitz, who had recently resigned as a review board member, also condemned the decision to index Frank Allan. He wrote that it was impossible to consider the entire series as one work. Zobeltitz had read fifty of these booklets and noted that each one was a self-contained story. Despite the ongoing presence of the same detective character and his assistant, the stories were independent of each other, focusing on different milieus and types of crime. He also disagreed with the board's view that the stories undermined morality. How could that be the case when the detective always brought the culprits to justice? He rejected their claim that the stories were sadistic. If these stories were sadistic, Zobeltitz wondered how James Fenimore Cooper's classic Indian tales or the endless number of popular war novels "dripping in murder and bloodshed" could be tolerated?[32] In another negative commentary published in Die Stimme der Freiheit, university professor Wolfgang Mittermaier warned that the Frank Allan decision showed "the danger of the worst sort of patronizing controls." For him, the Schund law was betraying itself in such decisions as "a legal monstrosity."[33]

The teacher Kuno Fiedler, who had been introduced to Frank Allan by his own pupils, launched the most forceful attack on the review board's decision to ban the popular detective. In "The Indexed Frank Allan: An Anti-criticism," also published in Die Stimme der Freiheit, Fiedler stated that forbidding a pulp series might seem like an insignificant event. In actuality, he cautioned, it was an important indicator or symptom of "the illness of these times – a sickness called reaction that itself issues forth from confused concepts as to the hopelessness of life."[34] What was the reason for the decision? Fiedler thought that there were actually two connected reasons: "The censorship is easily done and it demonstrates the review board's raison d'etre to the public... a public that wants to see action, even if it is senseless and foolish."[35]

He asked the review board if the heavy artillery it had decided to unleash was not out of proportion to the modest target it aimed to destroy. Was there not something suspect in this? Fiedler had misgivings about the whole review board set-up which, he thought, tended to generate a holier-than-thou attitude among its members that easily resulted in such blundering decisions. In another article in the same journal, editor Franz de Paola Rost showed how a fair judgment of Frank Allan had been severely undermined by a questionnaire that the Berlin Youth Agency distributed to pre-examining readers assigned to evaluate Frank Allan.[36] De Paola Rost pointed out that some of these hostile authorities later served as members of the review board itself. This meant that the same individuals making a case against Frank Allan later acted as judges on the review board: a grossly unfair and legally untenable situation.

Fiedler, like others, scornfully revealed the review board's hypocrisy when it berated Frank Allan for poor style, while its own opaque writing in the decision declarations included grammatical flaws and stylistic weaknesses.[37] It also applied unsound, circular logic when it argued that the wide-scale reading of Frank Allan bore witness to its very danger and was a main reason for its banning.

Fiedler himself found the booklets harmless and rather well-conceived, particularly in their logic. He condemned the reviewers for callously failing to recognize the consequences of their high-handed decision on the livelihood of pulp writers, publishers, and vendors. He warned the board members not to hide behind the usual excuse that they were doing it all for the sake of Germany's youth: "They are against you. They won't thank you for your protection – just as medieval witches were not grateful for the efforts of those who tried to tear their immortal souls away from the devil."[38]

Most of the flurry of articles defending Frank Allan and attacking the review board appeared in Die Stimme der Freiheit. In this defiantly liberal journal, a voice of reason stood up for the popular detective series. The review boards knew, however, that they could likely rely on broad approval from both political left and right. A curious example of this type of cooperation between left and right is Der Detektivroman der Unterschicht: Die Frank Allan Serie (The Detective Novel of the Underclass: The Frank Allan Series, 1930). The book was written by the young socialist scholar Hans Epstein under the guidance of his nationalist (later a Nazi) university professor Ernst Krieck. One of the first academic studies of pulp literature, the book begins with the argument that the publication figures alone (300,000 copies per weekly issue) call for a serious look at this slighted literature.[39] Profitability was high, explaining why Frank Allan was eagerly sold in tobacco stores, barber shops, alleyway bookstalls, and even grocery stores.[40] Epstein's study intended to be a first step towards understanding the contents of these stories and why they were so popular. He proposed to define a Frank Allan "typology" by examining twenty-five issues published between 1924 and 1929.[41]

Epstein was original in considering a detective pulp worthy of scholarly investigation, but his study is marred by typical prejudices against the genre and it seeks to explain the popularity of Frank Allan entirely by content analysis, without any reference to reader views or responses. Nevertheless, Epstein's analysis provides some valuable contemporary insights to the Frank Allan series. He argued that the series' appeal lay in its structural mixture of formulaic repetition coupled with content variation. The detective and his black assistant Sam always end up in the lion's den of a criminal mastermind, extricate themselves through the ingenuity of Frank Allan, and then apprehend the criminal and turn him over to the proper authorities. He succeeds where the police and the state fail, acting as a god-like instrument of justice. The reader can sit back, comfortably enjoy the suspense and horror, knowing that Frank Allan will always prevail.[42]

Epstein compared and contrasted the detective to his colportage forerunners. He resembled the highwayman in his striving for justice, but he was different in that the state sanctioned his activities (the detective is welcomed by government officials all over the world). Unlike the outsider status of the highwayman, Frank Allan enjoys the privileges of a pampered celebrity: "A transition has been made from the noble, but persecuted highwayman to the noble, amateur detective who is appreciated by practically everyone."[43] Epstein also noticed that while the stories avoided taking a political position, their superficially non-political status actually filtered a dangerous brand of conservative or reactionary politics into the minds of a largely uneducated readership.

Frank Allan's rescue missions usually help the rich. He himself prefers the company of the affluent, dining in expensive restaurants and driving a luxurious Maybach automobile. Allan always travels first class and lodges at top hotels. He places an order at the Junkers factory for a private plane which will allow him to combat international crime more effectively; it also provides him with another challenging, exclusive form of sportsmanship that can be linked to the sport of hunting criminals.[44] The rapport between Frank Allan and his black acolyte Sam idealizes the underling's obedience and willingness to sacrifice himself for the detective, whom Sam usually refers to reverently as "the master."[45] In numerous episodes, Sam's "black" fearfulness contrasts with Frank Allan's superior "white" self-control and dashing aloofness. Epstein criticized the series' authors for avoiding any critical portrayal of social class interaction. Their conservative political views were also reflected in their uncritical references to warfare (particularly gas warfare) and their repeatedly positive comments on the death penalty.[46] Epstein showed that, in Frank Allan, the death penalty is presented as a justifiable and fitting form of punishment for certain crimes.[47]

Although he offered no supporting evidence, Epstein claimed that the Frank Allan stories, like fairytales, fulfilled wish-fantasies of "a primitive, even childish" audience mostly composed of the lowest classes. He worried about the almost unnoticeable proliferation of anti-socialist, "reactionary" views through these extremely popular stories. While not bound to any distinct party line, the Frank Allan series effectively brainwashed hundreds of thousands of readers with anti-socialist messages.[48]

Hans Epstein held a doctorate from Frankfurt University and became a teacher of history and literature in 1932 at Frankfurt's Goethe Gymnasium. One year later he was forced out because of his Jewish background. He transferred to Frankfurt's renowned Jewish school, the Philanthropin. Epstein's study of detective pulps was mentored by Ernst Krieck, a professor of education, who joined the Nazi Party in 1932 and became a leading exponent of Nazi educational theory. While Epstein was subjected to a typical German-Jewish path of increasing ostracism and eventual emigration, Krieck briefly lost his position in 1932, but was reinstated as Rector of Frankfurt University in 1933. Three years earlier, in 1930, a young, leftist scholar and a middle-aged nationalist pedagogue could, remarkably, collaborate and share their interest and animosity for the pulp detective Frank Allan.

Krieck's hostility is revealed in the study's forward. In a pessimistic vein, Krieck felt that Schund entrepreneurs had already won the battle against anti-Schund educators because they were more in tune with the mentality and spiritual needs of their customers.[49] These needs were largely prompted for "a primitive social strata," according to Krieck, by the capitalist pulp industry.[50] He argued further that the publishers had a better idea of what this strata was like and what it wanted than the well-meaning, but misguided anti-Schund movement. For the Nazi educator, pulp publishers and writers had dangerously transformed themselves into the actual "educators of the public [Volkserzieher]."

Krieck distinguished two types of members of the lowest classes: the first could strive to reach a higher level of education if given an opportunity, while the second lacked such a capacity.[51] A "political-pedagogical influence" could lead the first group to "a higher rational level." The second group preferred to escape in their leisure time to a world of wishful fantasies: "The ideal of this reader finds fulfillment in the lifestyle of the highest social strata, which is reinterpreted into a fairy tale land. The hero moves about in luxury and riches: The 'avenger of the disinherited' is a great sportsman who also takes advantage of all sorts of technology. The presentation deliberately moves the rationality of events and thoughts to the foreground. But the magical-fairy tale foundation is everywhere evident."[52]

Krieck had pulled himself up from humble origins to become an elementary schoolteacher, a respected educational theorist, and, finally, a university professor. His writing betrayed ambiguous feelings about the lower classes or, as he (and Epstein) often anthropologically referred to them, "the primitive strata." He considered that in the past, popular culture had managed to produce its own distinct values and art: "The fairy tale… can have its 'truth' and artistic value, a fact that is also manifested in primitive collective poetry, in the folktales invented by minstrels and roving storytellers."[53] While a romanticized, past popular culture evoked an earlier age of organic harmony for Krieck, the modern age, with its mass-produced articles for consumption and profit, merited nothing but scorn. Krieck wondered if "the primitive strata," exposed to the onslaught of exploitative, mass culture, could somehow be redeemed and "refined" culturally.[54] Was it possible to design and invent an alternate literature that could act as an antidote and cancel the harmful effects of Frank Allan and his kind?

Krieck concluded his foreward by exhibiting a vitriolic language typical for the embattled Schundkämpfer. Like "daily drops of a narcotic that paralyzes the will," detective pulps were causing irremediable harm to their defenseless consumers.[55] The reader's "nervous system degenerated," while the publisher's "entrepreneurial profits soared" in a kind of parasitic symbiosis.[56] Although his right-wing, political concepts differed from his student's socialism, Krieck agreed with Epstein that the pulps were a source of great social and cultural harm, and that they were powered by the cold, remorseless forces of capitalism. In this Kulturkampf, the young, socialist teacher and his Nazi mentor found common ground.

It is unlikely that Krieck ever read a detective pulp. He built his arguments on the presuppositions and prejudices of others. Could he have tolerated pulp author Walther Kabel, a fellow conservative nationalist who, like him, joined the Nazi Party in 1932? Kabel's Harald Harst detective series was very successful and spanned the entire period of the Weimar Republic. In contrast to other popular detectives, Harst was neither English nor American, but German, and many of his investigations centered on Berlin. Harst's longevity and popularity was probably due to the original German twist of these stories, but it can also be attributed to the superior quality of the writing. A fluid style, an eye for detail, and an ability to depict believable, interesting characters characterized Kabel's writing. The local charms and flavors of Berlin and its provincial surroundings were sketched in vivid colors. Some of the plots were too elaborate, but over all, Kabel was a master at designing a crime story that neatly fit the sixty-four page format of the series (the simpler Frank Allan stories were only forty-eight pages long).

In the tradition of Sherlock Holmes and Watson, Kabel's fiction revolved around Harald Harst and his assistant Max Schraut. Like Holmes, Harst's ratiocinative genius allows him to unravel cases that stump the regular police investigators. His reputation is international and like other great detectives, he fights crime all over the globe. Scandinavia, India, and the United States (particularly 1920s crime capital Chicago) serve as stages for numerous Harst adventures, but he is always drawn back to his beloved Berlin which challenges him with many exciting assignments. Harst lives in a comfortable, quaint house with his mother and his housekeeper Mathilde, an authentic Berliner who speaks the city's dialect. Max Schraut, who narrates the stories, is an ex-pickpocket whom Harst has taken under his wing and is the fourth member of the Harst family. Harst's bride Marga Milden had been a victim of a homicide and it was her death that caused him to drop his career in the Prussian judiciary and turn instead to fight crime as a private detective.

In his office, Harald Harst keeps close track of daily events by reading newspapers and cutting out and cataloguing articles that might prove useful in upcoming cases. Schraut observes that Harst has "an ability to connect events that seemed to have nothing in common."[57] Harst fulfills a classic function of the detective character in being able to establish order in an apparently chaotic world. "Experience taught him," Schraut says, "that behind the most inconspicuous events, that might only reveal a trace of oddity, one could uncover a wide network of connections."[58] This eye for detail allows Harst, like Holmes, to pry open the most obstinate cases. Harst's exceptional memory is another strength. "He recalls every detail, number, and even the exact wording of sentences," Schraut writes in admiration and adds that Harst claims his ability is the result of "mental training."[59] Recalling contemporary fascination in occultism, his powers of concentration border on the supernatural: "The tone of Harald's voice, when he tied his deductions together, resembled the withdrawn speaking of a medium. The more he strained his mind, the more monotone his voice became."[60]

Harst is reserved, his thoughts hidden and impenetrable: "the less he speaks, the more he knows."[61] While logic and reasoning are the detective's main instruments, Harst also believes in intuition or a sixth sense "that is keener than the others."[62] Some of the superior powers that a great detective has in his arsenal cannot be learned, but, according to Harst, are inborn gifts.[63] In those rare moments, when Harst has no case to solve, he likes keeping his mind active by playing chess.[64] He is also a fine piano player who particularly enjoys playing compositions by Richard Wagner and Edvard Grieg. His reading interests reveal an intellectual bent. Philosophical works by Immanuel Kant, Friedrich Nietzsche, and Rabindranath Tagore are among his favorites. Occasionally, Harst dreams of leaving the hustle and bustle of the city and becoming a farmer in remote, rural East Prussia.[65] Harst's typically conservative idealization of agrarian life comes out in these daydreams.

Yet he is also fascinated and drawn to the modern metropolis. Chicago repeatedly appears not only as a focal point of the world's most sensational crime, but also as an architectural marvel with its "grandiose front of skyscrapers."[66] The city's extreme contrasts of wealth and poverty, its endless traffic, and "racing pulse," the illuminated advertisements on Michigan Avenue, the incredible mixing of nationalities and ethnic types make it more than a stage for crime stories: this Wunderstadt signals the very future of the world.[67] As Harst and Schraut end the case of "Der grüne Schatten" ("The Green Shadow"), they leave a Chinese immigrant's home and step out into the cacophony of Michigan Avenue which wraps around them with "the thousand sounds of this great, beautiful, broad city."[68] In sharp contrast to typical conservative or Nazi writers, as well as colportage authors, Kabel does not simply visualize the city as an evil Moloch, but he sees it as a place of intriguing complexity, of contradictions, of destructive crime and of creative opportunity. In "Der blinde Geiger" ("The Blind Violinist"), a storm passes over the skyscrapers as Schraut waxes eloquent about "the fabulous life tempo of this industrious, greedy, honest, dishonest, and so breathtakingly beautiful" metropolis.[69] Of course, Harst's business is to combat Chicago's notorious gangsters, and these also add something to the lure of the great city. In an act of inverse patriotism, Kabel claims that Berlin's crime is just as thrilling as Chicago's.[70]

Berlin is described as a "nerve-destroying Moloch," but it also has "ancient, picturesque corners" along the Spree that reveal "a romantic quality for which our time hardly has an understanding."[71] Harst, as a native Berliner, moves about with equal confidence in affluent Western neighborhoods like Zehlendorf or Dahlem, as well as in the crime-ridden areas of the Silesian Station and the "Scheunenviertel." With expert opinion, the reader is informed that the German metropolis "bids criminal elements the best opportunities in its peripheral places."[72] Kabel's intimate knowledge of the city allowed him to portray it from many angles with accuracy and the distinct flavors of its various quarters.

While Kabel's fascination with the modern metropolis went against the grain of the typical Weimar conservative author's attitude towards the city, his criticisms and disapproval of many facets of urban culture revealed his other side – the views of the cantankerous, cultural pessimist. As the hub of Berlin's fashionable, urbane lifestyle, the <u>Kurfürstendamm</u>, with its luxury stores, cafés, and restaurants, was a favorite target for sneering criticism from the nationalist right. Kabel joined the angry choir and scoffed at "the spruced-up provincials, the *nouveau riche*, and the con men [<u>Hochstapler</u>] who sought amusement" around the fabled avenue.[73] In the last issues of Harald Harst, dating from 1933-1934, the attacks on the effete <u>Kurfürstendamm</u> clientele become harsher, perhaps with the intention of pleasing the similarly critical Nazis: "These made-up little mugs with painted lips and shaved eyebrows are everywhere the same. You may meet them on Berlin's <u>Kurfürstendamm</u>, where they have a touch of the exotic."[74]

In <u>"Die Fremde in der Kakadu-Bar"</u> ("The Stranger in the Kakadu-Bar"), the upper echelons of Berlin society eat English oysters and drink French champagne. This "brash, pompous" class is, according to Kabel, a product of the war's disastrous outcome and it has parvenu allures of acting in a particularly "elegant and modern" way.[75] Its musical taste for "Nigger-Jazz" and Brecht's <u>Threepenny Opera</u> show to what low cultural levels it has sunk.[76] Harst's admiration for Wagner differs drastically with liberal republican musical fashion and raises his worries about the <u>Verniggerung der Musik</u> or music's black degeneration.[77] While sitting in his winter garden and enjoying coffee and chocolate ring cake, Harst turns on the radio to a station with light music. He moves the dial past any broadcast featuring "a squawking saxophone."[78] In his cozy alcove, Harst can keep modern times at bay, including raucous sounds generated by a racial other. In a sarcastic remark about American segregation, Kabel revealed his prejudices: "The freest republic on earth ruthlessly holds on to the old racial prejudice, perhaps justifiably, for the miscegenation of America [die Verniggerung Amerikas] would only be a matter of time if the white population did not so gruffly avoid any contact with the blacks."[79]

Kabel's descriptions of Jews include the usual stereotyped physical features found in colportage: hooked noses, big lips, fish eyes, and thick glasses. A greasy caftan and sleazy money-making schemes fill out the crude portrayals. Such is the description of the postcard vendor Moritz Seligfeld, who describes himself as "a poor yid," and helps Harst solve a jewelry robbery in the Swiss Alps.[80] Later on he proves not to be a Jew at all, but is a cleverly disguised English actor. In another story that involves a Jew as a central character, he too turns out to be a disguised figure. In <u>"Der ewige Jude"</u> ("The Eternal Jew"), an impostor plays the role of a revered Jewish mystic, who, the public does not realize, is no longer alive. The impostor takes advantage of gullible admirers seeking spiritual guidance. In an ingenious con scheme, "the prophet" exploits those who come for advice until Harst exposes the charade. Although Kabel notes that the genuine Jewish mystic would never have acted like the rogue impersonator, the imagery of a Jewish holy man stealthily robbing naïve, but affluent German burghers fit all too easily into the Weimar scenery of antisemitic scapegoating.[81]

4.2 *Film still covers for the detective series Harald Harstt*

4.2 To spice up the series, exciting movie stills were adopted for the final covers of Walther Kabel's Harald Harst (Berlin: Verlag moderner Lektüre, 1922-1934). Examples: *Der Mann der alles Wusste* (1933) vol. 364, D*ie Fremde aus der Kakadu Bar* (1933) vol. 351.

The story "Das Höllentor von Adagaru" ("The Hellgate of Adagaru") begins in Amsterdam's ghetto. Kabel indirectly criticized contemporary German society when he observed that children in the Jewish quarter still showed respect for elderly members of their own community.[82] Kabel took pleasure in transcribing part of this story with a Yiddish inflection and utilized the usual, stereotyped features – hooked noses, nickel glasses, greasy caftans – in describing Jewish characters. In this story too, not everyone who first appears to be Jewish is actually a Jew. Kabel used Jews to create an exotic effect in his stories but besides the commonplace stereotypes, the stories prior to 1933 lacked a vicious antisemitism, and rather expressed a mixture of admiration and repugnance, a curiosity and fear, similar to that found in the colportage novels of Ernst Friedrich Pinkert.

A less open-ended, angrier view of the Jews can be detected in some of the final issues of Harald Harst. In "Die Fremde in der Kakadu-Bar" (published May, 1933), reference is made to a character who arrived in Berlin from Cracow in 1920 dressed as a poor orthodox Ostjude. Three years later in 1923, the reader is told, the immigrant already owns a spacious apartment, and later he purchases a fine villa.

This Ostjude converts to Christianity. Kabel implied it was an all-too-typical Jewish story of success and sneaky assimilation taking place in the Inflation Period when many Germans lost their entire fortune. Baron von Weichert is the main villain in the story. He is the smug, aristocratic owner of the Kakadu-Bar. When Harst forces Weichert to admit his guilt in a case of murder and theft, the criminal reflects on the origins and causes of his evil ways. In an unusually clumsy passage, Weichert blames it all on his Jewish grandmother who raised him. She inculcated a selfish "ghetto mentality" that taught him to strive ruthlessly for money and power.[83] The fact that this story was published four months after the Nazi acquisition of power, makes it likely that this harder form of antisemitism was an attempt to get in step with the new regime in the hope of avoiding looming censorship. Kabel knew that his fellow Nazis had been among the most vociferous proponents of the Schund law. For them, detective pulps were a repugnant form of mass literature and another evil offshoot of Jewish media capitalism.

The review boards had become more aggressive and unbridled as democracy weakened in the years governed by emergency decrees. Kabel and his publisher realized that the 1930 indexing of Frank Allan, their major competitor, represented a serious menace for all pulp fiction. They also knew that it was only a matter of time before the full Harst series would be considered for a similar fate. This is the likely reason for the occasional, nastily antisemitic suppositions woven into the final narratives of 1933-1934. Did Kabel hope that a stronger antisemitic lacing of his stories might make them more palatable for a review board in the new era of Nazism?

Or was Kabel simply revealing ideas that were now more acceptable to the public and that he had previously kept to himself? Kabel's sensitivity to the bad reputation of popular literature and his humorous disdain for its critics was revealed in asides and comments throughout the stories. Sometimes simply the described setting and characters cast a light on who read the supposedly dreadful stuff. Harst's cook Mathilde is an avid reader of colportage. In "Der Mann am Trapez" ("The Man on the Trapeze"), she is reading installment fifteen of "Die Tochter der Verfluchten" ("The Daughter of the Accursed"). Harst gains some important clues for the case when he discovers that the colportage novel's author is the wife of a crook involved in the crime he is investigating.[84] In another story, a risqué French novel by Eugène Sue "inappropriately placed" on a bookshelf next to works by classic German writers Schiller and Goethe, is a key to solving the mystery because it contains a coded message. In "Die schwarzen Würfel" ("The Black Dice"), Sue is the favorite author of the cultivated, intelligent Erna Kaldenhoven who lived in an unhappy marriage with a "simple Landjunker, a rough man of instincts."[85] Harst asks a chaplain, who knew the deceased woman well, if she enjoyed reading the French author of many serial novels. The chaplain sighs and observes critically that Erna had a peculiar liking for Sue. Harst replies that one could argue about Erna's literary taste. In this discussion, Kabel uses his hero to defend the reputation of the author of Les Mystères des Paris (1843), the story that became Europe's most influential and imitated melodrama, the inspiration for hundreds of colportage novels. The chaplain's dismay with Erna's reading habits positions him in the camp of the Schund critics (who often were churchmen), while Harst's comment shows an appreciation for and willingness to speak on behalf of entertaining, popular literature. In the exchange, the chaplain concedes that Erna found Sue's writing relevant and meaningful: "Sue's garish depiction of moral depravity may have reminded her of the grief she suffered in her own marriage."[86] Throughout the Harst series, in short asides, Kabel constructed a defense of popular literature and admonished its haughty detractors. Its bad reputation was undeserved; its readers read not only for pleasure, but also because popular literature addressed them and their needs in a more direct and accessible manner than the old literary canon.

In "Die Kaschemme Mutter Binks" ("Mother Binks' Saloon"), Schraut speaks for Kabel when he says, "I am no literary writer [Literat]. I write 'Harst.' I write for those who want to learn to think, but who need light reading. Light reading does not need to be shallow."[87] In addition to the criticism of superficiality, Kabel disputed the accusation that the stories of popular literature were far-fetched and grossly unbelievable. In "Drei Löwen" ("Three Lions") the narrator reflects: "Life itself creates stories more fantastic even than those concocted by the popular fiction writer with the wildest imagination."[88] In "Der Kopf der nichts verriet" ("The Head that Didn't Betray Anything"), Schraut skeptically doubts Harst's hypothesis that a respected civil servant is a hard-boiled criminal: "A long-time civil servant is a criminal, possibly the leader of a criminal organization? This was the worst colportage kitsch," he first thinks, but then realizes: "Life writes the gaudiest stories. Whoever doubts it, doesn't know life."[89]

Kabel could also criticize certain popular fiction authors. Here and there, he made cutting comments on the immensely popular English crime author Edgar Wallace, finding his stories repetitive and predictable.[90] He also felt that "so-called purely literary intellectuals" might have less of an aversion for "so-called crime novels," if the crime writers were not as bent on making it easy for the reader to figure out the story's solution and overdoing the sensationalism.[91] While solving the case of "Pension Grollmatz," Harst tries to determine if there is an underground connection between two buildings and disparagingly refers to the shoddy literary scaffolding often used in inferior detective stories: "I can't stand the horrible expression 'underground corridor' that ruins so many bad novels. I also can't use terms like 'problem' or 'deduce' [kombinieren] and such other stock-in-trade of the detective factories."[92]

In the final Harst issues, published after 1932, Kabel increasingly made an effort to contrast himself with the authors of "asphalt literature," a favorite right-wing, derogatory term for Weimar's modernists. In Writing Weimar (2000), David Midgley notes that the right-wing press attacked Berlin "as the breeding ground of Asphaltkultur, of all that was seen as inimical to traditional German values."[93] Kabel could honestly claim to have ridiculed, criticized, and attacked Weimar's modernist culture all along. Urban housing projects seemed "terribly cold and sober."[94] Jazz was nothing more than Niggerlärm [nigger noise].[95] In "Die Kaschemme Mutter Binks," the recorder and writer Schraut serves as Kabel's proxy. Schraut claims that in the past a certain type of Asphaltliterat [modernist writer] had slandered him and tried to take him to court. Kabel thus presented himself through his alter ego as a victim of the Weimar Republic. Its authors wanted to silence him because his writing was "too manly, too forceful," it was also imbued with a nationalism they rejected. "I never denied my Germanness [Deutschtum]... and I got quite vicious when it came to beer table philistines, veterans' club maniacs, coffee house authors, magic mountains, Professor Unrats, and others. Sometimes, no, too often, my pen slipped too far to the right. Then I had to lay aside these writings which would have caused the whole Kurfürstendamm and Berlin West to scream with rage."[96] Kabel implied that his criticisms of cosmopolitan Weimar society, which indeed had been continuous and consistent, were also toned down and restrained so that he could publish in the hostile climate. As with his antisemitism, one has to ask whether this was all pandering to the new Nazi regime or the unveiling of a radical right-wing position that Kabel had felt obliged not to disclose completely before 1933. Along with the Nazi "harmonization" in these final issues one also notices a stiffening, deteriorating writing style.

Kabel's publisher, the Verlag moderner Lektüre, started openly trumpeting the Harst series' patriotism and nationalism in August, 1933. On the back covers, in an appeal to readers, the publisher recalled how the series had been launched in 1920 to offer German readers the chance to enjoy an alternative to all the glorified foreign detectives. Kabel was portrayed as a Frontkämpfer writer who had astutely managed to create a character with particular German sensibilities: "Thousands of letters from our readers, from all levels of society, have recognized our endeavor and expressed their approval."[97] In large, dark print the publishers emphasized how the stories promoted a German sense of family and friendship: "Only in German families can such a close relation between mother and son, and between friends, be built and strengthened. This, in turn, becomes a warm, homely foundation for a heartfelt community life. Author and publisher have sought to promote the moral and spiritual reconstruction of the German Volk and fatherland."[98]

To loyal Harst readers such claims surely must have seemed strained and distorting. The detective's affectionate ties to his mother were hardly a main theme of the series. Harst's friendship with Schraut was simply a by-product of their mutual adventures and a formula relationship of classical detective fiction. The publisher failed to mention the important role assigned to the many young women characters, who Kabel sympathetically portrayed as intelligent, independent, and very capable of promoting their own interests and desires. Such positive portrayals were hardly compatible with Nazi views of female subordination. Nazi ideology was more in line with the old colportage idealization of the angelic, self-denying, German woman who faithfully stands by her man's side through thick and thin.

The colportage or Nazi heroine was not the impertinent, stubborn, bright young woman who appeared in many Harst episodes of detective fiction. In "Ein Gast in der Nacht" ("A Guest in the Night"), the nineteen year-old Hella von Mauring drives up to Harst's house and asks him to investigate a case that involves her husband. A hand-written letter she had sent earlier to Harst suggests "a very energetic personality."[99] In "Die leere Tonne" ("The Empty Barrel"), Harst and Schraut stand in awe of the heroine Daisy Steenhope: "What this woman was capable of, what strength and adroitness she possessed, we now were finally going to notice."[100] She then kicks the villain in the eyes and blinds him. In "Das Schaltbild für sechs Röhren" ("The Circuit Diagram for Six Tubes"), Schraut himself gets punched by a woman. Harst remarks on his friend's female opponent, "Aloysia ... must once have been a boxer. Knocking you down with all your fatty cushions is not that easy."[101] In the same story, twenty year-old Anni Bartel tells Harst that she cannot tolerate injustice and proceeds to involve him in a difficult case in which she mysteriously and stubbornly resists his efforts to solve it.

Kabel's intrepid, independent young women were individualists who hardly seemed compatible with his conservative rejection of Weimar culture. In fact, the presentation of these usually sympathetic female characters was vitiated by many anti-feminist comments interspersed in the stories. Occasionally, he even slipped back into old colportage stereotypes of "satanic" or "demonic" women who are, as criminals, more evil and dangerous than males.[102] In one episode, Harst himself restrains a woman with physical force. When she breaks down, Schraut comments chauvinistically, "She was, after all, a woman."[103] Like conservatives and Nazis, Kabel detested the Bubikopf or bob hairstyle which symbolized Weimar's sassy, independent young woman.[104] Kabel's antifeminist mood, like his antisemitism and nationalism, became more pronounced in the last issues. In "Die roten Pantöffelchen" ("The Red Slippers," August, 1933), a wealthy widow of an industrialist is described contemptuously as "a cosmopolitan patron of modern women issues" with "an exaggerated intellect," but no understanding for the Volk.¹⁰⁵ Kabel also disliked women who insisted on using their academic titles.¹⁰⁶

Throughout the series, Kabel expressed resentment for the scoundrels and criminals who acquired wealth and prestige as a result of the lost war and the subsequent economic turmoil, particularly the Great Inflation. He called them "inflation hyenas."¹⁰⁷ Apparently he himself had made a bad commercial decision in selling a valuable property shortly before the Inflation and ended up as one of its many losers. Despite his great success as an author of popular literature, his income and lifestyle remained modest in the Weimar years. His publisher paid him one hundred marks for each Harst issue.¹⁰⁸ Like other former officers and underemployed academics, Kabel suffered a sense of status deprivation which he expressed in semi-autobiographical characters whose pent-up resentments simmer below the surface. In "Der schwarze Gast" ("The Black Guest") Harst meets a hotel detective. He is Count Gerhard von Pfuhl-Pfuhlberg, "a layed up naval officer." This former submarine commander ironically quips, "When in dire straits, the devil will even eat flies – I became a detective!"¹⁰⁹ In "Die Uhr ohne Zeiger" ("The Clock Without Hands"), the reader is told: "There are many well-educated chauffeurs these days. Hunger and need push some people into jobs that don't match their training and education."¹¹⁰ Harst too is a victim of the times and can hardly afford the cigarettes he enjoys smoking: "He only smoked his favorite Mirakulum brand, despite the fact that these sweetly smelling things cost more than he could afford. The war and its consequences had turned the millionaire Harald Harst into a modest pensioner."¹¹¹

Harst's Mirakulums were laced with a small amount of opium. Opium, morphine, and cocaine appear in many accounts, revealing a stressed society seeking escape from bitter realities. The users are often women. Harst quickly understands, by looking at a person's eyes, if they are cocaine addicts.¹¹² Berlin's organized crime traffics heavily in cocaine.¹¹³ In "Pfandleiher Immertod" ("Pawnbroker Immertod") a young female pilot smuggles cocaine into Denmark by air.¹¹⁴ In "Der Mann vom andern Ufer" ("The Man from the Other Shore"), Harst observes that he does not usually harbor feelings of hatred, but "when he hates, there is a reason."¹¹⁵ He hates the drug syndicates who "poison millions of people." Harst proceeds to explain:

> "The people cannot be enlightened enough about these pests. Until recently, the most common drugs were opium, morphine, and cocaine. Then someone invented the worst of all poisons, initially as an antidote to morphine addiction: heroin! Today these criminals earn billions on heroin."¹¹⁶

Kabel described the Weimar years as an "age of ferment, a time in the process of becoming a new epoch."¹¹⁷ Within this period of confusion, popular interest in occultism was great and detective stories often included occult themes. In general, Kabel loathed occultists, "these exploiters of human gullibility and weakness for the supernatural."[118] In several issues, Harst battles 'the Trias," an occultist mastermind criminal with access to ancient oriental secrets.[119] In "Der Bluffer" ("The Bluffer"), Harst meets former actress Emmy Bieler who "lived off of the stupidity of people by fortune-telling."[120] She had ingeniously modified an idea of the actual miracle doctor Heinrich Schäfer Ast (1848-1921) who diagnosed illnesses by examining a patient's neck hair under a microscope. Instead, Emmy uses neck hairs to tell fortunes: "To read the future from neck hairs, something new! She did it all exclusively by mail and made three hundred marks a month."[121] Kabel's fictitious soothsayer casts a light on an age of growing superstition and disorientation. Such figures were emblematic of the times and were meant to reveal the pitiful condition of contemporary German society.

Yet Kabel was not entirely immune to his age's fascination for the occult. In "Die Göttin der Wyndhiaberge" ("The Goddess of the Wyndhia Mountains"), Harst speculates on the possible uses of hypnosis and telepathy in controlling and shaping a person's unconscious actions.[122] In "Die Schildkröte vom Halensee," Harst determines that what first appears to be a hypnotic state experienced by Schraut and two others was actually caused by a tiny amount of a sprayed, hallucinogenic chemical.[123] While hypnosis and altered states of consciousness intrigued Harst, particularly their connections to secret oriental arts, the power of divining rods was something that he believed to be a substantiated fact. Kabel informed the reader, in "Die Versuche des Dr. Syme" ("The Experiments of Dr. Syme"), that the diviner is mistakenly viewed as a sort of miracle-maker, but there is no reason to consider his achievements in tapping water or metal resources as supernatural.[124] Harst explained that the diviner must be a person physically endowed with enough "personal magnetism" to be able to feel magnetic waves emitted from below the earth's surface.[125] As with other Weimar themes, Kabel's position was elusive and contradictory. While he embraced divining rods, most "occult sciences" seemed faulty or preposterous to him. The very popular "eye diagnosis," in which the physical and spiritual state of an individual could be discerned entirely by studying the iris, he deemed a real flop when applied to criminology.[126]

The whole complex of questions connecting occultism, popular superstitions, "cultural ferment," and the search for a new order became a topic of discussion in the November, 1933 issue "Der Mann, der alles wusste" ("The Man Who Knew Everything"). In a serious, studious manner, quite different from the lighter, more playful style antedating 1933, Kabel explained the spreading confusion and sense of cultural crisis that had afflicted Germany.

> The modern era is characterized by a dreary, omnipotent materialism. (Curiously, the 'inventors' of this movement hold fast, by way of blood, to ancient traditions

and religious precepts!) This age, which sought to reconfigure all moral concepts, found the greatest resistance among the middle classes, who instinctively resisted the destruction of all moral foundations. They eventually turned and fled into a sphere related to religion: mysticism, spiritism, occultism, astrology, palm reading, and similar, mostly supernatural endeavors to find truth and inner, spiritual satisfaction. The popularity in Germany of Indian Brahmanism, East Asian Buddhism, faith healing, and charlatan doctrines of salvation was only a reaction to omnipotent materialism. When highly educated men, politicians as well as scholars, were ready to seek out dubious fortune-tellers and follow their advice, one faced further evidence of a moral and spiritual rootlessness that ought to give cause for alarm.[127]

Kabel described a shaken, discombobulated society, and he outlined patterns of behavior that he felt deserved investigation. The initial parenthetical comment, however, showed that by 1934 he openly connected the spiritual crisis with a materialist culture that he ultimately blamed on the Jews. His pulp conservatism was transforming into Nazism. But all these attempts to either adjust his stories and ideas to the new system, or the making public of a previously private, right-wing radicalism, would not help in saving the series from the censor's axe. Paradoxically, Kabel suffered defeat at the hands of the Nazis whom he ardently wished to support, while he experienced his greatest success and popularity in the Republic which he scorned, ridiculed, and helped undermine.

As the author of a very popular pulp series, he could not disavow his ties to a media that the Nazis deemed incorrigibly rotten, a prime manifestation of mass culture, exploitation, and decadence. When the Berlin Review Board finally got around to considering the Harst series in April, 1934, it was performing its functions in a twilight state between Weimar law and Nazi rule by fiat. No longer beholden to parliament, nor concerned about criticism from a muzzled press, the review board could lash out with pinpoint brutality.

Between the banning of Frank Allan in 1930 and the censoring of Harald Harst in 1934, the series Tom Shark, der König der Detektive (Tom Shark, King of the Detectives, 1929-1939) had luckily managed to avoid censorship. It came up for review several months after the controversial decision to index the entire Frank Allan series. The Berlin Review Board, in its decision of July 25, 1931, observed that Tom Shark was very similar to Frank Allan, but they noticed some slight differences, which gave them a more favorable impression. The writing style was better, the greater length of the stories (sixty-four pages) somehow assuaged the typical pulp roughness, and the reviewers liked the stories' irony and humor.[128] They also welcomed the recurring inclusion of sport themes.[129] The decision not to censor Tom Shark allowed this detective series to continue until 1939 when the Nazi government peremptorily banned all detective pulp literature.[130] Whatever minor differences may have distinguished <u>Tom Shark</u> from <u>Frank Allan</u>, one thing was certain: the decision-making process was arbitrary and depended primarily on the composition of the particular review board in question. The SPD delegate Kurt Löwenstein's prediction, made during the parliamentary debates in 1925 about the <u>Schund</u> law, had proven true: the changing composition of the review boards would lead to inconsistent decisions that made no sense.

In April, 1934, Walther Kabel and his publisher appeared before the board to argue their case. They repeated the claims that their detective was uniquely German. They also brought a whole stack of fan letters to prove his popularity. The board haughtily dismissed the letters as irrelevant, pointing to the fact that the majority were written by adults, while the board's job was to protect youth.[131] Although they grudgingly agreed that Harst displayed some sympathetic and typically German traits, like his warm rapport with his mother, his cook Mathilde, and his friend Max Schraut, they "forcefully rejected" the author's view that the stories manifested "a national perspective." Indeed, they declared that Harst was "a personality who could not serve as a role model for our youth in the construction of Germany."[132]

Callously, the board found the <u>Harst</u> booklets to be "factory-produced mass ware without any psychological depth." In contrast to the <u>Tom Shark</u> decision, it could find no reason to handle <u>Harald Harst</u> differently from the precedent-setting case against <u>Frank Allan</u>.[133] The board flung the usual stigmas at the detective pulp and ascertained "the complete worthlessness of the novel." <u>Harald Harst</u> offered no "inner enrichment" and was merely "a cramped attempt to stretch the subject matter so as to throw more and more issues at the public."[134] Furthermore, some of the issues contained scenes that were simply abhorrent. The board referred to <u>"Der Fakir von Nagpur"</u> ("The Fakir of Nagpur") as an example. In it, a dying man's internal organs were visibly exposed like those of an anatomical specimen.[135] Kabel was also accused of concocting scientific and technical absurdities. Some of the hero's actions were impossible. In one story, Harst jumps from an airplane onto a moving train.[136]

The reviewers considered Kabel's writing style laughable and pompous. What probably incensed them most was that Kabel had dared to ridicule their colleagues on the film review boards. In <u>"Die goldene Schere"</u> ("The Golden Scissors"), Kabel referred to a couple of indecent films shown in Berlin and wondered why "the law against filth and trash remained silent?"[137] In <u>"Der Fall Tussi Gambys"</u> ("The Case of Tussi Gambys"), he had speculated that the film review board must have slept through a particularly risqué movie scene that was released uncensored.[138] Kabel's wit contrasted with the board's stuffy, irascible intolerance.

The largely obscure board membership reviewing <u>Harald Harst</u> was composed of two chaplains, two government administrators, a painter of ships and seascapes named Gustav Fenkohl, the writer Werner Schendell, the publisher

Reinhold Thieme, and the educator and Reichstag member Elsa Matz. As a DVP delegate, Matz had strongly endorsed the Schund law. Later, she had co-authored a manual explaining the new law with Ernst Seeger, Director of the Film Superior Review Board. She herself sat on both film and Schund review boards, and it was very likely her angry reaction to Kabel's ridicule of film censors that manifested itself in the board's caustic decision report.[139] For the dedicated Schundkämpfer Matz, her work as a reviewer and censor was no laughing matter.

Like other conservatives, Matz thought and argued in the terms of an idealist tradition permeated with nationalism. It was exactly the sort of heavy-handed, doctrinaire thinking that Siegfried Kracauer found inflated and dangerous, and peculiarly German. In her parliamentary speeches, Matz had declared that the moral status of German culture would determine Germany's fate. Of utmost importance was the cultural and ethical well-being of German youth. She argued that Weimar youth was split in two. There was a high-minded, patriotic youth "struggling for inner values" that encompassed all the different social classes and world views. Next to this positive youth was another type equally dispersed throughout society which caused her "to shudder at the thought that this should be the future of our fatherland."[140] This was a generation that lacked "the will to work, the will to self-discipline, the will to community, a youth that lived in boundless egotism."[141]

Turning to the SPD delegate Kurt Löwenstein during a 1925 parliamentary debate, she concluded, "You cannot deny that there is such a youth and for this reason we need a law to protect juvenile morality."[142] For Matz, the battle against Schund was part of a larger war to fend off the evils threatening German youth. She appealed for a kind of Burgfrieden (political ceasefire) between the parties in this sacred cause to save German youth: "Freedom may not be confused with disorder and the defiance written all over the faces of some of German youth," Matz argued.[143] Morality and national renewal could not be sacrificed or exchanged for freedom. Matz's angry speech inadvertently acts as a kind of prism through which one can see the contours of Weimar's wayward youth. This was a subaltern stratum that wanted to live a life free of Matz's strict moral code of Prussian military discipline and Lutheran self-denial. It resisted a conformism mandated by the political right as a patriotic panacea. This was a youth that wanted a freedom outside the tutelage of narrow-minded, self-proclaimed patriots and moral watchdogs. These were the young Bubikopf women and their dapper boyfriends who shimmied to the sounds of black musicians or smoked cigarettes and cheered at boxing matches. They were the German youths who went to the movies and read detective pulps. They lived a lifestyle that promoted and indulged individualism while being incorporated in new forms of consumerism and mass culture, a phenomenon that intrigued Kracauer and sometimes even gave him a sense of hope. But it marked a way of living that was anathema to Elsa Matz and Weimar's culture warriors of churchmen, conservatives, and Nazis.

Perched impossibly between the fronts, itself an ambivalent product of mass culture as well as its critic, Walther Kabel's detective series <u>Harald Harst</u> emblemized the contradictions and conflicts of Weimar society. A German detective who sneered at most everything modern and cosmopolitan was snuffed out by a review board of conservative cranks. Kabel's juvenile readers, who eagerly snatched up each new episode, enjoyed the stories when teachers and parents were not looking. They bought, sold, and traded the flashy booklets in a barely concealed market that both perplexed and menaced suspicious adult outsiders led by the graying fighters against "trashy literature."

4.3 Film still cover for the detective series Harald Harst

4.3 To spice up the series, exciting movie stills were adopted for the final covers of Walther Kabel's Harald Harst (Berlin: Verlag moderner Lektüre, 1922-1934). Final issue *Das Geheimnis um die "Marga"* (1934) vol. 372.

Kabel, strongly attached to his fictive hero, designed a fitting departure for him. In the last episode, <u>"Das Geheimnis um die 'Marga'"</u> ("The Marga's Secret," April,

1934), Harst attempts to assist a young woman who uncannily resembles his deceased wife. The detective's companion Schraut realizes this after he sees an aging photograph of her. Harst's prompted memory opens an old wound. Schraut notices an ominous change in his friend's behavior. Harst reads packets of timeworn letters, studies old photographs, and seems lost in reminiscences: "I could easily understand how his heart must have stood still when he saw her. First he didn't let anyone notice. Then the memories must have become ever more alive and he transferred this strong love... onto the stranger."[144] In a note foreshadowing departure, Harst confesses to his friend that lately his life "has received a precious gift of special meaning."[145] The detective in love can no longer be the infallible, rational machine. While pursuing this case, he makes a terrible mistake and drowns in the Baltic Sea. The author's own anguish at his hero's demise is expressed in the final words of the narrator: "I write the funeral song of a truly kind and warm-hearted man. His name was Harst and many loved him – far more than the general public realizes."[146] On the last page, he brings issue 372 and the entire series to an end: "I now say good-bye to my readers and friends forever."[147] Only a year later, the nationalist detective author Walther Kabel himself was dead. Perhaps the demise of his alter ego at the hands of a merciless censorship board was simply too much to bare.

Endnotes

1 Heinz J. Galle, Volksbücher und Heftromane Band 2 (Lüneburg: Dieter von Reeken, 2006), 46.
2 Ibid.
3 Ibid.
4 Willy Gensch, "Was liest unsere Jugend? Ergebnisse einer Umfrage," in Was liest unsere Jugend? (Berlin: R. von Decker's Verlag, 1930) ed. Hertha Siemering et.al., 62.
5 Ibid., 61-62.
6 Ibid., 63.
7 Ibid., 61.
8 Ibid., 64-65.
9 Letter from the Director of the Tübingen Trade School to the Ministry of Churches and Schools in Stuttgart (July 2, 1921). (HStA Stuttgart) E 151/09 277.
10 Gensch, 65.
11 Ibid.
12 Ibid., 55-56.
13 Ibid., 56.
14 Ibid., 82.
15 Siegfried Kracauer, "Eine kleine Leihbibliothek," in Schriften 5.2 Aufsätze (1927-1931) (Frankfurt: Suhrkamp, 1990), 360.
16 Ibid., 360.

17 Siegfried Kracauer, "Neue Detektivromane," in Schriften 5.2 Aufsätze (1927-1931), 44.
18 Ibid.
19 Ibid., 45.
20 Ibid.
21 Ibid.
22 Kracauer, "Hamlet wird Detektiv," Schriften 5.1 Aufsätze (1915-1926) (Frankfurt: Suhrkamp, 1990), 351.
23 Ibid.
24 PS Berlin [May 22, 1928] "Jack Nelson vom Tric Trac Tric Der Bund der Drei," (BArch) R 181.
25 Ibid.
26 PS Berlin [Aug.6, 1929] "Der blaue Weiher, Die Hölle der Verdammten" (BArch) R 181.
27 Ibid
28 PS Berlin [Aug.20, 1929] "Der Mann am Kreuze, Tawa Barru der verrückte, Henny Garlans Zauberschloss" (BArch) R 181, An appeal in Leipzig to overturn the decision failed.
29 Ibid.
30 Berlin PS [Jan.20, 1931] "Frank Allan," (BArch) R 181.
31 Herbert Lewandowski, "Nachwehen zum Frank-Allan-Urteil," Die Stimme der Freiheit, No. 8 (1930), 126.
32 Fedor von Zobeltitz, Letter regarding the Frank Allan case published in Die Stimme der Freiheit, No.7 (1930), 108.
33 Wolfgang Mittermaier, Letter regarding the Frank Allan case, dated June 19, 1930, published in Die Stimme der Freiheit, No.7 (1930), 107.
34 Kuno Fiedler, "Frank Allan der Indizierte," Die Stimme der Freiheit (1930) No.7, 103.
35 Ibid., 104.
36 Franz de Paula Rost, "Frank Allan!" Die Stimme der Freiheit (1930), No.6, 90.
37 Fiedler, 104.
38 Ibid., 105.
39 Hans Epstein, Der Detektivroman der Unterschicht (Frankfurt: Neuer Frankfurter Verlag, 1930), 3.
40 Ibid.
41 Ibid., 6.
42 Ibid., 11.
43 Ibid., 13.
44 Ibid., 30-31.
45 Ibid., 42.
46 Ibid., 49-50.
47 Ibid., 52.
48 Ibid., 35.
49 Ernst Krieck, Forward to Hans Epstein's Der Detektivroman der Unterschicht, vi.
50 Ibid., vi-vii.
51 Ibid., vii.
52 Ibid.
53 Ibid., viii.

54 Ibid.
55 Ibid.
56 Ibid.
57 Walther Kabel, Harald Harst (Berlin: Verlag moderner Lektüre, 1919-1934), "Der Mann vom anderen Ufer," [352], 11. The following citations are by individual title and series number.
58 Kabel, "Wen sucht Lord Trassy?" [344], 3.
59 Kabel, "Die Schildkröte von Halensee" [191], 54.
60 Kabel, "Der alte Gobelin," [272], 38.
61 Kabel, "Der schwarze Würfel," [278], 51.
62 Kabel, "Salon Geisterberg," [258], 22.
63 Kabel, "Der Vampir von Berlin," [347], 44.
64 Kabel, "Das Schaltbild für sechs Röhren," [275], 4.
65 Kabel, "Drei Löwen," [205], 5, and "Ein Gast in der Nacht," [197], 13.
66 Kabel, "Das Siegel Salomonis," [285], 17.
67 Ibid., 38-39.
68 Kabel, "Der grüne Schatten," [291], 64.
69 Kabel, "Der blinde Geiger," [286], 10.
70 Kabel, "Der schwarze Gast," [334], 16.
71 Kabel, "Die grüne Sanduhr," [365], 17, 30.
72 Kabel, "Allan Garps letzte Stunde," [343], 8.
73 Kabel, "Der Getreidespeicher der Morton-Bande," [350], 5.
74 Kabel, "Das Gespenst am Hardanger-Fjord," [367], 36.
75 Kabel, "Die Fremde aus der Kakadu-Bar," [351], 13-14.
76 Kabel, "Der Getreidespeicher der Morton-Bande," [350], 5, and "Die Fremde aus der Kakadu-Bar," 13.
77 Kabel, "Der Mann am Trapez," [322], 33.
78 Kabel, "Der alte Gobelin," [272], 26.
79 Kabel, "Das Siegel Salomonis," [285], 50.
80 Kabel, "Salon Geisterberg," [258], 7.
81 Kabel, "Der ewige Jude," [21], 29.
82 Kabel, "Das Höllentor von Adagaru," [206], 4.
83 Kabel, "Die Fremde aus der Kakadu-Bar," [351], 60-61.
84 Kabel, "Der Mann am Trapez," [322], 28-29.
85 Kabel, "Der schwarze Würfel," [278], 29.
86 Ibid.
87 Kabel, "Die Kaschemme Mutter Binks," [354], 39-40.
88 Kabel, "Drei Löwen," [205], 35.
89 Kabel, "Der Kopf der nichts verriet," [310], 57.
90 Kabel, "Die Königin der Orchideen," [358], 8 and "Einer, der die Freiheit haste..." [370], 31.
91 Kabel, "Der alte Gobelin," [272], 18.
92 Kabel, "Pension Grollmatz," [277], 34.
93 David Midgley, Writing Weimar (Oxford: Oxford Univeristy Press, 2000), 263.

94 Kabel, "Der Getreidespeicher der Morton-Bande," [350], 11.
95 Ibid.
96 Kabel, "Die Kaschemme Mutter Binks," [354], 39.
97 Kabel, "Die roten Pantöffelchen," [357], back cover. The same back cover appeal continued until the final issue in March, 1934.
98 Ibid.
99 Kabel, "Ein Gast in der Nacht," [197], 3.
100 Kabel, "Die leere Tonne," [66], 32.
101 Kabel, "Das Schaltbild für sechs Röhren," [275], 24.
102 Kabel, "Die Schildkröte von Halensee" [191], 62-64.
103 Kabel, "Die Uhr ohne Zeiger," [192], 53.
104 Kabel, "Die Schildkröte von Halensee," [191], 30.
105 Kabel, "Die roten Pantöffelchen," [357], 27.
106 Kabel, "Die weisse Schlange," [339], 7.
107 Kabel, "Der Mann von gestern..." [368], 17.
108 PS Berlin, "Harald Harst 1-331" [April 27, 1934], 2 (HStA Stuttgart) E 151/09 BU282.
109 Kabel, "Der schwarze Gast" [334], 8.
110 Kabel, "Die Uhr ohne Zeiger," [192], 39.
111 Kabel, "Der rote Zigeuner," [91], 7. See also "Die Schildkröte von Halensee," [191], 4.
112 Kabel, "Die Geschichte einer Irrsinnigen," [177], 12.
113 Kabel, "Der Vampir von Berlin," [347], 62.
114 Kabel, "Pfandleiher Immertod," [333], 5,56.
115 Kabel, "Der Mann vom anderen Ufer," [352]. 31.
116 Ibid., 32.
117 Kabel, "Der alte Gobelin," [272], 62.
118 Kabel, "Das Gespenst am Hardanger-Fjord," [367], 8.
119 Kabel, "Die grüne Sanduhr," [365], "Die Versuche des Dr. Syme," [366], "Das Gespenst am Hardanger-Fjord," [367].
120 Kabel, "Der Bluffer," [371], 31.
121 Ibid.
122 Kabel, "Die Göttin der Wyndhiaberge," [223], 14.
123 Kabel, "Die Schildkröte von Halensee," [191], 19.
124 Kabel, "Die Versuche des Dr. Syme," [366],32.
125 Kabel, "Die grüne Sanduhr," [365], 28.
126 Kabel, "Der schwarze Gast," [334], 44.
127 Kabel, "Der Mann der alles wusste," [364], 14-15.
128 PS Berlin [July 25, 1931], "Tom Shark,"2, (BArch) R 181.
129 Ibid., 3.
130 Christian Adam, Lesen unter Hitler, 205-206.
131 PS Berlin [April 27, 1934] "Harald Harst 1-331," 11, (HStA Stuttgart) E 151/09 BU282.
132 Ibid., 4.
133 Ibid., 3.

134 Ibid., 4.
135 Ibid., 5-6.
136 Ibid., 8.
137 Kabel, "Die goldene Schere," [230], 28.
138 Kabel, "Der Fall Tussi Gambys," [299], 14. Both episodes criticizing the film reviewers are discussed on page 10 of the Berlin Review Board's decision to index Harald Harst.
139 Ibid., 9-10.
140 RSR (June 16, 1925), 2344.
141 Ibid.
142 RSR (June 16, 1925), 2345.
143 Ibid.
144 Kabel, "Das Geheimnis um die 'Marga'," [372], 32.
145 Ibid.
146 Ibid., 55-56.
147 Ibid., 64.

Chapter Five. Nudism: Weimar Renaissance or National Degeneration?

On a sunny Sunday morning in March, 1931, Siegfried Kracauer joined a crowd of factory workers, white-collar office employees, and lower-echelon civil servants going to a matinée performance in Berlin's Grosses Schauspielhaus.

5.1 Cover of the nudist journal Die Schönheit

5.1 Sun, water, sport and nudity promise a joyful weekend on the outskirts of Berlin. Cover of Die Schönheit, one of the many nudist magazines that irritated Catholic and conservative politicians. Die Schönheit (1930) 9. Cover photo by Gerhard Riebecke.

The former Circus Schumann had been redesigned by architect Hans Poelzig as a giant expressionist theater and was renowned for its unusual decorative stalactites which hung down over the audience. On this morning, the people looked forward to a demonstration of nudist exercises performed by Adolf Koch's Körperkulturschule [physical development school].

Kracauer facetiously entitled his article "Battle Against the Swimsuit." In the theater's foyer, a young girl wearing pigtails approached visitors and tried to sell them a nudist magazine. She asked, "Sirs, have you gotten our newest edition of Freude am Körper (Physical Joy)?" The journalist ironically observed that she sold "physical joy [Körperfreude] in the same tone of voice as one would sell matchsticks, shoe laces, or flowers."[1] Inside, the theater was packed with curious spectators. Adolf Koch explained that nudism originated from a small sect around the year 1900 and, thirty years later, had blossomed into a mass movement. Koch discussed socialist Freikörperkultur [nudism], a word that bothered Kracauer. He thought the clumsy compound word revealed something of the movement's own confusion and questionableness. While Kracauer could support its aims of improving proletarian health through exercise and hygiene, he flinched at Koch's claim that socialist nudism was a new world view. He suspected there was something amiss here in Koch's insistence that naked exercises could open the door to an ethereal, transcendent realm. In the nudist performance and in its enthralled audience, he saw a strange, misconceived combination of social engagement and popular distraction. As in other Weimar endeavors, a proposed solution to modern ills was merely a distorted expression of social malaise. The May, 1931 edition of the nudist journal Das Freibad took a friendlier perspective of the Koch School's matinée. The journal's anonymous author heralded the presentation as the nudist movement's greatest success in Germany to date.[2] Among the 4,000 spectators in the Grosses Schauspielhaus, there were over one hundred political representatives from Berlin's city assembly, the Prussian Landtag, and the Reichstag. Fifty reporters from German and international newspapers observed the nudist spectacle which had been sold-out for a month in advance. All kinds of organizations declared their support for Koch's brand of socialist nudism, including the Prussian Institute for Sexual Sciences, the League for the Legal Protection of Expectant Mothers, and the Association of German Lung Disease and Tuberculosis Patients.

The Freibad writer noticed that conservative papers avoided reporting about the matinée because of its obvious public approval. The Center Party, however, did not let popularity stymie its relentless campaign against Koch. Any public institution that cooperated with the Koch School came under Catholic scrutiny. An appeal had been made to the Ministry of Transportation and the National Railroad Office to ban Koch's publications from train station bookstores and kiosks. In a second article, Das Freibad reported that the unexpected triumph at the Grosses Schauspielhaus on March 29, 1931, had increased the alarm bells sounded by the Center Party and its publications in the capital. In a letter to Adolf Koch, Germania's editor Lorenz Zach explained why he had become his implacable foe. "If I am correctly informed," he wrote, "it is the opinion of the movement you represent, that any sense of shame

[Schamgefühl] caused by an encounter between two members of the opposite sex is unnatural. As a convinced Catholic, I am of a contrary opinion."³ Zach informed Koch that he had no interest in interfering in nudism when it took place in a closed area off limits to the public. The problem was that Koch's nudist publications were displayed all over Berlin in highly trafficked areas where one could hardly avoid seeing them. This, he felt, posed a grave moral danger to youths. Zach concluded by observing that "...in recent times, the journals have had an influence on Berlin's cityscape out of all proportion to the movement's actual size. Thus you are the one who is limiting the freedom of others. One cannot avoid places and streets where these publications are exhibited... Two world views intersect here that are simply incompatible."⁴

The conflict, in some ways, resembled the debate over Schund and the political divisions it generated. Conservatives again suggested that there was too much freedom in Germany and not enough morality. The SPD had opposed the Schund law and now took the side of Koch and his socialist nudists. Regarding the controversial issues of "trashy literature" and nudism, Catholics vehemently opposed Social Democrats. These two parties, whose cooperation was vital for the survival of the Republic, found themselves at loggerheads over cultural differences and clashing moral codes. Here there truly was a problem of incompatible values and world views. While Germania attacked Koch, the SPD's Vorwärts called on city administrators and the national government to promote and support the kind of healthy, restorative nudism practiced by the Koch schools.⁵

In the nudist question, Catholics joined conservatives and Nazis against Social Democrats and Communists. The nudists themselves were divided into three groups: a bourgeois right; a socialist left; and a neutral, unpolitical nudism in the middle. H.E. Kieslich, in a 1930 article published in Magnus Hirschfeld's journal Die Aufklärung, ridiculed, like Kracauer, all the ideological claptrap associated with nudist organizations: "Unfortunately, nude bathing is mixed up with some sort of Weltanschauung in all too many designated nudist areas. Here they require the otherwise ordinary member to endorse blue-blonde racial purity and 'German convictions,' elsewhere they expect allegiance to orthodox marxism. In between are the various shades advocating reformism, vegetarianism, or youth movement ideals. Very few associations simply accept decent people without pestering them about a world view."⁶ Kieslich considered the pompous shrouding of nudism with lofty philosophical ideas an uncalled for form of special pleading: "Glossing over nudism with a world view opens the whole endeavor to suspicion. It all grows from the fear that one might think that co-educational nude bathing is an end in itself. For God's sake, no one should think that! No, nudism serves a world view, a völkisch German, a socialist, or a reformist one. It was created for that purpose. No one bathes in the nude because it's fun or because they like to see good-looking, naked people around them. Wouldn't that be something!"⁷

Kieslich's honest insights and criticisms of Weimar nudism were aimed against the same sort of pseudo-intellectualism that Kracauer noticed in his neighborhood lending library when bourgeois women frowned on his penchant for crime novel reading. In a number of film reviews, Kracauer had taken Weimar's film companies to task for shying away from the production of straightforwardly enjoyable and entertaining movies like those of Harry Piel or Hollywood fare. Haughtily aspiring to art, they ended up producing kitsch. In a parallel manner, Kieslich referred to the pretentious forms of nudism as "awful twaddle" [übler Schmus] and as "high-class kitsch" [Kitschigedel].[8] Weimar's popular culture was filled with swagger that covered deep-seated insecurities.

5.2 Cover of the nudist novel Ist Nacktheit Sünde?

5.2 "Is nudity a sin?" asks the title of Egbert Falk's novel *Ist Nacktheit Sünde?* Egbert Falk was the pseudonym of Georg Fuhrmann. (Stuttgart: Otto Mieth Verlag, 1922). Cover illustrator unknown.

Very revealing of the strivings and intentions of Weimar nudism were two nudist novels: Georg Fuhrmann's Ist Nacktheit Sünde? (Is Nudity Sinful? 1922, written under the pseudonym Egbert Falk) and Anton Putz zu Adlersthurn's Insel der Nackten (Island of the Nudists, 1927). While Adolf Koch hoped to free the working class from the physical and moral damage inflicted by capitalism, bourgeois nudists originally viewed themselves as a radical elite who would help break the dangerous chokehold of modern urban civilization and establish an alternative utopia. The nudist novels revealed the confluence of heady ideas originating in the reform and youth movements, and in an artistic, Bohemian counterculture that rejected prevailing Wilhelmine conventions in the years before World War I. For the nudists, a deep sense of alienation resulted both from a modern materialist economy and what they considered a Christian religion hostile to the human body. Capitalist materialism leveled and quantified all livelihoods, rendering work empty and meaningless. At the same time, Christianity's teachings harmed man by cutting him off from vitally important ties to the regenerative, harmonizing energies of nature.

The main character in Ist Nacktheit Sünde? is Hans Fischer. He and his fiancé Lucie are part of Berlin's reform movement subculture. They enjoy the company of theosophists, natural healers, and vegetarians. Lucie designs graceful, loose clothing, following the precepts of the reformers and rejecting the unhealthy products manufactured by the modern, fashion industry. Lucie's youthful idealism does not blind her from the fact that the battle against fashion wear is uneven since it is backed by powerful capitalist interests, while the reformers have to subsist on the margins of society.[9] Hans and Lucie attend a meeting of reformers who plan to start a nudist lodge.[10] One of Hans' friends, the painter Christensen tells the group that he can insure its purity and internal harmony by weeding out unsuitable candidates, screening them phrenologically and graphologically: "He was able to detect the smallest, most hidden characteristics of strangers by studying the formation of the face, the head, and the hand...."[11] The carefully selected individuals are expected to share a common longing for "beauty, purity, truthfulness, transcendence, and love of nature [Naturfreude]."[12] The group wishes to discuss topics like popular medicine, natural healing, marriage reform, women's rights, Isadora Duncan's modern dance, the dreamy art of Fidus, and the future prospects of breeding and racial refinement.[13]

The nudist lodge views itself as a small elite, an avantgarde that will explore new possibilities later to be emulated by the masses. All of this is explained by the elected leader of the group, the author Friedrich Richter. He proposes that the lodge's main goal is the search for a new, higher human being who can best be realized by means of "an unerotic and naked togetherness."[14] He challenges the group to discuss whether it wishes to require nudity from its members immediately or prefers a gradual turn to nakedness. Richter theorizes that the act of dropping one's clothing removes all barriers of caste and money. Nudity also fosters open and honest communication between the group's members. Richter believed that in this "exceptional community" one would "learn to read the language of the body."[15] This nudist skill would somehow assist couple's in figuring out if they were a good match or not.

A skeptical Kracauer had suspected that the shiny apple of nudism contained a worm. In fact, the original nudist synthesis of idealism and Social Darwinism was a dangerous blend of countercultural experimentation and a program for eugenically-designed racial improvement. In Ist Nacktheit Sünde?, nudist racism is propounded in a speech by the lodge's expert on the "racial problem," Hermann Niethammer, an anthropologist who resided in Ceylon and Java for many years. He tells the lodge's members that it is pointless to make restrictive rules on vegetarianism, temperance, and smoking. What really counts is racial purity.[16] He himself will become a member only on the condition that the group consists of pure Aryans. The lodge needs to guard against homosexuals and it should not accept physically handicapped people [verkrüppelte Gestalten] either.[17] Niethammer's outspoken prejudices – which reflect the actual views of early nudist theorists like Richard Ungewitter and Heinrich Pudor – are uncritically supported by most of the lodge's members who warmly applaud his speech. The painter Christensen seconds Niethammer's position on homosexuals, "foreign races," and "the physically ugly."[18] He reminds the audience that through phrenological examination one can weed out anyone who should not belong to the group.

Hans Fischer then moves the discussion to another important topic and lets the group know that its success hinges on its ability to recruit female members. Only if they join, can the lodge establish "an island of beauty in the midst of purely material life."[19] He makes a special appeal to women listeners. He knows that the taboo against nakedness presents a greater obstacle for women than men. On the way home, Lucie tells him that she is not ready to appear naked before strangers. Hans understands and respects her decision. He feels that he owes her an explanation for his own commitment to the nudist cause: "I am hungry for the extraordinary. Maybe it has no other meaning than to increase my sense of self-esteem, to test boundaries, and to enrich my life."[20] Hans' honest confession reveals a quest for fulfillment that characterized much of Weimar's popular culture. The engagement in subaltern activities frowned upon by mainstream society, be they nudism, occultism, or reading "trashy literature," gave the individual a chance to experiment, to fantasize, and to boost self-esteem. These apparently unrelated activities gave disenfranchised people a sense of meaningfulness or empowerment otherwise lacking in their lives. Alternative values and new moral codes set them off from a daily life characterized by mediocrity and a gnawing sense of disorientation.

Hans and Lucie face continual financial hardship as they try to build themselves an agreeable countercultural niche. Hans is offered a job as editor of a nudist magazine that operates on a shoestring budget. But his main challenge is to recruit women for the lodge. Several willing women step forward and overcome initial feelings of embarrassment by posing as "marble statues" of Greek goddesses. These manifest Hellenic ideals and give their audiences a chance to contemplate aesthetic and physical perfection. The nude ensemble is meant to inspire and to educate. In this context, nakedness loses its sexual, erotic qualities and transposes itself to a higher spiritual realm. The nudist ideology claimed that <u>Schönheit ist nicht pikant</u> [beauty is not piquant]. Yet, in an unintentionally funny scene, Hans admits that it would be dishonest to pretend nudism lacked any sensuality at all. As he waits for a newly initiated "goddess" to undress, he "notices with astonishment how he is seized by an inexplicable restlessness, a completely strange feeling, an exciting expectation... The feeling of expectation sends a tingle up his spine which cannot be prevented even by the strictest self-control."[21]

5.3 Cover of the nudist novel Die Insel der Nackten

5.3 Nudism and exoticism offer a promise of freedom to world-weary Europeans in Anton Putz zu Adlersthurn, *Die Insel der Nackten* (Wien: Czerny, 1927). Cover illustration by Willy Mernsinger.

Such frank admissions were rare in nudist literature because they could easily be exploited by anti-nudist critics and used to reinforce conservative arguments that nudism was a perversion. For them, it was simply another form of modern moral decay, certainly not the source of moral renewal it purported to be. Nudists disputed these views by claiming that only through nudism could one effectively overcome the decadent eroticism that represented a real danger to society. They argued that the church-going bourgeoisie hypocritically preached chastity and marital fidelity, while it engaged in prostitution and extra-marital affairs. It was the seemingly upright burgher who frequented debauched nightclubs where skimpily-clad or naked dancers excited the perverse fantasies of male spectators. These partially clothed or stripped performers appealed to base instincts; in contrast, the nudist's body manifested honesty, moral purity, and aesthetic ideals.

While Georg Fuhrmann's Ist Nacktheit Sünde? offered an insight to the prewar origins of reform movement nudism in Berlin, Anton Putz zu Adlersthurn's Die Insel der Nackten transposed nudist life to the near future. The story begins with a convention of utopian literature. A shipwreck casts two wealthy Germans, Arabella Schliemann and her suitor Achilles von Soesten, on a remote Pacific island. Bauro is inhabited by south sea natives and a thriving colony of German nudists. The survivors show gratitude to their island rescuers, but are shocked by their unusual alternative lifestyle, so different from the rich, snobbish society they unexpectedly left behind. While Arabella reacts with scorn for the nudists, Achilles' curiosity is piqued and he is intrigued by the strange ways of his hosts. Arabella lectures her native hostess Omagege that it is shameful to stand naked before a male stranger like Achilles.[22] Omagege tells her that shame is a concept foreign to her.[23] Using a typical nudist argument, she says her body is a part of nature and she sees no need to hide or cover any part of it. Arabella is further outraged when the leader of the German nudists, the darkly tanned Knapproth, comes to meet them unclothed and addresses them in the familiar "du" [you] form. He lets them know that nudism is the island's law and that the formal "Sie" is not used. These ways underline Bauro's equality. The German nudists and the original islanders share a mutual respect for each other. No one on Bauro seeks to force their ways or customs on anyone else. Knapproth contrasts Bauro's enlightened nudist tolerance with European intolerance. If his people visit Europe, he surmises, they would be required to wear clothes, but the utopian islanders do not require guests like Arabella and Achilles to go naked.[24]

Knapproth explains that before the war he had been a teacher in a southern German village. Accepted and supported by pupils and parents, his liberal methods were viewed with suspicion by the Catholic Church. At this time he first came into contact with the nudist ideas of Richard Ungewitter.[25] After serving in the war, he moved to the city and joined the nudist movement. He and his nudist friends discussed reformist topics of interest such as nutrition, clothing, race, and religion. Constantly harassed by Church and state authorities, Knapproth and his fellow nudists petitioned England to give them an island in the South Pacific where they could settle. England granted them the island of Bauro, and in return, the nudists promised to establish a productive community and to pay annual taxes.

The nudists let the local inhabitants know that they wished to live in harmony and respect, they had no colonial intention of forcing European customs on them. Instead, they threw overboard all the empty formalities, social hierarchies, and hypocritical morals of western civilization. They wanted a new society based on nature's own laws. Knapproth made it clear that the kind of civil strife suffered in Germany would not be transplanted to the island paradise.[26] Bauro would have no social classes, nor would it allow political parties. Nudity eliminated such tensions.

As Achilles gets to know the islanders, he learns about their goals and views. One nudist tells him that the typical European shuns nudity because without clothes, he loses "the whole masquerade of his lying self. This explains his great fear of nakedness. It is nothing but shame and fear of oneself."[27] When Knapproth accompanies Achilles to the nudist settlement, the visitor feels awkward in his clothes and decides to remove them. An initial feeling of self-consciousness quickly vanishes. He also starts experiencing nature's elements with new intensity: "He had never felt so light and free. The wind was so much cooler, so much more refreshing. Slowly, we settled into a natural state of ecstasy [Naturrausch]."[28] The atheist Achilles is easily converted to nudism, but the situation is very different for the devout Catholic Arabella.

Her stubborn opposition reflects the Catholic Church's hostility to the nudist world view. For Arabella, the naked German islanders make a mockery of themselves and all western values. They have, from her perspective, adopted the ways of heathen savages. The concept of original sin has been discarded in favor of a wild worship of nature, a cardinal error that can only lead to perdition in the eyes of Catholics. Arabella equates the nudist disrobing with the casting away of morality. She rejects Omagege's equation that what is natural must be moral. She dismisses the island woman's views as sophistry, condescendingly asserting that "a naturist cannot learn German logic."[29]

The concept of original sin clashes with the nudist idealization of the body as a site of natural purity and innocence. A religious authority on the island, the hermit Reginhardt, tries to convince Arabella that the Roman Catholic Church distorted and perverted the teachings of Christ when it defined the body as sinful. He asks, "When did Christ damn the naked body? When did Christ express a word against the wishes and rights of nature, against the erotic needs of man? Never!"[30] Reginhardt calls for a revised pre-Church understanding of Christ's teachings. This view of an original Christianity in harmony with nudism was widely shared by nudists of the 1920s and 1930s. Arabella's own resistance to the nudist ideology slowly erodes. Experiencing the peaceful harmony and happiness of island society, she finds herself questioning her own values and attachment to Catholic teachings. She does make one last meek criticism of the nudist island's Social Darwinist, euthanasia program. A utopian guide explains that denying life to the unwanted is an act of "higher humanity," it defends the population from contamination, and is a measure rarely used since the healthy, beautiful islanders normally produce "a noble progeny."[31] Utopian racial engineering protects the island population from degeneration because it denies a place for "a weakling, or someone who is ill."[32] This argument briefly unsettles Arabella, but she and her utopian companion quickly move on to another, less disturbing subject.

In the end, Arabella, like her shipwrecked friend Achilles, is converted to the nudist way. Her "convent school education" and denial of the physical self is overcome as she embraces and joins the nudist society.[33] A refreshing nude swim in the island's pristine waters helps wash away her last objections and inhibitions. Arabella throws away her make-up kit, a last vestige of decadent Europe. She chooses instead to let water and wind naturally beautify her. Accepting nature and her body as part of this larger whole allows her to overcome her resistance to public nudity and to embrace this noble way of living.[34]

In 1924, Hans Suren, one of Weimar's foremost nudist leaders, reported that, "There still exists today a settlement on Tahiti founded on organic [naturgemässen] life, ruled by pure, noble motives."[35] While Putz zu Adlersthurn dreamed of an exotic nudist paradise, Suren converted nudist ideas into practice. His treatise, Der Mensch und die Sonne, published in more than seventy editions during the 1920s, became the nudist Bible. A former officer and physical education instructor for a Prussian military institute, Suren provided useful advise on healthy exercises and athletic games, while exalting nudism as a new value system and lifestyle capable of redeeming mankind.

Suren advocated nudism as an inexpensive antidote to all the physical and spiritual evils emanating from western civilization. He viewed the city through expressionist spectacles and saw it as the Moloch machine that consumes endless numbers of men: "Like tottering slaves, they drag heavy chains of labor... far away from the sun – far away from nature, in the prisons of the cities.[36]" Der Mensch und die Sonne offered these slaves a way out of their predicament through a rediscovery of nature and a new sense of their own physical being. As an example, Suren described a nudist cross-country run that he organized for a group of men as a collective act of joyful liberation.[37] It cost nothing, he noted, and recommended that it be done in all kinds of weather so as to strengthen the body. The participants wondered how it was possible that only a short time before they had been hunched over documents (Suren's followers were middle class Angestellten or white-collar workers, not proletarians like many of Koch's followers). Exposed to wind and weather, and united in naked equality, the nudists exulted in their new-found freedom: "What gives us the strength? What makes us feel so fortunate and happy that we want to pass this on to all our fellow humans? It is nakedness and nature! The work of the sun on solar humanity!"[38] This sense of bursting free from the strictures of an artificially confined society was typical of Weimar nudist writing. Suren incorporated such scenes into his Manichean universe and liked to contrast Mother Nature with her degraded antagonist, "the prostitute civilization."[39]

This dichotomy translated into a further opposition between nature's instinct and civilization's intellect. Suren felt that intellect had led mankind into a blind alley where it was trapped in alienating, exploitative work and a culture of decadent hypocrisy. Instinct could free man. A return to nature meant purification and liberation. Cold-hearted science, materialism, egotism, and loneliness stood on one side.[40] On the other, one found fulfillment, peace, and harmony: "Carry the torch high so as to show mankind the gate that leads out to nature, to sunshine, and to the path towards happiness and peace. Every one of you has the right and power to be part of the great, noble work... Your torch is enthusiasm! The people should be sparked by your enthusiasm so that they too rush out into nature and sunshine, and experience themselves. And this experience will give them the push they need to overcome the rigors of daily life."[41]

Youth, the one part of society not yet entirely corrupted by civilization, easily took the lead in following its natural instincts toward liberation. Suren approved of German youth's rebellion against an overly academic system of education. He argued that school hours needed to be shortened so that more time was available for physical exercise.[42] Suren's anti-academic, anti-intellectual views were linked to his aspirations for a coming German resurgence: "It is better to train fewer intellectuals, then to let national power [Volkskraft] go under."[43] Exercise and exposure to the sun and elements was the key to national revival regardless of whether it was military or economic.[44] According to Suren, both the Spartans and Athenians had recognized how important the physical as well as the moral condition of each individual was for the Volk as a whole.[45] He argued that Germany's military power depended more on physical health and endurance than on material factors like supplies and armaments.[46] He wanted to save the younger generation from the fate of the city's frivolous, stylish poser [Modejüngling] with his hanging shoulders and pale skin. He needed to be replaced by "the tanned young man with broad chest and sparkling eyes."[47]

Like the nudist novelists, Suren presented ancient Greece as an inspiration and an ennobling model for contemporary nude culture. Knowing the high regard in German society for all things Greek, the nudists presented themselves as Germany's truest admirers of Hellenic civilization. If Olympian athletes competed in the nude, how could nudism possibly be wrong? Nudity and gymnastics, according to Suren, were the foundation of Greek civilization and power.[48] He observed that Greece had succeeded in defeating the numerically superior forces of Persia, hinting that a similar destiny might await Germany too.

Suren contrasted the value of Greek sports, designed to foster harmony, with modern sports that destructively forced athletes to chase after records. The latter was a product of a sensationalist press and a fawning public. Suren maintained that the pentathlon typified the Greek idea of sport. It built the whole body and the whole man, while modern athletes were forced to specialize so they could win a single event for which they were physically predisposed. This was contrary to the holistic, spiritual approach of Körperkultur which meant to revive the Greek ideals of beauty and harmony.[49] In modern sport competitions, the spectators worshipped champions.[50] "How different was the ancient Olympic spirit that prevailed in Greece," lamented Suren. "An unhealthy desire," he continued, "for sensational achievements will not allow for a thoughtfully planned, harmonious building of the physical abilities of the individual or the masses."[51] Ancient Greece was indifferent to "sensation and cheap thrills."[52] The Greek audience "calmly observed, technically considered, and aesthetically judged the competitor's harmony in form and achievement." Suren predicted that the Germans would one day follow their Greek mentors, but to do so, he insisted, it was first necessary to embrace nudism in sports.[53]

Suren wrote that for the time being nudists would have to accept the fact that they were small in numbers. They could, however, take heart in recognizing their elite status and that it was their mission to teach and lead the masses.[54] He himself did not foresee how quickly this development would take place and how important his book Der Mensch und die Sonne would be in the process. Nudism's popularity spread so rapidly that powerful conservative institutions, especially the Catholic Church, felt threatened and called upon to respond.

The Jesuit Philip Küble attacked Suren in his tract Nacktkultur (Nudism, 1926). For him, Körperkultur was a hoax, a huge exaggeration that threatened the well-being of Germany. Youth was particularly endangered by the siren's call of nudism. Küble warned that the longed-for regeneration through sun worship was a nefarious deception.[55] Rebirth and purification could only come from the Creator. Only Christianity could harmonize body and soul, and usher in an age of national resurgence. Nacktkultur's appeal for public nudity was not a path to liberty but the road to perdition.

Küble ridiculed Suren's idealization of the tanned body and viewed it as a form of primitivism: "Whoever wants to develop into a Negro may want to lie naked in the sun, should he have nothing better to do. A reasonable person asks if he thereby really makes a significant contribution to his health."[56] Instead of evolving to a higher level of being, as the nudist's claimed, Küble argued that their activities meant devolution to a lower state, one that he liked to identify with dark-skinned Africans.

His own racial prejudices and nationalism were fully revealed when he associated sexually transgressive behavior with blacks by discussing the "Black Horror on the Rhine," (a widely reported nationalist topic in which French colonial soldiers had supposedly raped and abused German women in the occupied Rhineland). Küble scoffed at the nudist proposition that cultures which wore little or no clothing were actually less prurient than cultures that wore lots of clothing. He sarcastically hypothesized that in such a case centuries of nakedness and sunshine ought to have quelled the African sex drive: "We have experienced something else in the Rhineland. It's not possible... to complain about the black disgrace on the one hand, and on the other, to praise Negro culture as the highest form of culture."[57]

According to Küble, the nudists' goal of purifying man by a return to nature was self-destructive. By telling modern man he needed to emulate primitive cultures, if not the animal kingdom, the nudist ideology promoted a regression to a dangerous state of wildness and immorality. In nudism, Küble did not envision a utopia of frolicking "natural" humans, but an apocalyptic, bestial world far worse than that of the animals. Free reining instincts in animals were naturally self-limiting, but this, unfortunately, was not the case for the human species: "In truth, the most brutal animal behaves better than a brutal man!"[58] Nudism eliminates the main restraints that put a check on man's destructive instincts: "The chains of control were up until now the Schamgefühl and the moral law, with its sanctioning concepts of heaven and hell. All of this falls away, but without avoiding the dangerous possibility that man might place his reason and imagination in the service of his drives."[59] Inadvertently, the nudists opened Pandora's box. The unleashed sex drive would inevitably transform man into a beast.

While the nudists argued that the Schamgefühl was an obsolete, culturally-learned attribute that needed to be discarded, Küble explained that it was at once God-given and natural. It was the cornerstone to individual moral behavior. Everything else – love, marriage, family, and society – depended on it. For nudists, Schamgefühl manifested the falseness and rot in modern society. Instead of straightforward honesty and acceptance of one's entire body, including the genitalia, a decaying society tried to hide and stigmatize an essential part of man. Raising children and youths in nakedness meant progress towards a life of harmony with nature and reality. Nudists were moral because they accepted themselves completely instead of building a system of deceit and repression. For Küble, the idea that one could lift morality through nakedness was a pipe dream of the worst sort.

The Jesuit's frustration with the growing popularity of nudism, even within Catholic ranks, became apparent in his criticism of the German nation for its naïve credulity: "In this Volk one only needs pretty thoughts about some topic and they are already accepted as true. Oh what pretty thoughts, we are already in paradise!"⁶⁰ A return to earthly reality required sensible thinking about the complex matter of Schamgefühl: "Let us leave fiction aside for the moment and let us examine what is true. Determining the right concept of Schamgefühl is of central importance."⁶¹

Would the population listen? Or would the nudists succeed in converting ever more followers? Would the Church's battle with nudism suffer setbacks similar to those suffered in the struggle against occultism and "trashy literature?"⁶² Such questions haunted the defenders of traditional values and the Catholic forces that helped prop up Weimar's precarious patchwork hegemony in the years from 1924 to 1930.

Küble asked his readers to place their trust in reason, not nudist fantasy. Over and over, he reiterated that reason alone could evaporate the clouds of confusion misleading many of his contemporaries. His analysis of Schamgefühl intended to show how wrong nudism was in trying to knock down an essential pillar of civilization. "What does Schamgefühl want in general?" Küble asked. "It seeks to protect human dignity... whoever openly shares with anyone his most personal, holy side is throwing himself away and loses his dignity."⁶³ Küble extended this line of reasoning to man's sexual nature. Public nudity equaled a loss of dignity. The genitals should not be seen in public, just as intercourse ought not be visible for all to see.⁶⁴ It was the nudists' cramped attempt to obfuscate sexuality in their strange form of pantheism that was unnatural, not the Church's teachings.

According to Küble, one feels shame for the same reason that one feels hunger, cold, or pain.⁶⁵ It is inborn and not culturally or historically acquired as the nudists mistakenly claimed. God has given man this sense for a very good reason: "If Schamgefühl is a protective instinct defending personal dignity, it must express itself most forcefully against an instinct that most seriously threatens human dignity: the sex drive."⁶⁶ Küble proceeded to elaborate his argument theologically. The body only became associated with shame after the commitment of original sin.⁶⁷ It caused what could generally be called "the evil desires" or the flesh's rebellion against the soul.⁶⁸ The sex drive is only a part of "the evil desires" but not identical to them as the nudists falsely think. Man's feeling of shame originates in these developments and not, as the nudists claim, in "the rotten fruit of false Christian asceticism."⁶⁹

Küble's defense of Schamgefühl also disputed an antisemitic, nudist view explaining its origins. He angrily rejected the proposition that the sense of shame was a Jewish invention. The nudist ideologue Carl Heinrich Stratz had blamed the Jews for inventing Nacktscham [shame of nakedness]. According to Stratz, Küble recounted, Moses sought to stimulate male fertility in his community by ordering women to cover their physical charms in a seductive manner. This preposterous hypothesis Küble called "mean-spirited slander."⁷⁰

The nudist adulation of ancient Greece also met with nothing but scorn from Küble. He argued that Greece's decline could be traced to the historical moment when Greek athletes began exercising in the nude. Küble noted that numerous passages in the <u>Odyssey</u> showed that the Greeks originally possessed a sense of shame, but later lost it with the introduction of nude sports and training. This loss resulted in such immoral, shameless behavior as "the Greek vice" of pederasty.[71]

Küble prognosticated a similarly inevitable downward trend for Germany's nudists.In actuality, he held the nudists in greater contempt than the Greeks for the ancients had balanced physical exercise with intellectual education. Suren, instead, heavily favored the former while declaiming intellectualism as a chief factor for Germany's decline. The Greeks, at least, practiced a religion and paid homage to their gods, Küble continued, while the nudists drifted into a sinful state of atheism. The nudist's cult of the sun went hand-in-hand with deification of the body or what Suren called the "holy temple of <u>Körperkultur</u>."[72] Instead of worshipping God, Küble admonished, Suren had turned the sun and body into false idols. He had the audacity to reverse God's will by subordinating soul to body. Since Suren preached "pure, lasting pleasure of the natural," how could he deny or set limits for the satisfying of sexual desires?[73] If Christian ethics had become superfluous, Küble rhetorically and facetiously asked, "Has Mr. Suren become my lawgiver? Mr. Suren should realize that 'today's frightening materialism' cannot be driven out by an even more frightening materialism. With <u>Körperkultur</u> alone we will not achieve a spiritual renewal, but instead create spiritual enslavement."[74] Küble concluded by noting that Germany already had an abundance of problems. It did not need another in the quixotic form of nudism: "What no one has accomplished since Adam, we will achieve if we follow Mr. Suren. By cultivating nudity, we will save poor chastity!"[75]

Küble's stinging attack on nudism elicited an immediate response from the nudist camp. Writing under the pseudonym Theologus Christianus, Josef Seitz published <u>Nacktkultur? Darf und soll der Mensch nackt leben? (Nudism? Should Man Live Naked?</u> 1926). The pamphlet was subtitled "An Answer to Father Ph. Küble, S.J." Seitz argued that Küble's intolerant views were entirely un-Christian and revealed the prejudices of a priestly caste misrepresenting true Christian values. Küble perverted Christianity when he stamped the body with sin, instead of hallowing it as God's greatest gift. The nudists endeavored to unite body and soul in a new purity. Nudism elevated morality by making the naked body an accepted part of everyday life, not an object of craven desires.

Seitz felt that Küble unintentionally lowered the standard of morality by equating chastity with the wearing of clothes. "Poor virtue! ...What a strange opinion you have of virtue, of will, of the soul of man!! My virtue should depend on a piece of cloth, on a mass-produced article of clothing? No, Father Küble, my virtue is different and I hope that virtue in general is different. My virtue has its seat in the will and its foundation in the recognition of good and evil."⁷⁶ Seitz challenged Küble to provide evidence that cultures who lived naked were unchaste. He also asked him to see for himself what the nudists were like: "Let the nudists carry out their experiment; observe their family bathing areas, the outdoor swim areas along rivers and lakes; you will find that these people are as decent and chaste as the people wearing clothes."⁷⁷

Another pamphlet responding to Catholic anti-nudism, <u>Freiheit dem Leibe!</u> <u>(Liberating the Body!</u>, 1927) was published anonymously by "a Catholic theologian." This ostensible Catholic attempted to reconcile nudism with Catholicism using the usual argument that the body, as God's creation, could not be deemed sinful and that nudism stood for a religiously inspired idealization of physical beauty and cosmic harmony. Framed in an anti-materialist discourse, the writer claimed that nudism searched for a way out of the modern, mechanical predicament and echoed the call for inward, moral improvement and religious revival. The nudist education of youth towards "chaste nakedness" deserved recognition as a "cultural achievement."⁷⁸ The classical homage to beauty would be blended with Christian spirituality in a new mystical age or Third Reich: "We used to consider this a poetic vision. Today we feel that the pressure of modern civilization has forced us onto a path of reform that leads towards the Third Reich."⁷⁹ The calls made by "a Catholic theologian" and "Theologus Christianus" for the Catholic Church to rethink and modify its position on nudism went unheard. The Catholic backlash persisted.

A follow-up to Küble's sweeping condemnation of nudism was Joseph Mausbach's tract, <u>Über Sittlichkeit und Badewesen</u> (<u>On the Ethics of Bathing,</u> 1930). Mausbach, Professor of Moral Theology at the University of Münster. had been a Center Party delegate to the Weimar Constitutional Convention in 1919. His booklet was the printed version of a speech he gave at a 1930 Cologne conference discussing the local archbishop's concerns about the disturbing new trends in public bathing.

The Catholic Rhineland was a region vulnerable to invasion by urban nudists, particularly on weekends and holidays. The river and its tributaries offered plenty of bathing sites and these were often adjacent to villages and towns. In the Rhineland the two worlds clashed dramatically when holy processions marched past riverbanks filled with nudists.⁸⁰

Mausbach observed, "Unfortunately, today it is not unusual for young men and ripe girls to ride together in a boat completely naked, to swim together, and to return to shore."⁸¹ Such unsupervised, "wild bathing" was not much worse than the kind of bathing that took place in the supposedly ordered public bathing facilities administered by local communities.⁸² Mausbach bemoaned the fact that these official establishments condoned mixed gender swimming in scanty swimsuits only a stitch away from nakedness: "The moral feelings of any normal person does not therein see the nobleness of nature, but rather a complete aberration that will inevitably destroy the Schamgefühl, and along with it, moral dignity and chastity."[83] Naked and semi-naked bathing in the Rhine was not only blasphemous, it was also an affront to national pride in this cradle of German culture and patriotism.[84] Mausbach further noted that it made a generally bad impression and even drew complaints from foreign tourists.[85]

Not all foreigners, however, were offended. French journalist Roger Salardenne visited Germany because he was interested in nudism. Along the banks of the Rhine, he witnessed the tensions between Catholics and nudists. In the town of Worms, two conservative Catholic acquaintances, named Wilfried and Johann, shared their experiences and views on nudism (while Salardenne tactfully kept his favorable opinion private). When Wilfried saw the nudists, he got off his bicycle, went down to the river's edge, and told them what he thought of their shamelessness: "I shouted words like 'pigs, bandits, sadists.' A woman thumbed her nose at me. Oh, what filthy elements."[86] His friend Johann listened to the story, then exploded in anger: "If I had been in your place, and if I had my shotgun with me, I would have shot right into this depraved horde! One ought to slaughter them like wild dogs, one ought to shoot them down one after another!"[87]

Salardenne himself had observed another tense encounter between these incompatible groups. Some weekend nudists congregated on a river island easily visible from a path just beyond the town of Worms. "The philistines take their Sunday walk along the riverside," Salardenne wrote, "they can see the nudists at play. The outraged philistines throw stones and other objects at the nudists."[88] The Church sympathized with public outbursts of anti-nudist ire. Küble wrote approvingly of an incident in an Austrian village where outraged inhabitants had attacked and beaten a group of nudists with switches. The Jesuit warned that if state institutions failed to handle the issue of nudism properly, German Christians might have to take the matter into their own hands and resort to mob rule [Volksjustiz].[89] In his nudist rebuttal to Küble, Nacktkultur? Darf und soll der Mensch nackt Leben?, Seitz took Küble to task for these impious views.[90]

Mausbach felt the Catholic Rhineland was being threatened by a debased urban population that infested the banks of the Rhine on weekends and holidays. The theologian recalled a speech by Cologne's Mayor Konrad Adenauer in which he diagnosed all national evils as emanating outward from the large cities into the countryside.[91] Mausbach agreed, noting that in the cities all of God's commandments, all the rules of the Church and long-standing customs were being dragged in the dirt. Germany's renewal inevitably would have to originate in the devout countryside and would eventually succeed in repairing the social-cultural damages inflicted on the nation by the cities. In military imagery, Mausbach imagined cordoning off the morally polluted cities until they could be reconquered by the righteous legions of the countryside. The Rhineland had turned into a cultural battlefield because here discordant provincial and urban inhabitants met, intermingled, and clashed at various places and even at different times of the week or year. Unlike the seaside, where bathers were a large, anonymous, cohesive crowd, along the Rhine, small towns and villages lay clustered together adjacent to the swimming areas favored by nearby city residents with their alien ways. Here, Mausbach warned, village children at play could encounter scenes of nudist profligacy.[92] The city also extended its tentacles and captured more prey when innocent Catholic country youths visited the urban centers in their free time and copied its bad habits.

Unlike Küble, Mausbach framed the battle against nudism within a larger war against Kulturbolschewismus [cultural Bolshevism]: "Germany is called upon to act as a strong bulwark against the onslaught of a godless, immoral atheism."[93] Such combative language was indistinguishable from National Socialist appeals and indicated a terrain of common interest offering tempting political allegiances for Germany's embattled churchgoers. Like Küble, Mausbach called on Catholics to become more militant and aggressive. After all, the enemy showed no mercy in this conflict. Anti-religious, Communist graffiti had been painted in red on Catholic churches.[94] The less crude Social Democrats were equally dangerous. They had dared to establish a red Kinderrepublik, or socialist summer camp, in the Rhine Valley, the heartland of German Catholicism. Children in this camp practiced sports, played games, and were indoctrinated with an anti-religious ideology. Just as disturbing as the socialist encroachment on the traditional Catholic homeland was the confused response of some young Catholics to the new swimming fashions and habits. Many were unsure and even some priests, Mausbach fretted, made the mistake of giving in to the "loud and strong supporters of modern bathing."[95]

Mausbach acknowledged that the war and its aftermath had created such a tremendous sense of oppression that the people needed some forms of compensatory release. Unfortunately, these forces were not being channeled into constructive action. Instead popular needs for entertainment and distraction were being exploited by the twin evils of "individualism and naturism." Like Küble, Mausbach saw the erosion of the sense of shame as a particularly dangerous development which even threatened to ruin the delicate marital ties that sustained the family.[96] Along with many other perceived crises of the Weimar Republic, the Ehekrise, or crisis of marriage, caused alarm and received much media attention. Mausbach was convinced that infidelity and nudism were related and he tied them to the general decay of Weimar society: "How small liberties, erotic conversations, naturist beauty worship, modern dance can imperceptibly lead into shameless nudism! Even more disturbing, on account of their biological impact, are the consequences in matrimonial sex life. We are experiencing today the step-by-step desanctification of a marriage blessed by God. In this new form, woman loses her dignity, all motherliness is stripped away, marriage is loosened and can be dissolved at any time, newly conceived life can be destroyed, children can be systematically killed, and youths can be seduced and Bolshevistically brutalized."[97]

These disastrous trends were the result not only of nudism, but also of Weimar's pervasive egotism and individualism: "What contemporary erotic individualism preaches is an assault on the deepest foundations of the family and national health."[98] Socialism was no answer to this trend because it was itself vitiated by "skeptical individualism."[99] The only force that could rescue the nation in crisis was Christianity. Mausbach acknowledged that the Church had suffered a serious loss of support during and after the war, but this could not shake his belief that only the Christian religion offered solutions for the modern world's myriad problems. The Church's values were eternal and the Church would know how "to rescue the age even against its own will."[100]

Such determination revealed the paternalist, authoritarian streak in Mausbach's thinking, but in another passage he seemed willing to accommodate to the rule of the people. Ordinances from above, he admitted, would not work in an age of democracy.[101] Mausbach's pamphlet was published in 1930 shortly before the nation was governed by emergency decree and the democratic system dismantled in piecemeal manner. Mausbach's and other Catholic leaders' feelings of being in a state of siege inclined them to support rule by decree. Catholic Chancellor Heinrich Brüning resorted to such measures and his even more conservative Catholic successor Franz von Papen would rule in a draconian manner as Germany's democracy dissolved into dictatorship.

Among the first decrees issued by Papen's Prussian Minister of the Interior Franz Bracht was a ban on nude swimming in public, and a much-derided Zwickelerlass [Spandrel Edict], stipulating that henceforward only swimsuits that covered most of the body would be tolerated. Both Franz Bracht, former mayor of Essen, and Chancellor Franz von Papen were politically in line with the right wing of the Center Party. Mausbach, who died on January 31, 1931, would have applauded the conservative backlash against naked bathing and "revealing" swimsuits. The ordinances were issued in the summer of 1932. At the same time, the Schund review boards were stepping up their campaign against colportage, detective pulps, and nudist magazines. Conservative paternalism and morality politics preceded and foreshadowed the turn to National Socialism. With the general population torn by confusion and strife, conservative circles, including the Churches, felt the time had come to make decisions on their behalf.

The authoritarian approach to resolving Weimar's culture wars was endorsed by the arch-conservative journalist Wilhelm Stapel. As editor of the pro-Nazi journal Deutsches Volkstum, he agreed with Mausbach that nudism was principally a problem caused by the cities. He disparaged the views of Hans Suren, who advertised nudism as the best antidote to urban evils. In an anti-nudist article of 1926, Stapel mentioned a popular Hamburg burlesque about a white-collar nudist named Hulda.¹⁰² Stapel used the fictional character as an ideal type and incorporated her into his sarcastic critique. Hulda and her fellow office workers leave the city behind on weekends and venture out into the lovely Lüneburger Heide [Lüneburg Heath]. Stripping off their clothes, they pose in the natural environment and take photographs of each other. Straining to imitate statuesque versions of Greek deities, they hope to have their pictures published in one of the many popular nudist magazines.

Stapel poked fun at Hulda for having graced the pages of the journal Schönheit, despite her "peasant ancestry and her rather robust bone structure."¹⁰³ This did not deter her from standing like "an Aphrodite born from the foam, gazing upwards into the radiant light of the sun god, which lets one recognize the seriousness of the matter."¹⁰⁴ He admitted that all of this could be considered an innocent game were it not for the fact that the nudists claimed to be espousing "a new world view."¹⁰⁵ In some ways recalling Kracauer's reactions, Stapel's mild irritation turned to sarcastic anger when the nudists proclaimed that their exercises and health concerns were the foundation of a new world view. "Whoever lives according to nudism, " Stapel commented with barely suppressed rage, "undresses not for concrete, objective reasons, but for philosophical ones. He longs to be lifted up from darkness into light, from matter to spirit."¹⁰⁶ Stapel considered such inflated claims laughable as well as dangerous. Unlike Kracauer, who merely found the nudist call for a new world view bombastic, Stapel, as a self-proclaimed guardian of German culture, considered it an intrusion into his professional territory and caustically warned that he had no tolerance for amateurs.

He derided nudist suggestions that embracing nature signified a return to a prelapsarian state of harmony, honesty, and innocence. Scornfully, he told the nudists, "Unfortunately, the Garden of Eden is not nature, but metaphysics. That is why it is not so easy to play Adam and Eve before the Fall in [Berlin's] Grünewald."¹⁰⁷ Stapel discussed the problem of Schamgefühl, but, in contrast to the Jesuit Küble, he did not associate it with original sin nor did he view it, like the nudists, as a culturally conditioned aberration. For him, it was a "fundamental phenomenon of moral life" present in all cultures, albeit in different forms.¹⁰⁸ The child knows no shame, but once it grows into a moral subject, the 'Schamgefühl' is awakened and, in Western culture, expressed in clothing and by covering parts of the body. Stapel condemned the nudist endeavor to get rid of the sense of shame. He believed that removing it was an act violating an individual's need for privacy. Kracauer had also taken issue with the nudist attack on Schamgefühl. According to him, each person had a right and a need for some privacy. Just as it is normal that a part of one's personal life should be kept private, so, too, should a part of one's body not be exposed to public viewing: "Does one expose one's soul and does one talk about everything to everyone? Rightfully, one does not do so. Just as rightfully, one does not usually go around in the nude," Kracauer reasoned.¹⁰⁹ Both Kracauer and Stapel insisted that their views of propriety were not prudish.

They were not opposed to nude bathing per se or when it was possibly appropriate. What they opposed was public nudism and nudism as a doctrine or a pretentious system of ideas.

They differed, though, in the way they condemned nudism. Kracauer felt sorry for the socialist nudists performing at the Berlin matinée. He saw them as misled and following the delusions espoused by their leader Adolf Koch, a danger more to themselves than anyone else. As an all-too-typical Weimar phenomenon, Kracauer observed, they did not confront reality but escaped from it. Stapel also viewed them as escapists, but from his unforgiving, intolerant perch, he depicted them as both naïve and malicious. Like other cultural pessimists, he fit the nudists into the hated context of urban modernity and liberalism. They were simply another degenerate product of the city. He associated them with a soft, unmanly aestheticism, part of the sickly postwar society that was unwilling to take on the Herculean tasks facing the nation. Furthermore, they were crafty and knew how to exploit lewd, popular interests in their lifestyle by flooding the print market and plastering every corner newspaper kiosk with nudist magazines. Stapel concluded his anti-nudist diatribe by mocking the vanity of the movement's leaders. "The prophets and apostles of mankind are convinced that they can lead mankind out of the misery of the times," he wrote. Actually it was all "self-deception."[110] Nudism stood not for reconstruction [Wiederaufbau], but for disintegration [Zersetzung].[111]

Six years later, in 1932, Stapel returned to the question of nudism but this time extended the topic to include a discussion of Bracht's edicts against nudism and modern swimsuits. The new requirements were attacked in the liberal and socialist press, but for conservatives, they were a welcome sign that a return to morality and propriety were high priorities on the government agenda. Stapel contended that the need for such action showed to what reprehensible moral levels everyday life and culture had sunk. This he blamed on the lack of adequate role models produced by the Weimar Republic. In a typically arrogant manner, he blamed the SPD leadership for lacking the cachet to distinguish between proper and improper social behavior. This, he deduced, was a consequence of the leadership's lowly social origins. Unsure of themselves, they often followed and were led astray by the dictates of effete intellectuals [Zivilisationsliteraten] or the loose morals propagated by the liberal press.[112]

Stapel entitled his short article "Mosse und Ullstein als Verteidiger der Nacktkultur" ["Mosse and Ullstein as Defenders of Nudism"]. These two Berlin publishing houses were among the largest newspaper companies in the Weimar Republic. Both were owned by Jewish families. Stapel, the self-styled judge and defender of proper decorum, blamed Jews in particular for not knowing how to follow bathing resort etiquette and for promoting nudism. Going bathing, Stapel declared, was more a matter of social countenance than of caring for one's hygiene or health. The prevailing rules of bathing life had been shaped mainly by "the German-European world."¹¹³ Stapel thought that "a certain elegance, lightness, and decency" was needed to participate in the appropriate routines of the seaside bather.¹¹⁴

Intruders into this refined world who failed to follow its unwritten rules, he declared, "must unfortunately be forced" to conform to them.¹¹⁵ According to Stapel, the Jews lacked the cultural-historical background necessary for assimilating into a dignified bathing society: "They think that because one wears less clothes, while on a bathing holiday, that this means the bathing lifestyle is footloose and fancy-free. Heavily made-up and smoking cigarettes, their clothing reduced to a minimum, they sit around among the general population and act as if they were in a nightclub [Nachtcafe]. They encourage the unreliable members of other races to imitate them."¹¹⁶

Another bad influence on seaside society came from nudism. Here, too, Stapel's conservatism revealed its racist prejudices. Nudism, he contended, "opens opportunities for all sorts of subhumans."¹¹⁷ Recalling imagery used by Küble, he continued with a stereotyped contrast: "What is fitting for a Negro in the jungle, is not fitting for a German at a bathing resort."¹¹⁸ Like the conservative leadership in the Papen government, Stapel disapproved of nudism and of the smaller, more revealing bathing suits that had become popular and acceptable during the 1920s. Having an exposed navel was commonplace for men wearing swim shorts, as well as for women wearing two-piece outfits. Stapel found them both inappropriate and wanted the navel covered.

With an air of antisemitic disgust, Stapel painted the picture of a detestable figure he imagined blemishing the resort beach. This time he was not angered by the nudist Hamburg secretary Hulda, but by an obese, Jewish vacationer lying in the sand and wearing a swimsuit that was much too small: "In the middle of an extensive sand fortification, lies a fat, old man. His swimsuit is pulled down below the navel and his hairy body bids itself not only to the sun. The walls of sand are garnished with little black-red-gold flags upon which 'a German newspaper of world-repute' has printed advertisements. Is this black-red-gold naked bear aware of the affect he is having on the republican society?"¹¹⁹ Stapel's hairy, overweight sunbather crudely represented a flaccid Jewish physiognomy supposedly typical and emblematic of the undignified, uncouth Weimar Republic. But the beachside republican brute offended more than Stapel's sense of bathing resort decorum. The declining standards on the beach reflected a wider national decline and were the result of the intertwined influences of nudism, Jewry, urbanism, libertinism, liberalism, and socialism. Stapel's criticism turned cynical and sinister when he proposed the Nazis as the ones who could clean up the mess. He self-servingly interpreted the rise of National Socialism as an expression of a national will that wanted to return to older German virtues, to tried-and-true ways that conformed to his own conservative, elitist sense of what was "fitting and proper."

Kracauer little realized the prophetic nature of his 1930 title "Battle Against the Swimsuit." By 1932 the battle for or against the swimsuit had become a reality and a flashpoint in Weimar's culture wars. Communist Peter Leyendecker published a pamphlet in which he viewed the Bracht swimsuit edict as a significant indicator of the new Papen government's intentions and future policies (Franz von Papen served as chancellor from June 1 to December 3, 1932). Leaning entirely on the Weimar Constitution's emergency clause, Papen lacked an adequate political base and sought to elicit conservative support by trumpeting his program to restore German morality: "Hardly have von Papen and Schleicher erected their administrative dictatorship and chased away their Social Democratic competitors in Prussia on July 20," Leyendecker wrote, "they start the great process of the 'moral' renewal of the German Volk."[120]

While they professed to defend the lost honor and dignity of womanhood and to revive Christian values by issuing orders about bathing attire, at the same time, they ignored barely disguised advertisements for prostitution in Hugenberg's conservative dailies. Nor did they proscribe dress guidelines for high society's upcoming ball season. Leyendecker's complaints underlined the class prejudices and political affinities of Papen's program. A Nazi owner of a Berlin nightclub did not have to worry about government interference in his club's lewd presentations.[121] Prussian Interior Minister Bracht's moral reforms, Leyendecker maintained, were aimed exclusively against proletarian culture. In working class Moabit, a gymnasium was closed because exercising women were supposedly not properly dressed. A Communist holiday retreat on the Grosser Plötzensee was forced to close on account of illegal, public nude bathing.[122]

The Bracht measures left it up to the "dutiful" local constable to decide whether bathing suits were appropriate or not. They alluded to swimsuits that would "disturb" a hypothetical "reasonable man" but avoided the problem of clearly depicting or defining an unacceptable outfit.[123] A similar can of worms had been opened in the "trashy literature" controversy. There, too, political conservatives and some moderates felt a publication could be branded if "no sensible father would place this book in a child's hands." Too many parliamentary lawmakers failed to recognize how subjective these far-ranging laws were, how open to interpretation, and how open to abuse. They relinquished clarity for such cloudy constructs as the "reasonable man" or "sensible father." Here, too, nationalist morality politics translated into an extension of state power and curtailment of individual freedom.

Leyendecker was incensed by the paternalism and uncalled for oversight manifested in the swimsuit and anti-nudist ordinances. The Papen government, he felt, obviously looked down upon the people as immature rabble. The police would now determine if someone was dressed properly or not. On September 28, 1932, the so-called Zwickel edict was issued to address questions about correct bathing attire and to make the new rules more precise. Sub-clause three declared that a male swimsuit was required to have a Zwickel or spandrel. The word Zwickel, like its English equivalent, is uncommon and hardly anyone knew what it meant. A dictionary definition referred to "the space between two bending lines." Simply put, the edict required that the crotch be covered. Much of Weimar's press lampooned the whole effort to renew German morality by targeting swim attire. Especially liberal and left-wing papers seized the opportunity to pour scorn on the new, self-styled custodians of propriety. Police officers could now come snooping and checking bathers' crotches, they laughed. The word Zwickel lent itself to all sorts of puns and plays on words.[124] Leyendecker joined in the sport: "With the decree there is a new difficulty. We have all ended up in a Zwickmühle [a catch-22 situation]. Who knows what a Zwickel is?"[125] Funny as the controversy seemed to be, the Communist Leyendecker reminded liberals and Social Democrats to sober up. The Zwickel edict needed to be seen in context. It was part of a stepped up culture war against the left. Papen's reactionary school policies and his efforts to give the Churches more say in cultural matters were all part of a flimsy plan to win popular support for the conservative government.[126]

Leyendecker extended his criticism to all parties except the Communists. They all had colluded against the working class and its progressive proletarian culture, derisively labeling it "cultural Bolshevism." The Schund law had been the brainchild of Democratic Minister of the Interior Wilhelm Külz. This law was being perverted to attack left-wing, especially Communist publications. Long before the Schund measures, Soviet films like the world famous Battleship Potemkin had been censored. Berlin's SPD chief-of-police had ordered his forces to ban Communist activities and to arrest Communist writers on charges of blasphemy. Leyendecker accused the SPD of betraying working class interests by partnering with reactionary Catholics.[127] Worst of all, though, were the Nazis. While Catholics wanted stricter enforcement of Schund und Schmutz rules, Nazis used extortion and threats to achieve their aims. Leyendecker warned that the Nazis considered themselves an "assault force" fighting to rid Germany of "red subhumans."[128]

Leyendecker was not surprised by which three Berlin dailies praised the unpopular Zwickel edict: the Nazi Angriff, the Catholic Germania, and Hugenberg's conservative Nachtausgabe.[129] These forces together formed what Leyendecker called "the cultural reaction" or "cultural fascism." The use of such defamatory terms and catchwords showed how Weimar's cultural disputes had intensified. Reactionary epithets like "cultural Bolshevists" or "materialists," in turn, were transformed into badges of honor by calumniated leftists. Likewise, right-wing conservatives and Nazis accused of barbarism transformed leftist slander into a compliment by agreeing and priding themselves on being modern-time barbarians. This reminting of slanderous terms into accolades revealed that a point of no return had been reached in Weimar's culture wars.

Recalling leftist criticisms made during the parliamentary Schund debates of the mid-1920s, Leyendecker noted that the left was not so much concerned about useless intangibles like rescuing the soul, but rather with hard facts that really made a difference in people's lives, like the housing shortage, widespread poverty, hunger, the reduction of welfare and unemployment benefits.[130] These were matters where cultural action ought to complement political struggle. Instead of measuring hemlines of swimsuits, the government ought to focus on the real-life problems. Was it moral for the Papen administration to cut benefits and salaries, Leyendecker asked. And the new government even had the audacity to insinuate that its policies were ordained by God. Was it moral to let a large part of the population languish in poverty, while the rich benefited from tax breaks, investment stimuli, and subsidies for heavy industry and agriculture?[131] A final manifestation of the conservatives' warped sense of morality was their saber rattling and eagerness to militarize German youth. True morality, Leyendecker explained, would try to do away with the Stahlbad (bath of steel, or modern warfare) instead of the Freibad (public, outdoor swimming pool).[132] True morality could be demonstrated in fighting capitalism instead of discussing foggy metaphysical concepts like original sin.[133] For Leyendecker, society needed collectivization and Soviet-style reforms, not state intervention on swimsuits and spandrels.

Adolf Koch traced his nudist ideas to the prewar youth movement and Wandervogel. In these groups that enjoyed hiking, it would happen that on a hot day, a lake or river would tempt participants to take off their clothes and jump in for a refreshing swim. Koch had a similar experience while leading a group of school children on a summer camping trip in Brandenburg. Once the children spotted water, there was no stopping them. Koch recalled that afterwards the children insisted, "From now on, we will only swim naked!"[134] This incident caused a flashback in Koch's mind and he thought about the time when he and a group of soldiers on the Western Front had taken a break from warfare by swimming naked in a lake. Koch did not elaborate, but the two events seemed to coincide in his mind as moments of freedom and cathartic purification.[135] To turn these experiences into something lasting and liberating became his mission. As a Berlin teacher he was assigned to working class Moabit. Moabit's underprivileged proletarian children became the first objects of his grand reform endeavor.

With the approval and permission of parents, and the benign tolerance of his principal, Koch organized an after-school program of nude exercises for more than a hundred pupils. Physical education of this experimental sort quickly became caught up in political confrontation. In January, 1924, a conservative representative in Prussia's Landtag sounded an alarm about the supposed abuse of two hundred school girls "dancing naked" in a Berlin school.[136] Berlin's conservatives were calling for early elections and the news from the Moabit school, cleverly distorted and shaped into a scandal by the right-wing media, was just what they needed.[137] The Center Party called for an official investigation. Berlin's socialist school administration was put on the defensive despite an SPD counterattack that declared "rhythmic-gymnastic exercises" had long ago been accepted as part of the educational reform movement.[138] Only conservative obscurantism and ignorance, the SPD argued, could equate sound pedagogical exercises with the lascivious "nude dancing" exhibited in Berlin's red light district.

The association of vaudeville strip-tease with nudism was an oft-repeated strategy used by conservatives and churchmen to stigmatize the growing nudist movement as a symptom of modern decadence. Nudists liked to turn the tables by maintaining that actually it was a sick consequence to conservative sexual repression that led so many people to attend Berlin's disreputable naked revues. Nudists stood on a higher moral plane. They were steeled against decadent enticement because they lived in harmony with their bodies and had a healthy, moderated approach to sexuality. Koch's medical partner Hans Graaz observed that it was not principally urban residents who visited Berlin's dens of iniquity, but the city's provincial guests.[139] It was hypocritical conservative Christians who patronized "naked dancing," not Berlin's nudists.

Koch's new pedagogy had little regard for conservative sensibilities and fanned the flames of conflict by insisting on co-educational nude exercises. Through such exercises, in all stages from childhood to adulthood, one actually reduced the modern individual's exaggerated, unhealthy interest in all things sexual.[140] "He who is acquainted with the naked body," Koch wrote, "cannot be tantalized by silk stockings or fashion wear. Once viewing naked persons becomes habitual, a cultivated exterior purity transforms itself into inner purity."[141] What outsiders did not understand, but participants themselves knew from experience, was that repeatedly seeing nude bodies of the opposite sex actually had a gradual chastening, rather than stimulating, effect.[142]

Not nudity, but the strategically revealing, partly covered body excited the salacious imagination. The problematical body was not the naked one, but the one where a swimsuit "revealed more than it covered."[143] Koch explained: "Each accentuated covering awakens curiosity and thus creates a source of stimulation."[144] When genitalia are taboo, children and youths develop an unhealthy, exaggerated interest in them. An excited sensation is associated with anything sexual and this "blocks the growth, usually for a lifetime, of a deeper sense of respect and responsibility for sexual things."[145] Nudists believed that an open approach to nakedness, an acceptance of nudity and a promotion of nude exercises, game-playing, and swimming, would create a more well-rounded person, accepting his own physical self and disinclined to brood about or show an excessive interest in the opposite gender's physical appearance or sensual attraction.

Koch's nudism entailed the obvious physical frankness of naked interaction, but it also promoted a reasonable, tempered approach to libido. Youths were cautioned not to engage in sex at an early stage of physical maturation and that masturbation ought only be practiced in moderation. Koch's sexual education program was meant to make adolescents feel confident and good about themselves, while overcoming destructive reactions caused by traditionally repressive attitudes to sex. Koch also believed his program for youth games, exercises, and hiking was a healthy alternative to typical, covert youth pastimes of visiting amusement parks, reading erotic literature, and sneaking into adult bars and clubs.[146] Koch wanted youths to be proud of their bodies. His co-educational method was meant to further physical well-being, while also increasing willpower and self-control. Promiscuity was frowned upon, but socialist nudism showed understanding for non-traditional, open-ended relations and did not preach monogamy. Koch's nudism conceived of man as a natural being but not the savage beast, unfettered from ethical rules, alarmingly envisioned by many clergymen. Koch maintained that socialist nudism espoused ethics as much as the Churches did, but its ethics were compatible with nature while theirs were not.[147]

Siegfried Kracauer had made light of Koch's endeavors when he entitled his critical article "The Battle Against the Swimsuit" ["Kampf gegen die Badehose"]. For Koch the battle against the bathing suit was no laughing matter. Besides heightening erotic curiosity, the bathing outfit hindered nudist health aims and physical therapy. It was essential that the body should be fully exposed to the warming, healing rays of the sun. Nudists thought ultraviolet light could not penetrate clothing, thus any clothing at all impeded the stimulating, enhancing effects of the sun's rays on the epidermis. Koch and his followers devoted a lot of time to studying and explaining the central importance of the skin in the life-sustaining exchange between the body's surface and the surrounding environment. Hans Graaz observed that the skin of his urban patients was pale and bloodless.[148] Skin degenerates if it is not exposed to sun and air, the doctor wrote. Often ridiculed for their fanatical insistence on nudity, the nudists felt that their great project of individual physical renewal and collective hygiene was crucially undermined by the wearing of any clothes. From a different angle, Gustav Heidecke, another Koch collaborator, argued that the swimsuit, by covering rump and lower spine, made it impossible for physical educators to detect or correct bad posture affecting the lower spinal column or the pelvis.[149]

Koch criticized bourgeois nudists for neglecting gymnastics and treating physical education in an amateurish way.[150] Even Suren's extensive program did not satisfy him. While Suren's exercises helped muscular development, they did not form "a system aimed at unifying body and soul."[151] Many of his exercises seemed rather cramped. Koch criticized Suren for orienting himself mainly towards males, and also for publicizing his program as "German," a stance that indirectly called into question the national character of other physical programs. In fact, socialist and nationalist nudism often shared similar aims. Koch's partner Graaz, for example, propagated eugenic views which maintained that only healthy, efficiently productive individuals ought to be allowed to reproduce.

Kracauer had faulted Koch for not limiting himself to physical exercise and the rejuvenation of the individual body. But the ex-teacher, like his medical associate, wanted much more and ambitiously aspired to reform the whole person and society. The Koch method required teamwork and cooperation between a gymnastic teacher and a medical doctor. Together they carefully studied each individual through physical examination and personal health questionnaires, and then placed him or her into the most beneficial program. Both teacher and doctor served as counselors, aiming to discuss life's many problems, including career decisions and sexual difficulties. They were expected to be teacher, friend, and socialist comrade all rolled into one.[152]

Becoming a participant in Koch's school first required integration in a group of eight to twenty members. These small groups gave a feeling of belonging and purpose, and were supposed to develop an intimacy in which members felt comfortable enough to exchange ideas and discuss personal problems.[153] "The path to nude gymnastics, which in the widest sense is free body culture [Freikörperkultur], requires a practical sense of community," wrote Koch in 1929. He added, "It requires understanding for the other, it seeks to build and not to judge."[154] The goal was all-around improvement, an educational endeavor that, Koch proudly maintained, went far beyond bourgeois nudism. Paired with specially designed group exercises, his method of personality development induced group communication as well as personal introspection or the discovery of hidden feelings. The latter process completed the socialist-nudist endeavor which Koch referred to as "inner nakedness."[155]

In this system, nudity became the means for achieving multiple types of harmony. Physical nakedness harmonized the body with nature and restored or fortified one's health. Nakedness in a group setting promoted honesty and opened communication with fellow nudist comrades. One chasm that nudism could not bridge was that of class differences and conflict. Koch labeled bourgeois nudist claims of erasing class barriers as superficial and absurd. Co-educational nakedness, however, helped overcome unnatural, religion-induced feelings of embarrassment and shame, and created a more respectful, honest interaction between men and women.

A final successful bond propagated by nudity could take place between the generations, between children and adults. This union, though, had to be handled with care since it could be easily misconstrued. Hamburg teacher and Koch collaborator Jenny Gertz recorded an innocent and exhilarating experience of intergenerational harmony, not unlike that of Adolf Koch's initial moment of inspiration. She was hiking with some of her pupils on a hot, July day. Coming to a river, the children decided to take off their clothes and dived in. As on previous, similar occasions, the children spontaneously called on their teacher to join them, but she had not dared to because she thought they were not ready for such conviviality. This day was different. She felt the moment was right: "The sun burned, the water enticed, the children's eyes appealed – I felt I must. I slipped out of my clothes and

I went into the river as the children cheered endlessly. A calm, happy sparkle from their eyes hit me. I knew: now I have become one of them, we are now comrades, and no meanness in the world could destroy the purity in us or around us."[156] Jenny Gertz felt liberated and unified with her children as she swam naked in the river. The conventions and taboos of society were washed away and exchanged for a singular feeling of freedom. Gertz later became a well-known dance teacher, working primarily with proletarian children. In his study of dance and nudism, Empire of Ecstasy, Karl Toepfer described Gertz's contributions: "Nudity was central to her pedagogic method, and photographs of her nude students performing outdoor movement choir improvisations are among the most beautiful images of group action produced during the Weimar Republic."[157]

While nudist pedagogy was accepted by most Social Democrats and Communists, Weimar's conservatives, Catholics, and right-wing politicians viewed such activities as examples of perverse hedonism and the end of all civilized standards. When the Koch "nude-dancing" scandal broke in January, 1924, the Catholic press jumped on the conservative bandwagon and used the opportunity not only to attack Koch but to smear Berlin's reformist educational leaders and their progressive secular schools.

The Center paper Germania (January 29, 1924) asked, "How was it possible for presentations that make a mockery of every moral sensibility to take place?"[158] The paper honed in on the non-denominational views of Koch and Berlin's reformist superintendent Wilhelm Paulsen.[159] The article speculated that Koch and his nudist program may have counted on approval or sympathy from the well-known, leftist superintendent. Germania reminded its readers that upon Paulsen's selection in 1921, Berlin's Catholics had protested vehemently because of his non-denominational background. With the unfolding of the Koch scandal they felt a sense of vindication and revealed their anti-republicanism: "Although we have here the deviance of a single person, it demonstrates something about the bankruptcy of a system, the final fruit of a mistaken revolution, that should have been done away with long ago."[160]

In actuality, Paulsen had known nothing of Koch's experiment. The children had participated in the program with parental approval as an extracurricular activity. Koch had managed to get his principal's approval to use school facilities for after-school exercises and had convinced his superiors that the program not only had parental support, but would surely be admired by the city's progressive school administration.[161] The decision to let Koch lead his exercises on school grounds was a cardinal mistake because it made it easy for political opponents to recast the story and make it seem like the city had given official approval and sponsored nude gymnastics. The political backlash in the press was intense. An investigation was called for and Koch was suspended from his teaching duties for the duration. Although he was eventually rehabilitated, severe damage was done to the city's educational reform efforts. Koch decided to leave his teaching career and instead established his own private nudist gym schools. For Koch, the scandal had a positive side in that it drew the national media's spotlight on him and popularized his ideas. It helped rally progressive support for his cause. Koch's private school would flourish in Berlin and he was soon able to start branch institutes in Breslau, Barmen Elberfeld, Hamburg, and Mannheim.

The most acrimonious attacks on Koch and the Berlin school board came from newspapers affiliated with conservatives, Nazis, or völkisch splinter groups. The conservative Deutsche Tageszeitung (January 30, 1924) called Koch "a child abuser" and sarcastically described the nude exercises as "new republican romanticism."[162] The antisemitic leader of the Deutschsoziale Partei (German Social Party) Richard Kunze, called Koch an Edelkommunist [a refined Communist] and he excoriated fellow Berlin assemblyman Richard Weyl, who had dared to defend "Koch's abuse of two hundred completely naked school girls," as an SPD Jew.[163] Kunze, who later dissolved his party and became a Nazi, was able to question Superintendent Paulsen directly during an assembly meeting in February, 1924. He got a lot of laughter by asking Paulsen if he would be willing to lead the city's representatives in nude dancing so as to improve their health.[164] Kunze elicited even more derisive laughter and the trampling of feet when he suggested that not so much moral harm could be inflicted on the honored assembly's ladies and gentlemen as on innocent, school children.[165] He continued with sarcastic, antisemitic criticism of Weyl and concluded that "it is not a German spirit that surrounds the German people" but rather a Jewish one: "So ladies and gentlemen, I ascertain that all these signs of decline are nothing more than the consequences of Jewish decomposition within our own people [Volkstum]. It is a pigsty, but it has become a Jewish pigsty."[166]

The Berliner Börsen-Courier (January 30, 1924) tried to bring some objectivity to the story and accused right-wing papers of making a mountain out of a molehill: "These articles gave the impression that entire school classes, led by an unclothed teacher, presented themselves naked in public."[167] The article then gave a factual account of how Koch's exercises had been moved to private rooms after some parents complained. The paper characterized Koch as a fanatic whose convictions were fundamentally honorable and idealistic. Although it was unfair to portray him as lewd or perverse, he and his supporters needed to realize that "the capital is not the right terrain for such experiments."[168] The Vossische Zeitung (January 29, 1924), one of the Republic's most venerable papers, both defended and criticized Koch:

> Whoever has heard him speak in public has gained the impression of a fanatically enthused young man who is determined to follow what he considers to be the right path. Despite warnings from friends, he is unusually extreme and has often damaged the cause for which he fights.[169]

The author of the article, Paul Hildebrand, hoped that Koch would not end as a martyr and wished that he would behave less radically because his aims "could easily be misinterpreted."[170]

The SPD's Vorwärts (January 30, 1924) echoed Hildebrand's concern and complained that "the opponents of secular schools now found the longed-for pretext to condemn the hated schools and to profit politically from the whole affair."[171] This conflict showed the volatility of politics in the capital and how bellicose the two camps were. The conservative, nationalist, and religious right claimed the republican and leftist parties were responsible for the nation's decline and all the moral rot in society. The left, in turn, viewed the right as ceaselessly creating obstacles to badly needed reforms and blocking the road to progress and national renewal.

The more polarized the political constellations of the Weimar Republic became, the less chances there were for compromises in the middle. An accompanying tendency was the declining size and strength of the moderate parties. The Catholic Center Party had played a crucial role in brokering Weimar's coalition governments, but it was moving rightwards. The Koch controversy and the popularization of nudism alienated conservative Catholics. Incidents like this one and other cultural conflicts, such as the "trashy literature" controversy, made it increasingly unlikely that Catholic politicians would seek cooperation with liberal or socialist parties. How could Catholics forge alliances with parties fundamentally hostile to Christian values and partly responsible for the Church's weakening hold on the faithful?

In a second article on the nude exercises published in Germania (January 30, 1924), the reporter maintained that 99% of the German population would find such exercises immoral: "One often talks about declining morality in the metropolis. Can it be otherwise when such 'peculiar' teachers influence the education of our children?"[172] The writer expressed astonishment that any parents would allow their children to participate in Koch's program: "Although the case regards only non-denominational children and parents, it shows once more how closely related a lack of religion is to a state of immorality. Catholic parents will draw a lesson from this incident and understand why we hold so tenaciously to denominational schools. We can no longer have a point of contact with a world view that systematically rips purity out of a child's heart, as happened in the present case."[173] Catholic and nudist concepts of purity were miles apart. Koch felt that purity could only be attained by removing one's clothes and embracing nature. It was through nudism that one purified oneself from the evils of the modern world. The physical inhibitions and psychological deformations affecting millions, Koch and other nudists believed, were promoted by the guilt-inspiring and anti-natural teachings of the Catholic and Protestant churches.

Despite the polarizing conflict, there were some revealing, underlying similarities between purity-adulating nudists and some puritanical Protestants. Like Luther's followers, who espoused an unencumbered fundamentalism in which a man and his Bible were all that was necessary to return to a direct, honest rapport with

God, so the nudists believed, in their own fundamentalist manner, that by reducing oneself to nakedness and directly experiencing nature, one could reintegrate man with a pantheistic universe. Some observers commented on what they perceived as the religious ardor in the nudist "worship" of nature and their peculiar tendency to refer to the body as a temple. When Hans Graaz first watched Koch's pupils exercise, he missed the primal pleasure that, he felt, ought to come with a naked physical workout. It all looked more like a very serious "dogmatic, Protestant cult ceremony," Graaz wrote.[174] Siegfried Kracauer would have likely agreed since he repeatedly complained that Weimar's alternative, countercultural movements were simply distorted reflections or curious copies of the despised original.

5.4 Adolf Koch proudly announced the opening of his "nudist paradise" in 1933

5.4 Adolf Koch proudly announced the opening of his "nudist paradise" in 1933, described in *Das Nacktkultur-Paradies von Berlin* (Leipzig: Ernst Oldenburg Verlag, 1933). The Nazis promptly closed his socialist-nudist schools and parks in the same year. Cover design by "Wernicke."

It is also interesting to note that sometimes the Nazis and their <u>völkisch</u> allies could be found on both sides of the fence. They attacked occultism but, at the same time, derided academic science and called for a corrective in a new, contrarian German science (itself shot through with occultist precepts).[175] Schund was anathema to them, but some of their own execrable writing came up for embarrassing review, and liberal and leftist critics designated Nazi writing as the worst kind of "trashy literature." Koch's nudism the Nazis generally attacked, but occasionally defended.

They sided with conservatives when they maliciously named the Moabit school scandal a case of "nude dancing." But the Völkischer Kurier of Leipzig applauded a Koch presentation and declared that his clean, purposeful nudism ought to sweep aside the salacious filth depicted in effete magazines like Reigen, Der Junggeselle, and Berliner Leben.[176] This same Nazi newspaper, four weeks earlier, had lashed out at Koch as part of its pre-election propaganda campaign.[177] Obviously, the views of the far right were malleable and opportunistic, but they were also contradictory and confused, showing how the radical right could easily turn from ally to enemy or vice versa. A youth movement rally organized to support Koch, on February 29, 1924, included a remarkable mixture of political persuasions and social types: "The giant hall is overflowing – workers, members of the youth movement: from swastika to Soviet star! Here and there, almost embarrassed, fashionably dressed women from the Kurfürstendamm."[178] At this rally, Koch spoke and elaborated on the value and virtues of his program. Not only was it designed to restore health but in words clearly aimed against his Church detractors, Koch announced that free people do not recognize "false shame, but rather pride in their bodies."[179] Koch's supporters duly noted a declaration of sympathy by representatives of the völkisch organizations.

Eight years later, President Hindenburg's appointment of Franz von Papen's cabinet, in the summer of 1932, brought further trouble for Adolf Koch and his brand of nudism. The nudist magazine Figaro complained that Reichskommissar Franz Bracht and his Berlin police chief were applying restrictive bathing and anti-nudist laws mainly against leftist organizations like the Koch School, while neglecting right-wing nudism.[180] The capital's municipal administration ordered a strict separation of youths by gender in activities like swimming and exercising. Koch protested against this directive which went against the heart of his program. The Prussian Landtag's SPD delegation offered a supporting petition, but the Figaro reporter noted it would have little effect since Bracht "high-handedly ignored the Landtag's resolutions."[181]

Bracht wanted all public nudist events banned and his subordinates tried to categorize as public as many of the Koch School's activities as possible. The police department notified municipal authorities that they considered the school's "socialist bathing evenings" to be public events despite the fact that the hundreds of participants were card-carrying members of the private school.[182] A police decree of September 29, 1932, was aimed against the school's popular matineés. An official explanation justified the decree by patronizingly arguing that many spectators attended not out of personal interest but simply for sensual delight.[183]

While Koch had always counted on support from the left and defined his form of nudism as socialist, he did not reject support from the radical right. In his last Weimar publication, <u>Das Nacktkultur-Paradies von Berlin</u> (<u>The Nudist Paradise of Berlin</u>, 1933), Koch discussed the repeated efforts to close his schools. In December, 1932, the Prussian <u>Landtag</u> voted to keep the Berlin school open. Votes in favor came from Social Democrats, Communists, and Nazis.[184] Shortly thereafter, however, the Nazis in power shut down his schools. The recently opened Selchow nudist park that Koch portrayed with much pride and enthusiasm in his 1933 publication was also forced to close.

Hans Suren, on the other hand, carved out a comfortable sinecure for himself in the Third Reich as the Agriculture Minister Walther Darré's "special plenipotentiary for physical exercise beneficial to the farming population." Practically everyone active in Weimar's popular culture and entertainment enterprises scrambled to adjust to the new regime, some with success, others without. While the pulp author Walther Kabel accentuated his nationalist anti-cosmopolitan side and unsuccessfully advertised his character Harald Harst as a patriotic German detective, Suren revised his nudist Bible <u>Der Mensch und die Sonne</u> to fit the new times and changed the title to <u>Mensch und Sonne: Arisch-olympischer Geist</u> (<u>Man and Sun: Aryan-Olympic Spirit</u>). Christian Adam, in his <u>Lesen unter Hitler</u> (<u>Reading Under Hitler</u>, 2010) calls it one of the Third Reich's "most curious bestsellers," noting that over 200,000 copies were published.[185] All of Koch's publications, on the other hand, were placed on the Nazi censorship index. Suren's male-oriented, militaristic nudism could find a place in the new Nazi world, while Koch's socialist, co-educational nudism could not. Any efforts that Koch undertook to accommodate his nudism to the new system were refused, though his services as a physical therapist were later needed to help rehabilitate the scores of wounded and mutilated soldiers. In 1942 Suren tripped up his promising Nazi career when he was arrested for "causing a public nuisance."[186] He spent the remainder of the war in jail.

Endnotes

1 Siegfried Kracauer, "Kampf gegen die Badehose," in ed. Andreas Volk, <u>Berliner Nebeneinander</u>, (Zürich:Edition Epoca, 1996), 75.
2 anonymous, "Nacktheit und Körperfreude," <u>Das Freibad</u> (May 10, 1931), 93.
3 anonymous, "Neuer Kampf gegen uns," <u>Das Freibad</u> (May 10, 1931), 96.
4 Ibid.
5 "Nacktheit und Körperfreude," 93.
6 H.E. Kieslich, "Kritisches zur Nacktkultur," <u>Die Aufkärung</u> (November, 1930), 181.
7 Ibid.

8   Ibid., 180.
9   Georg Fuhrmann, Ist Nacktheit Sünde? (Böblingen: Otto Mieth, 1922), 179-180.
10 Ibid., 30, 34.
11 Ibid., 56.
12 Ibid., 58.
13 Ibid.
14 Ibid., 59.
15 Ibid.
16 Ibid., 61. For the connections between reform movement, vegetarianism, and antisemitism, see Corinna Treitel, Eating Nature in Modern Germany (Cambridge: Cambridge University Press, 2017) pages 84-93.
17 Fuhrmann., 62.
18 Ibid.
19 Ibid., 64.
20 Ibid., 66.
21 Ibid., 110.
22 Putz zu Adlersthurn, Insel der Nackten (Wien: Rudolf Cerny, 1927), 19.
23 Ibid., 24.
24 Ibid., 19.
25 Ibid., 55.
26 Ibid., 71.
27 Ibid., 91
28 Ibid., 103.
29 Ibid., 29.
30 Ibid., 126.
31 Ibid., 151.
32 Ibid.
33 Ibid., 116-117.
34 Ibid., 116.
35 Hans Suren, Der Mensch und die Sonne (Stuttgart: Dieck, 1924), 58.
36 Ibid., 10.
37 Ibid., 120.
38 Ibid.
39 Ibid., 51.
40 Ibid., 10.
41 Ibid., 12.
42 Ibid., 72.
43 Ibid.
44 Ibid., 33.
45 Ibid., 116.
46 Ibid.
47 Ibid., 117.

48 Ibid., 90.
49 Ibid., 92-95.
50 Ibid., 95.
51 Ibid., 95-96.
52 Ibid., 96.
53 Ibid.
54 Ibid., 49-50.
55 Philip Küble, Nacktkultur (Düsseldorf: Jugendführungverlag, 1926), 18.
56 Ibid., 14.
57 Ibid., 116.
58 Ibid., 112.
59 Ibid., 113.
60 Ibid., 73.
61 Ibid.
62 See Corinna Treitel, A Science for the Soul (Baltimore: Johns Hopkins University Press, 2004), 197-200.
63 Küble, 75.
64 Ibid., 125.
65 Ibid., 76.
66 Ibid., 78.
67 Ibid., 94.
68 Ibid., 95.
69 Ibid., 85.
70 Ibid., 88.
71 Ibid., 25.
72 Ibid., 144.
73 Ibid., 148.
74 Ibid.
75 Ibid., 165.
76 Theologus Christianus [Josef Seitz], Nacktkultur? Darf und soll der Mensch nackt leben? (Munich: Verlag von J.M. Seitz, 1926), 4.
77 Ibid., 5.
78 Anonymous, Freiheit dem Leibe! (Stuttgart: Dieck, 1927), 20.
79 Ibid.
80 Joseph Mausbach, Sittlichkeit und Badewesen (Köln: Gilde-Verlag, 1930), 35-36.
81 Ibid., 25.
82 Ibid.
83 Ibid.
84 Ibid., 36-37.
85 Ibid., 37.
86 Roger Salardenne, Bei den nackten Menschen in Deutschland (Leipzig: Oldenburg, 1930), 71.
87 Ibid., 71-72.

88   Ibid., 69.
89   Küble, 46-47.
90   Theologus Christianus, 5.
91   Mausbach, 30.
92   Ibid., 33.
93   Ibid., 34.
94   Ibid.
95   Ibid., 21, 28.
96   Ibid., 23.
97   Ibid., 14.
98   Ibid., 16.
99   Ibid.
100 Ibid., 24.
101 Ibid., 27.
102 Wilhelm Stapel, "Die Lichtbekleideten," in <u>Deutsches Volkstum</u> (1926), 497.
103 Ibid.
104 Ibid.
105 Ibid.
106 Ibid., 498.
107 Ibid.
108 Ibid., 502.
109 Kracauer, "Kampf gegen die Badehose," in <u>Berliner Nebeneinander</u>, 78.
110 Stapel, "Die Lichtbekleideten," 503.
111 Ibid.
112 Stapel, "Mosse und Ullstein als Verteidiger der Nacktkultur," <u>Deutsches Volkstum</u> (1932), 719.
113 Ibid.
114 Ibid.
115 Ibid.
116 Ibid.
117 Ibid.
118 Ibid.
119 Ibid.
120 Peter Leyendecker, <u>Von Zwickeln und Muckern</u> (Remscheid: Selbstverlag, 1932), 1.
121 Ibid., 5.
122 Ibid.
123 Ibid., 2.
124 Ibid., 6.
125 Ibid., 3.
126 Ibid., 6.
127 Ibid.
128 Ibid., 7.
129 Ibid., 8.

130 Ibid., 10.
131 Ibid., 9.
132 Ibid., 12.
133 Ibid., 13.
134 Adolf Koch, Das Nacktkultur-Paradies Berlin (Leipzig: Oldenburg, 1933), 30-31.
135 Ibid., 32.
136 Ibid., 37.
137 Ed. Adolf Koch, Körperbildung Nacktkultur (Leipzig: Oldenburg, 1924), 126-127.
138 Ibid., 127.
139 Hans Graaz, Nacktkörperkultur (Berlin: Verlag der Syndikalist, 1927), 21.
140 Hans Graaz, "Nacktgymnastik," in ed. Koch, Körperbildung Nacktkultur, 57.
141 Ed. Koch, Körperbilding Nacktkultur, 27.
142 Gustav Zepmeisel, "Schamgefühl bei Kindern?" in ed. Koch, Körperbildung Nacktkultur, 64.
143 Koch, Das Nacktkultur-Paradies von Berlin, 89.
144 Ed. Adolf Koch, Nacktheit, Körperkultur, und Erziehung (Leipzig: Oldenburg, 1929), 29.
145 Ibid., 30.
146 Ibid., 132
147 Ibid., 136.
148 Hans Graaz, "Nacktgymnastik," in ed. Koch, Nacktheit, Körperkultur, und Erziehung, 52-53.
149 Gustav Heidecke, "Schule und Körperkultur, " in ed. Koch, Nacktheit, Körperkultur, und Erziehung, 79.
150 Ed. Koch, Nacktheit, Körperkultur, und Erziehung, 122.
151 Ibid. 29.
152 Ibid., 122.
153 Ibid., 50.
154 Ibid.
155 Ibid., 112.
156 Jenny Gertz, "Das Ringen um den Leib," in Körperbildung Nacktkultur, ed. Adolf Koch, 99.
157 Karl Toepfer, Empire of Ecstasy (Berkeley: University of California Press, 1997), 303.
158 cited in ed. Koch, Körperbildung Nacktkultur, 133.
159 Ibid., 134.
160 Ibid., 134-135.
161 Andrey Georgieff, Nacktheit und Kultur (Wien: Passagen Verlag, 2005), 59.
162 cited in ed. Koch, Körperbildung Nacktkultur, 137, 139.
163 cited in ed. Koch, Körperbildung Nacktkultur, 130.
164 Koch, Das Nacktkultur-Paradies von Berlin, 45.
165 Ibid., 46.
166 Ibid.
167 cited in ed. Koch, Körperbildung Nacktkultur, 144.
168 Ibid., 145.
169 Ibid., 146.
170 Ibid.

Chapter Five. Nudism: Weimar Renaissance or National Degeneration? 211

171 Ibid., 149.
172 Ibid., 143.
173 Ibid., 143-144.
174 Hans Graaz, "Kritik," in ed. Koch, Körperbildung Nacktkultur, 206.
175 See Eric Kurlander, Hitler's Monsters: A Supernatural History of the Third Reich (New Haven: Yale University Press, 2017).
176 cited in ed. Käte Hütt, Freunde und Feinde der Körperkulturbewegung (Berlin: Vorwärts, 1924), 11.
177 Käte Hütt, Introduction to ed. Hütt, Freunde und Feinde der Körperkulturbewegung, 11.
178 Anonymous, "Streusandbüchse," (Feb. 29, 1924) cited in ed.Koch, Körperbildung Nacktkultur, 166.
179 cited in ed.Koch, Körperbildung Nacktkultur, 166.
180 Anonymous, "Bracht gegen die Körperkulturschule Adolf Koch!" Figaro (1932) Heft 21, 809.
181 Ibid.
182 Ibid., 809-810.
183 Ibid., 810.
184 Koch, Das Nacktkultur-Paradies von Berlin, 70.
185 Christian Adam, Lesen unter Hitler (Berlin: Galiani, 2010), 107-109.
186 Maren Möhring, "Nacktheit und Leibeszucht," in ed. Paula Diehl, Körper im Nationalsozialismus (München: Wilhelm Fink, 2006), 215.

Epilogue

Cultural conflict in the Weimar Republic sometimes resulted in surprising allegiances or unexpected rifts. Theodor Heuss, the young luminary darling of liberals, received loud applause from conservative and nationalist representatives during his parliamentary speech defending the Schund law. Right-wing media also focused much approving attention on his endorsement of the controversial measure.

The liberal editor of the influential Berliner Tageblatt, Theodor Wolff, demonstrably resigned from membership in the Democratic Party because of Heuss's position.[1] Heuss, in return, resigned as chairman of the Schutzverband Deutscher Schriftsteller [Protective Association of German Writers]. Offended by the attack of numerous authors, Heuss noted in his memoirs that his resignation from the writers' association was meant to show them that they were mistaken in considering him as "their representative."[2] Politics could get hot and confused when it came to disagreement in matters of culture.

Liberal Frankfurt journalist Siegfried Kracauer's criticism of Adolf Koch's socialist nudism paired him, on this issue, with Wilhelm Stapel, the nationalist publisher of Deutsches Volkstum. Both critics vehemently disagreed with Koch's thesis that by ridding mankind of Schamgefühl, or a sense of shame, one smoothed the individual's development through puberty and made the mature adult impervious to erotic temptations. Both Stapel and Kracauer related Schamgefühl to a universal need for individual privacy and intimacy. For them, it was just as inappropriate to make all one's personal feelings public as it was to walk around naked. Both Stapel and Kracauer ridiculed the nudists for their ill-begotten attempt to reconstruct an earthly paradise and derided Koch's assertion that nudism represented a new world view. Kracauer's criticism went a step further than Stapel's in suggesting that nudist attempts to overcome sensuality might actually overshoot their aims with unintentional, harmful effects on sexual relations.[3] Despite the controversies around Koch's nudism, his movement could sometimes unite the most seemingly incompatible groups. The Berlin demonstration organized in his favor on February 29, 1924, included Communists, Nazis, and "fashionably dressed women from the Kurfürstendamm."[4]

Another unusual cooperative endeavor between left and right, between a socialist, Jewish student and his nationalist (later Nazi) mentor, was the critique of detective pulps Der Detektivroman der Unterschicht.[5] This surprising partnership revealed a common thread in the battle over one particular form of popular culture. Weimar's political establishment and elite almost uniformly condemned "trashy literature." Colportage's readers, writers, publishers, and vendors had little chance to have their voices heard or their interests defended. The Schund law came close to including a clause that would have allowed censorship of popular literature for adult readers. Conservative delegates argued that the state needed to protect adult readers as well as youths. A large part of this readership was composed of the lower social classes. Only the tiny liberal journal Die Stimme der Freiheit spoke up for these readers and contested individual cases of review board censorship. While these embattled liberals condemned many of the review boards' decisions, one of the most talented writers of the trade, Walther Kabel, continued to espouse the views of the conservative, nationalist right. A right-wing review board repaid him by indexing his life work: the Harald Harst detective series.

Occultism fared better than Schund in the Weimar years, despite some attempts at government intervention. Potsdam Judge Albert Hellwig, for one, had raised the possibility of censoring occultist literature. He must have been surprised when his attempt to convict August Drost, the psychic detective of Bernburg, for fraud met with fierce criticism from the Vossische Zeitung, one of the Republic's most respected papers. A major liberal newspaper siding with occultism against Hellwig's empiricism cannot be easily explained and shows the complexity of cultural conflict in the 1920s. Siegfried Kracauer, like Hellwig, recognized the dangers of occultism but felt that censorship against it was uncalled for. When film censors forced the producers of Somnambul (1928) to cut key portions of the movie, thereby changing the plot, Kracauer warned that it was not the censor's job to act as society's guardian.

In the original version, psychic detective Elsbeth Günther-Geffers used her clairvoyant powers to assist a wrongly accused suspect in proving his innocence. "We too are highly skeptical about applying uncontrolled supersensory methods," Kracauer wrote, "and do not think that the policeman's craft ends where the clairvoyant's craft begins."[6] He realized that the censors were worried that the original story could influence spectators "to believe in the power of the medium and to lose faith in the police." Still, Kracauer observed, "That might be undesirable but was not grounds for forbidding or mutilating the film."[7] When it came to censorship, Kracauer's liberal views coincided with those of Die Stimme der Freiheit.

Occultism was itself a complex phenomenon not as easily amenable to control as was "trashy literature." There were many forms of occultism and the fascination with it crossed all social barriers. Although ridiculed by the left and condemned by the churches, its appeal was difficult to combat or contain, and occultists did not face the wall of hostility confronting Schund. Some occultists even ventured into politics, dreaming of representation in the Reichstag. "Why shouldn't mesmerists sit in the Reichstag?" asked writer Joseph Roth somewhat facetiously.[8] He had noticed the strange posters of an obscure occultist party called the Nationale Freiheitspartei. Nudists also imagined electing delegates to the Reichstag. One nudist wrote in 1924 that "it is not utopian to suggest that in the near future the followers of nudism will use their right to send representatives to the parliament for the benefit of their Volk."[9]

6.1 Elsbeth Günther-Geffers in the film Somnambul

6.1 Günther-Geffers was supposed to play a key role in the film Somnambul (1928), but the censors would not allow it. In a review in the Frankfurter Zeitung (March 22, 1929), Siegfried Kracauer wrote that they had no right to remove controversial plot elements, such as the idea that a psychic detective might solve a crime more swiftly than the police. *Illustrierter Film-Kurier* 1092 (1929).

While neither occultists nor nudists would realize these political ambitions, they would both continue to flourish as long as Weimar democracy provided the freedom for fringe groups to conduct their experimental or utopian activities.

Once the Nazis gained power, popular culture, like everything else, was subjected to Gleichschaltung or subordination to the Nazi mission. Adolf Koch's nudism was an early target for a number of reasons. Koch openly aligned his movement with the political left, promoting new gender relations, declaiming the Schamgefühl as unnatural and harmful, and publishing articles by sexologist Magnus Hirschfeld (a favorite target of Nazi calumnies) in its journals. Koch's nudism had been endorsed by high-ranking SPD leaders like Reichstag delegate Clara Bohm-Schuch. His private schools were closed down, but the Nazis shared mutual goals with nudists by promoting strong bodies, by sponsoring outdoor exercise, and by planning to improve the race through eugenics. Koch's socialist nudism would be stamped out, but the nationalist nudism of Suren adjusted and thrived.

Adaptation to the new system also became a priority for the producers of popular literature. Schund publishers tried to jump on the Nazi bandwagon by quickly issuing series of fawning pro-Nazi stories. The Freya Verlag (publishers of Heinz Gronau's colportage novel Der Hiesel) issued two adventure series in 1933-1934 entitled Sieg-Heil! and Ein Hitlerjunge Erlebt.[10] In the same years, the Neues Verlagshaus für Volksliteratur (publishers of the first two colportage novels indexed by the review boards) produced forty-four issues of Die Fahne hoch!, which glorified Nazi street fighters and martyrs like Horst Wessel, Hans Maikowsky, and Herbert Norkus.[11] But these efforts backfired. Instead of flattering the Nazis, these pamphlets were eyed by the new potentates with revulsion and labeled "national kitsch". From the Nazi perspective, such literature commercialized and stained what ought to have been revered as a hallowed, supremely patriotic moment in German history. Nazi struggle and strife was not an appropriate subject for cheap, mass-produced reading material and these series were short-lived.

Even before Hitler's appointment as chancellor in early 1933, the political hurricane unleashed by the electoral gains of the NSDAP in October, 1930, had changed the climate of political and cultural discourse. Social Democracy and liberalism were in retreat, hammered by constant attacks from the far right and their many conservative allies. Nazis and nationalists were now setting the tone. A nudist writer's shrill acclamation of Adolf Koch in 1932 illustrated the new stentorian style: "Adolf Koch is cut from the same wood that great popular leaders are carved from. Courageous, when necessary even ruthless, obsessed with the cause that he has made the essence of his life, he follows his path."[12] Would Koch have approved of such a fashionably Hitlerized portrayal?

While right-wing imagery and slogans dominated the scene in the Republic's two final years, all the left's accomplishments were questioned. Kurt Löwenstein,

SPD Reichstag delegate and Schund law opponent, felt called upon to defend the popular summer camps for the Red Falcons (the SPD's youth organization). The Kinderrepublik, as these camps were called, had long irritated Catholics and angered conservatives. In a 1931 booklet promoting the camps, Löwenstein wrote that "the literature about us by our opponents is almost more plentiful than our own publications."[13] Bavaria's DNVP Minister of Culture wanted to ban the camps using a new law that forbade political indoctrination of children. Löwenstein pointed out the hypocrisy of this position. No measures were taken against the strong monarchist influences children were subjected to in Bavarian schools, despite the fact that the schools were supposed to educate children to support the Republic.[14]

Löwenstein rejected accusations that distorted SPD pedagogy, claiming it undermined the family and taught children the virtues of "free love."[15] The real emphasis in the Kinderrepublik was to learn the importance of collaboration and collective work.[16] Social Democrats taught their children that systems of communal production would eventually supersede the capitalist system based on profit.[17] To prepare children for the future, they needed to learn how democracy worked and how to practice it. This was a necessity, even in the face of authoritarian family structures, which Löwenstein admitted, existed not only in bourgeois households but in many working class SPD families as well.[18] Löwenstein also defended the SPD's insistence on co-education. He denounced the "shameless lies" of a Catholic priest who contended that sexual diseases pervaded socialist summer camps.[19] Instead of attacking the Kinderrepublik, Löwenstein suggested conservatives would do better to supervise their own schools more carefully.[20] He made reference to a religiously affiliated boarding school that was under investigation because several female pupils had contracted sexual diseases. In another religious boarding school, boys had been molested by their teachers.[21]

Löwenstein concluded his defense of Social Democratic educational and youth activities by underlining the subaltern status of proletarian children: "Everywhere they are merely the tolerated ones from whom one can demand everything, but who themselves have nothing to demand."[22] The SPD empowered these youths in the Kinderrepublik. "In the group setting," Löwenstein proudly wrote, "our children are not proletarians, but Red Falcons. Here they are not belittled, they are not in the way. Instead they make decisions themselves... they make plans and carry them out themselves. In this Kinderrepublik they experience a new socialist state."[23]

Anti-nudist theologian Joseph Mausbach deemed the Kinderrepublik one of the evil emanations of the city that threatened religious mores in the Catholic province.[24] Weimar's cultural conflicts were often polarized within a scheme pitting an ostensibly pristine and morally pure countryside against the decadent city. Berlin was portrayed as the capital of immorality. This is why Else Matz, in a speech given in the Reichstag on July 16, 1925, recommended that the film boards be staffed by more representatives from the provinces. She observed that "the cultural standard and view from Greater Berlin is not really always in line with other parts of the Reich."[25]

Wilhelm Stapel complained bitterly in 1930 that the capital's "cultural standard" was all too often widely and eagerly copied. The publisher of Deutsches Volkstum decried the mindless aping of Berlin taking place in Germany's smaller cities and towns: "One feels refined if it smells a little like the Kurfürstendamm on main street [Hauptstrasse]...".[26] Stapel warned of Berlin's nefarious, alien qualities that threatened national standards: "Mixed in with the population of Berlin are all too many Slavs and unrestrained, pushy Ostjuden."[27] Stapel also attacked Berlin's large publishing houses Ullstein and Mosse for supporting nudism. The conservative and right wing press liked to connect the capital's supposed decadence with what they deemed to be a spineless Social Democracy. During the Adolf Koch scandal of 1924, the SPD daily Vorwärts reported on the proliferation of nationalist propaganda that wrongly mixed everything up and then suggestively tied it all together: nudism, nude dancing, moral decline, and Social Democracy. The headline "Nude Dancing" was used over and over again to get the readers' attention. Then one showed "the faithful readers what 'a depraved lot' these Social Democrats are: ...Thousands of papers and local rags spread [the swindle in the province], some in good conscience, some with malicious intent for election purposes. And now one knows what's happening in socialist Berlin."[28] Typical of this kind of muckraking was a local paper in Brandenburg's rural Ostpriegnitz. The paper's anonymous writer blamed Social Democrats for "nude dancing" and workers' associations for sponsoring degenerate sports events. He called for a return to Turnen, or the kind of old-fashioned, traditional group physical exercises which alone could help the cause of "German liberation."[29]

An SPD paper in the province of Anhalt turned the usual argument around by illustrating how sometimes the countryside surprisingly could be more tolerant and accepting of progress than Berlin itself. While the Koch scandal caused a furor in the capital, a demonstration of socialist physical exercise in the town of Bernburg, where the psychic detective August Drost had been put on trial, met with widespread public approval. The reporter wrote that the rhythmic group movements and dance routines were warmly applauded and "the free exercises in the nude by gymnasts were a true aesthetic delight."[30] Among the visiting guests were the mayor, the district's governmental administrator, and numerous local school teachers. In a final note, the SPD reporter observed that even in the little backwater town of Ketzin, in contrast to Berlin, nude exercises could be performed without public complaint. He made light of Berlin's reputation as the source of all moral decay: "Oh! Poor den of iniquity Berlin!" [O! Armes Sündenbabel Berlin!].[31] Koch's medical collaborator Hans Graaz wrote acerbically that the most numerous visitors to Berlin's notorious dens of iniquity were not its own (supposedly decadent) inhabitants, but the curious visitors from the provinces.[32]

Berlin's decadence was trumpeted in the right-wing press in continual reports about sex, crime, corruption, and moral decay. In a sarcastically entitled article "What Berlin 'can be proud about'," Wilhelm Stapel accused the Aschingers' restaurant chain and the huge Fürstenhof Hotel (located on Potsdamer Platz) of promoting typical Berlin filth.[33] He had picked up a copy of an Aschingers publicity bulletin stamped with the hotel's address (probably material made available to guests in the hotel lobby). It contained news about Berlin's latest hedonist attraction: a Wittenberg Square bookstore specialized in "sexual science." The advertising bulletin announced that a curious crowd regularly assembled before the store's display windows and the store's manager coyly did not want to hide the fact that the police had already stopped by on a number of occasions. The bookstore sold erotic novels, books on "sexual science," and sexual paraphernalia.[34] The article concluded that Berlin could "finally be proud to have Germany's leading bookstore for the sexual sciences."[35] The same bulletin contained a second article that also incensed Stapel. It suggested that tourists ought to visit a lesbian bar where they could voyeuristically watch "women with a certain something get together. It will be an exciting experience to be able to observe this interesting sort of life."[36] Stapel was willing to accept the fact that large cities invariably harbored some vice, but he became indignant when Berlin's largest newspapers could dare to criticize "people of education and taste" for expressing their disapproval.[37] Posing as a watchdog for bourgeois respectability, Stapel crusaded against urban vice and made sure it would not become socially acceptable. He was outraged that the popular Aschingers and the prominent Fürstenhof Hotel were themselves involved in what he claimed to be the promotion of vice.

Like many others, Stapel wanted a return to Prussian values, to the manliness, hard discipline, and the military prowess that supposedly had made Germany strong. For conservatives, the Republic had feminized, sensualized, and weakened Germany's moral fabric. The publisher of <u>Deutsches Volkstum</u>, influenced by a long tradition of cultural pessimists like Julius Langbehn and Paul de Lagarde, theorized that there was an essential difference between Volk and the institutions of the state. He elaborated this distinction in his writing and he advised civil servants that their first duty was to the Volk, serving the state was only a secondary matter. He went on to suggest that state disloyalty sometimes could be a virtue. By making such points, he legitimized the right's superficial accommodation to the Republic: like ill-suited clothing, democracy could be cast off at an opportune moment. The Republic would then be replaced by a form of government more appropriate to the character of the German people. In the meantime, for the right, the province was the repository of the Volk's virtues; it needed to be defended from the dangerous decay and corruption emanating out of socialist Berlin. The specter of national pollution haunted the right-wing imagination throughout the Weimar years. Although they were confident that Germany's outward form eventually could be changed, what would happen if the inner national character had been contaminated beyond repair? It was this hysterical fear of a mutilated national soul that produced the rabid attacks endlessly generated by the right in Weimar's culture wars.

New media like the movies exacerbated the cultural dangers. Conservative critic Hermann Hass argued that, thanks to salacious films, even "the naïve burgher" now was exposed to corrupting amusements that in the past would have been limited to a few urban hedonists patronizing a Berlin cabaret.[38] In his scathing attack on Weimar culture, <u>Sitte und Kultur im Nachkriegsdeutschland (Morality and Culture in Postwar Germany,</u> 1932), Hass presented the defeat of 1918 as primarily a moral debacle and cultural catastrophe.[39] He made the Versailles order and Weimar democracy directly responsible for opening the floodgates to man's worst instincts and initiating a period of relentless hedonism in Germany. Where once the martial spirit of Potsdam and Prussia had guided the nation, now a film cult of stars ruled. Gigantic film contracts and salaries catapulted young starlets into the highest ranks of society. The revered officer corps, which had stood for duty, discipline, and patriotic sacrifice, had been cast aside to make way for film divas, who made deplorable role models.

Empty sensationalism joined with vile libertinism to undermine culture and morality. German youth and Germany's future were imperiled. Urban youth in particular, Hass wrote, was subjected to a barrage of moral turpitude: erotic advertisements, exhibitionist fashion, and "overpriced, whipped-up merrymaking."[40] How could one avoid youth's exposure to all the modern means of promoting corruption? "If in every little stationery store and at every kiosk nakedness is visible, if promiscuity is a main theme of the lyrics in all popular songs and hits... so it is unavoidable that these things become accepted as normal..."[41] Even worse than suggestive magazines and songs were the "sexual science" publications. Too expensive to be purchased by young readers, they were loaned out by the private lending libraries that Kracauer had noticed sprouting up all over the city and which he used to procure the latest detective stories. Hass observed that these libraries had no qualms about spreading "the pornographic plague."[42]

Hass's conservative lament against Weimar culture was accompanied by similar Nazi tirades. <u>Entfesselung der Unterwelt: Ein Querschnitt durch die Bolschewisierung Deutschlands (The Underworld Unchained: A Cross-section through Bolshevized Germany,</u> 1932) was a Nazi attack on the "bolshevization" of German culture. The authors meticulously catalogued and criticized all sorts of leftist publications, never failing to connect leftist views with general moral decay. At one point in their study, the authors sketched out what they considered the likely implications for a typical German youth's exposure to a single pornographic photograph. Their hypothesis reveals more about Nazi fears and hysterical sensibilities than Weimar youth's actual vulnerability to pornography: "He experiences a shock that tears down the barrier of character. In pours a spring flood of elementary desires. At one blow, his underworld is unleashed: he falls into the depths of sin."[43] Writing in a style only slightly less hyperbolic, Hass perceived Germany's cultural problems in a similar manner. He too felt that German youth was defenseless against contemporary culture's overpowering forces of corruption. According to nationalist critics, what made matters worse was that many youths had lost their fathers and other male role models in the war.[44] The German army was no longer available to fill the gap by teaching such military virtues as patriotic service and soldierly obedience.[45] Conservatives preferred seeing 1918 as a collapse of moral will rather than a military defeat. It ushered in an age of cultural upheaval.

With the fall of the officer corps, an entire social ethos and sense of honor had been dismissed.[46] The spirit of sacrifice and duty to the nation inculcated by Prussian militarism was replaced by remorseless individualism. The defeat changed the German nation from "an organically organized whole into the sad heap of ruins of an aimless, leaderless mass."[47] The goal of Hass's cultural critique was to help steer the nation back to the cherished old values. In stark opposites he framed the nation's future and asked his fellow Germans whether they preferred: spirituality or licentiousness, sense of community or atomization, Christ or anti-Christ?[48]

Hass chimed in with other right-wing writers that Germany in 1932 was now prey to the menace of cultural bolshevism. It lurked behind many of the disturbing phenomena of the times, including the erosion of the family. The marriage crisis [Ehekrise] was a consequence of proposed alternative forms of gender relations, but it also could be attributed to the defeat and the ensuing wave of selfish egotism. Traditional monogamous marriage and the nuclear family were under attack. Hass lamented that the upper class had become a particularly bad example cherishing a profligate lifestyle and practicing divorce as if it were a sport.[49] Indignantly, he recounted the story of one baroness vacationing in Biarritz. She had cultivated a liaison with a black chauffeur and spent her evenings with him in "shady bars."[50]

Hass's crescendo of moral outrage mixed with a fear of racial contamination. He regretted that adultery, miscegenation, prostitution, and homosexuality had all become acceptable in Weimar's permissive society.[51] Hass looked back nostalgically to the old traditional, patriarchal family of Wilhelmine times.[52] Only a new, strong leader could put the national house back in order.[53] The leveling effects of modern democracy stymied German culture and left the nation without a mission.[54] Typical of this situation was the press's neglect of serious artists and its preference for spotlighting entertainers like Josephine Baker, who "made all of Europe happy with the obscene movements of her brown body."[55]

The newspapers eagerly printed her autobiography in installments. Unlike the crude attacks by many right-wing critics of nudism who identified it with "nude-dancing," Hass gave credit to the nudist movement for rejecting and distancing itself from lascivious exhibitionism like Baker's erotic dance. He also approved of Hans Suren's anti-intellectualism and the call for a new race of tanned Hellenes. In contrast, he repudiated Adolf Koch's "democratic-socialist nudism."⁵⁶

Suren's male-oriented, nudist exercises reminded Hass of military training or <u>Zucht</u> [a term that alludes to physical toughening as well as breeding]. Hass also wanted a turn to spiritual <u>Zucht</u> or superior moral cultivation. To illustrate the point, he called for new, stricter censorship boards led by strong, soldierly leaders. "Only those soldiers remain united in battle," Hass wrote in a typical military analogy, "who have a strict, goal-oriented leader."⁵⁷ The chief censor, like a combat officer, needed to act forcefully in order to carry out his mission: "Moral <u>Zucht</u> instead of liberal relativism! [<u>Geistige Zucht statt liberalen Relativismus!</u>]"⁵⁸ Such rigorous measures would help put an end to the insufferable sense of inner strife, moral decline, and cultural conflict that characterized the postwar years.⁵⁹ Western concepts of freedom needed to be discarded in favor of a German mission and a renewed national ethic.

In conservative eyes, Weimar democracy only produced and promoted upstarts, snobs, and parvenus.⁶⁰ Film stars, SPD politicians, and wealthy Jews typified this lot. They congregated in Berlin, a city where, Hass explained, Americanism, Bolshevism, and old Prussian values converged in an unblendable mix. Democracy allowed such strange and dangerous pluralism, giving everyone an unsettling feeling of insecurity.⁶¹

The impending chaos could only be avoided by a resurrection of the officer corps and the <u>Frontkämpfer</u> spirit. While Potsdam, just beyond the capital city's limits, stood for the old Prussian martial values, the unhealthy pulse of Weimar culture beat most strongly on Berlin's <u>Kurfürstendamm</u>. If Berlin was the cauldron in which contrary forces swirled about, Potsdam and the <u>Kurfürstendamm</u> were the geographical antipodes around which Prussian militarism and Weimar cosmopolitanism clustered. The broad avenue in West Berlin, with its many cafés, restaurants, and fashionable stores, symbolized everything that the right-wing critics or cultural reactionaries (as leftist writers called them) despised.

Siegfried Kracauer's famous 1932 essay "<u>Strasse ohne Erinnerung [Street without Memory]</u>" is an analysis of the continual erasure of history happening on this quintessentially modern avenue: "Usually the past sticks to the places which it at one time inhabited; on the <u>Kurfürstendamm</u> it withdraws without leaving a trace."⁶² Places like a tearoom and a gaudy café that Kracauer patronized a short time before are gone, their customers and ambiance swallowed up as if they had never existed at all. Stores, objects, and people on the <u>Kurfürstendamm</u> are imbued with a quality of transitoriness. Kracauer reflected on the rootless, improvised nature of this boulevard and how it captured an essential quality of the modern condition. Kracauer's fascination with modernity included critical views but contrasted with the tedious hostility of conservative, nationalist cultural critics. They longed for that past which modernity was erasing here in the heart of Berlin with relentless speed. They bemoaned whatever was transitory, ephemeral, or not firmly anchored; they longed for tradition and for things that grew in an incremental, historical process; finally, they hated the Kurfürstendamm.

In a 1931 essay, "Der Kurfürstendamm als Siegesallee, [The Kurfürstendamm as a Victory Avenue]," Kracauer reflected on the same social clash that Hass adumbrated and lamented upon in his anti-Weimar diatribe. Berlin's erstwhile glorification of the officer had given way to the spotlighted film diva. Kracauer began this essay by writing that the Kurfürstendamm was "the modern victory avenue" but instead of being lined with marble statues of kings and generals, it was dotted with photographs of society's celebrities.[63] What did all these artistically conceived photos in display windows, on walls, and in passageways signify? Many of them were of rich women with aristocratic titles.[64] They exuded an air of cosmopolitanism, which Kracauer defined by using the English word "high life." The photographically portrayed men were distinguished by birth, money, or intellect. Kracauer ironically wrote that "we live in a democratic country," duly noting that aristocratic, monocled generals were displayed beside "commoners" who had made a name for themselves by the pen, like the writers Heinrich Mann, Alfred Döblin, and even "the revolutionary poet" Ernst Toller.[65] The photographers made sure to give them an air of importance by using shadow and light effects to emphasize certain features: "If they were made of stone or bronze, they would stand on pedestals and be visible at a great distance."[66]

These photographs distinguished society's most prominent members but "society receives its real source of light from the stars."[67] Divas like Marlene Dietrich, Gerda Maurus, and Lee Parry posed photogenically at race tracks or film premieres wearing fairy tale gowns. These were the ultimate role models and Kracauer felt that the glow they gave off even enhanced those who happened to stand next to them.[68] In the Weimar Republic, the Kurfürstendamm, not Potsdam, set the tone. Kracauer asked, "Marble has been transformed into photo – but where have the dashing lieutenants gone?"[69] This last part of Kracauer's essay touched on a particularly sore point for conservatives and nationalists. The snappy lieutenants who had strolled past the old Siegesallee had been replaced by "a sort of fashionable young man."[70] These fit into the new victory avenue as smoothly as the lieutenants had fit into the old: "they could be most accurately described as male Girls [männliche Girls]."[71] Tastefully dressed, with bleached, curly hair, Kracauer somewhat snidely described them as high quality ware: "They are a pleasure for the girls, whom they hardly notice, and even more so for the men, who come looking for them."[72] They have an easygoing, carefree attitude. Some have traveled to distant parts of the globe simply for adventure. They enjoy writing down what they have observed: "Or they go to the movies; or they live, without doing anything."[73] Such a life of pleasure and idleness, with its hints of homosexual flirtation, androgyny, and individualism clashed with the nationalists' strictly defined gender roles and idealized image of the stalwart Prussian officer cadet.

These free-wheeling, cosmopolitan inhabitants of Berlin's cafés lived lives seemingly without a mission or moral compass and were an affront to the self-proclaimed guardians of national morality. Nothing could have upset the right-wing culture critics more than the sight of these stylish do-nothings freely promenading down the Kurfürstendamm or languidly observing life go by from a café terrace.

Endnotes

1 Theodor Heuss, Erinnerungen 1905-1933 (Tübingen: Rainer Wunderlich Verlag, 1963), 343.
2 Ibid.
3 Siegfried Kracauer, "Kampf gegen die Badehose," Frankfurter Zeitung, (March 31, 1931), in Berliner Nebeneinander (Zürich: Epoca, 1996), 78.
4 Anonymous, Streusandbüchse (Feb.29, 1924), cited in ed. Adolf Koch Körperbildung Nacktkultur (Leipzig: Ernst Oldenburg Verlag, 1924), 166.
5 Hans Epstein, Der Detektivroman der Unterschicht (Frankfurt: Neuer Frankfurter Verlag, 1930).
6 Siegfried Kracauer, "Ein Hellseher-Film," in Kleine Schriften zum Film 6.2 (Frankfurt: Suhrkamp, 2004), 231.
7 Ibid.
8 Joseph Roth, Der Drache (March 25, 1924), in Berliner Saisonbericht (Köln: Kiepenheuer und Witsch, 1984), 243.
9 F.H. Thies, "Die Körperkulturbewegung," in ed. Koch, Körperkulturbewegung Nacktkultur (Leipzig: Ernst Oldenburg Verlag, 1924), 92.
10 Heinz J. Galle, Volksbücher und Heftromane, Band 2 (Lüneburg: Dieter von Reeken, 2006), 258.
11 Ibid., 260.
12 Bernhard Hagedorn, "Tagebuch des Figaro," Figaro 1932 (Heft 1), 5.
13 Kurt Löwenstein, Freie Bahn den Kinderfreunden (Berlin: Reichsarbeitsgemeinschaft der Kinderfreunde Deutschlands, 1931), 3.
14 Ibid., 13.
15 Ibid., 18.
16 Ibid., 20.
17 Ibid., 21.
18 Ibid., 22.
19 Ibid., 24.
20 Ibid., 30.
21 Ibid.
22 Ibid., 40.

23 Ibid., 41.
24 Joseph Mausbach, <u>Sittlichkeit und Badewesen</u> (Köln: Gilde-Verlag, 1930), 30, 34.
25 Reichstag Stenographic Reports [June 16, 1925], 2345. The conflict over urban and provincial morality, or different regional norms is discussed at length in Kara L. Ritzheimer, <u>"Trash," Censorship, and National Identity in Early Twentieth-Century Germany</u> (New York: Cambridge University Press, 2016). See pages 241-259.
26 Wilhelm Stapel, "Der Geistige und sein Volk," <u>Deutsches Volkstum</u> (1930) cited in ed. Joachim Meyer <u>Marbacher Magazin 35: Berlin-Provinz</u> (Marbach: Schillergesellschaft, 1985), 10.
27 Ibid., 11.
28 Anonymous, "Nackttanzschwindel," <u>Vorwärt</u>s (Feb.12, 1924), cited in ed. Koch, <u>Körperbildung Nacktkultur,</u> 160.
29 Ibid., 160.
30 Anonymous, <u>Volkswart</u> (Jan.28, 1924) cited in ed. Koch, <u>Körperbildung Nacktkultur</u>, 168.
31 Ibid.
32 Hans Graaz, <u>Nacktkörperkultur</u> (Berlin: Verlag der Syndikalist, 1927), 21.
33 Wilhelm Stapel, "Worauf Berlin 'stolz sein kann'," <u>Deutsches Volkstum</u> (1932), 816.
34 Ibid.
35 Ibid., 817.
36 Ibid.
37 Ibid.
38 Hermann Hass, <u>Sitte und Kultur im Nachkriegsdeutschland</u> (Hamburg: Hanseatische Verlagsanstalt, 1932), 180.
39 Ibid., 173.
40 Ibid., 50.
41 Ibid., 30.
42 Ibid., 37.
43 Adolf Ehrt and Julius Schweickert, <u>Entfesselung der Unterwelt: Ein Querschnitt durch die Bolschewisierung Deutschlands</u> (Berlin: Ekart-Verlag, 1932), 47.
44 Hass, 30.
45 Ibid.
46 Ibid., 108.
47 Ibid., 107.
48 Ibid., 87.
49 Ibid., 80.
50 Ibid., 66.
51 Ibid., 83.
52 Ibid., 91.
53 Ibid., 185.
54 Ibid., 9.
55 Ibid., 101.
56 Ibid., 99-100.
57 Ibid., 185-186.
58 Ibid., 186.

59 Ibid., 140.
60 Ibid., 124.
61 Ibid., 142.
62 Siegfried Kracauer, "Strasse ohne Erinnerung," in Schriften 5.3 Aufsätze (1932-1965) (Frankfurt: Suhrkamp, 1990), 173.
63 Siegfried Kracauer, "Der Kurfürstendamm als Siegesallee," in Schriften 5.2 Aufsätze (1927-1931) (Frankfurt: Suhrkamp, 1990), 318.
64 Ibid., 319.
65 Ibid.
66 Ibid.
67 Ibid.
68 Ibid.
69 Ibid., 320.
70 Ibid.
71 Ibid.
72 Ibid
73 Ibid.

Bibliography

Primary Sources

Anonymous: *Freiheit dem Leibe?*, (Stuttgart: Dieck, 1927).
Anonymous: *Das Rätsel von Konnersreuth*, (Düsseldorf: Gesellschaft für Buchdruckerei und Verlag, 1927).
AST [pseudonym]: *Das "Wunder" von Konnersreuth*, (Wien: Freidenkerbund, 1928).
Berghoff, Karl-Heinz: *Rigo Muratti*, (Dresden: Mignon, 1924).
Bernfeld, Siegfried: "*Das Kind braucht keinen Schutz vor Schund! Es schützt sich selbst,*" in *Die literarische Welt*, Jg. 2, Bd.49 (Dec.3, 1926), P.369.
Bry, Carl Christian: *Verkappte Religionen*, (Gotha: Perthes, 1925).
Dessoir, Max: *Vom Jenseits der Seele*, (Stuttgart: Ferdinand Enke, 1931).
Deutsch, Josef: *Konnerseuth in ärztlicher Betrachtung*, (Paderborn: Bonifacius-Druckerei, 1932).
Drost, August: "*Wie ich zum Hellsehen kam,*" in Uhu, Jg. 2, Heft 4 (Jan., 1926), PP. 26-34, 90-97.
Ebertin, Elisabeth: *Sterndeuter, Hellseher, Wahrsager und Zunftgenossen*, (Hamburg: Dreizack, 1931).
Ehrt, Adolf und Julius Schweickert: *Entfesselung der Unterwelt*, (Berlin: Ekart-Verlag, 1932).
Epstein, Hans: *Der Detektivroman der Unterschicht*, (Frankfurt: Neuer Frankfurter Verlag, 1930).
Fiedler, Kuno: "*Frank Allan der Indizierte,*" in *Die Stimme der Freiheit*, Jg.2 (No. 7, 1930), PP.103-105.
Fuhrmann, Georg: *Ist Nacktheide Sünde?* (Böblingen: Otto Mieth, 1922).
Gaudlitz, Walter: *Okkultismus und Strafgesetz*, Dissertation Universität Leipzig (Leipzig: Moltzen, 1932).
Gerlich, Fritz: *Der Kampf um die Glaubwürdigkeit der Therese Neumann*, (München: Natur Verlag, 1931).
Gerlich, Fritz: *Die stigmatisierte Therese Neumann von Konnersreuth*, (München: Kösel und Pustet, 1929).
Graaz, Hans: *Nacktkörperkultur*, (Berlin: Verlag der Syndikalist, 1927).
Gronau, Heinz: *Der Hiesel*, (Heidenau: Verlagshaus Freya, 1933).

Haspinger, Alois: *Die Wildschützen der Tiroler Grenze*, (Dresden: Adolf Ander, 1922).
Hass, Hermann: *Sitte und Kultur im Nachkriegsdeutschland*, (Hamburg: Hanseatische Verlagsanstalt, 1932).
Hellwig, Albert: *Jugendschutz gegen Schundliteratur*, (Berlin: Stilke, 1927).
Hellwig, Albert: *Okkultismus und Verbrechen*, (Berlin: Hanseatischer Rechts und Wirtschaftsverlag, 1929).
Hepner, Maria: "Beschreibung des wesentlichsten Eindrucks des Schriftbildes," in Die Zukunft, Jg. 8, No. 6 (June 1932), PP. 242-244.
Heuss, Theodor: *Erinnerungen 1905-1933*, (Tübingen: Rainer Wunderlich, 1963).
Hütt, Käte (Ed.): *Freunde und Feinde der Körperkulturbewegung*, (Berlin: Vorwärts, 1924).
Kabel, Walther: *Harald Harst*, (Berlin: Verlag moderner Lektüre, 1919-1934).
Kieslich, H.E.: "*Kritisches zur Nacktkultur*," in Die Aufklärung (Heft 10/11, Nov. 1930), PP.180-182.
Koch, Adolf (Ed.): *Körperbildung Nacktkultur*, (Leipzig: Oldenburg, 1924).
Koch, Adolf (Ed): *Nacktheit, Körperkultur, und Erziehung*, (Leipzig: Oldenburg, 1929).
Koch, Adolf: *Das Nacktkultur-Paradies von Berlin*, (Leipzig: Oldenburg, 1933).
Koch, Adolf: *Wir sind nackt und nennen uns Du!*, (Leipzig: Oldenburg, 1932).
Keun von Hoogerwaerd, Harald: "*Blick in das Jahr 1933*", in Der Querschnitt (Heft 12, Dec. 1932), P.887.
Kracauer, Siegfried: *Berliner Nebeneinander: Ausgewählte Feuilletons 1930-1933*, (Zürich: Epoca, 1996).
Kracauer, Siegfried: *Frankfurter Turmhäuser: Ausgewählte Feuilletons 1906-1930*, (Zürich: Epoca, 1997).
Kracauer, Siegfried: *Kleine Schriften zum Film, Bänder 6.1-6.3, 1921-1961*, (Frankfurt: Suhrkamp, 2004).
Kracauer, Siegfried: *Schriften: Aufsätze, Bänder 5.1-5.3, 1915-1965*, (Frankfurt: Suhrkamp, 1990).
Küble, Philip: *Nacktkultur*, (Düsseldorf: Jugendführungsverlag, 1926).
Kühr, Erich Carl: "Physiognomische Beurteilung des Bildes," in *Die Zukunft* (No.6, June 1932).
Lambert, Rudolf: "*Der Insterburgerprozess gegen die Hellseherin Frau Günther-Geffers,*" in *Zeitschrift für Parapsychologie* (April 1929), PP. 232-233.
Lewandowki, Herbert: "*Nachwehen zum Frank-Allan-Urteil,*" in Die Stimme der Freiheit, Jg. 2 (No.8 1930), P. 126.
Leyendecker, Peter: *Von Zwickeln und Muckern*, (Remscheid: Selbstverlag, 1932).
Löwenstein, Kurt: *Freie Bahn den Kinderfreunden*, (Berlin: Reichsarbeitsgemeinschaft der Kinderfreunde Deutschlands, 1931).
Mausbach, Joseph: *Sittlichkeit und Badewesen*, (Köln: Gilde-Verlag, 1930).
Mumm, Reinhard: *Der Christlichsoziale Gedanke*, (Berlin: Mittler und Sohn, 1933).

Oestreich, Paul: *"Schutz der Jugend vor Schund und Schmutz?"*, in Die Stimme der Freiheit, Jg.3 (No.7/8 1931), PP.121-124.
Olden, Rudolf: *Das "Wunder" von Konnersreuth*, (Frankfurt: Fravo-Bücherei, 1927).
Olden, Rudolf: *Propheten in deutscher Krise*, (Berlin: Rowohlt, 1932).
Pelz, Carl: *Die Hellseherin*, (Stolp: Pfeiffer, 1928).
Pelz, Carl [pseudonym: Fred Karsten]: *Vampyre des Aberglaubens*, (Berlin: Deutsche Kultur-Wacht, 1935).
Petzet, Wolfgang: *Verbotene Filme*, (Frankfurt: Sociatäts Verlag, 1931).
Pinkert, Ernst Friedrich [pseudonym: Leonore von Stetten]: *Grossstadtmädel*, (Leipzig: Marien Verlag, 1926).
Pinkert, Ernst Friedrich: *Ihr Junge*, (Niedersedlitz: Münchmeyer, 1932).
Pinkert, Ernst Friedrich [pseudonym: Leonore von Stetten]: *Mädchenhändler*, (Leipzig: Marien Verlag, 1925).
Pinkert, Ernst Friedrich: *Mein Sonny-Boy*, (Niedersedlitz: Münchmeyer, 1930).
Pinkert, Ernst Friedrich: *Schwarze Natascha*, (Niedersedlitz: Wolga, 1927).
Putz zu Adlersthurn, Anton: *Insel der Nackten*, (Wien: Rudolf Cerny, 1927).
Rost, Franz de Paula: *"Frank Allan!"* in Die Stimme der Freiheit, Jg.2 (No. 6 ,1930), P. 90.
Roth, Joseph: *Berliner Saisonbericht*, (Köln: Kiepenheuer und Witsch, 1984).
Salardenne, Roger: *Bei den Nackten Menschen in Deutschland*, (Leipzig: Oldenburg, 1930).
Schlesinger, Paul [pseudonym: Sling]: *"Bernburger Hellseher Prozess,"* in Vorwärts (articles Oct. 13-Nov. 6, 1925).
Schneider, Rudolf: *"Horoskop des Nationalsozialistischen Führers Gregor Strasser,"* in Die Zukunft, Jg. 8, No. 6 (June 1932), PP. 237-239.
Schumacher, Artur: *"Blick in das Jahr 1933,"* in Der Querschnitt, Jg. 12, Heft 12, (Dec. 1932), PP. 887-888.
Seeling, Otto: *Der Bernburger Hellseher-Prozess und das Problem der Kriminaltelepathie*, (Berlin: Linser, 1925).
Seitz, Josef [pseudonym: Theologus Christianus]: *Nacktkultur?* (Munich: Verlag von Josef Seitz, 1926).
Siemering, Hertha [Ed.]: *Was liest unsere Jugend?* (Berlin: R. von Deeker's Verlag, 1930).
Suren, Hans: *Der Mensch und die Sonne*, (Stuttgart: Dieck, 1924).
Wingender, Hans: *Erfahrungen im Kampfe gegen Schund- und Schmutzschriften*, (Düsseldorf: Selbstverlag, 1930).
Wunderle, Georg: *Die Stigmatisierte von Konnersreuth*, (Eichstätt: Geschäftstelle des Klerusblattes, 1927).
Yogananda, Paramhansa: *Autobiography of a Yogi*, (New York: The Philosophical Library, 1946).

Zenz, Reinhold: *Ist Hellsehen Möglich?* (Königsberg: Verlag der Königsberger Allgemeinen Zeitung, 1928).

Zobeltitz, Fedor von: *Die Papierne Macht*, (Bielefeld: Velhagen und Klasings, 1902).

Bibliography: Secondary Sources

Adam, Christian: *Lesen unter Hitler: Autoren, Bestseller, Leser im Dritten Reich*, (Berlin: Galiani, 2010).

Aschheim, Steven: *Brothers and Strangers: The East European Jew in German Jewish Consciousness, 1800-1923*, (Madison: University of Wisconsin Press, 1982).

Bering, Dietz: *Kampf um Namen: Bernhard Weiss gegen Joseph Goebbels*, (Stuttgart: Kletta, 1991).

Brooks, Jeffrey: *When Russia Learned to Read: Literacy and Popular Literature, 1861-1917*, (Princeton: Princeton University Press, 1985).

Brooks, Peter: *The Melodramatic Imagination*, (New Haven: Yale University Press, 1995).

Buckler, Julie A.: "Melodramatizing Russia", in McReynolds, Louise (Ed.), *Imitations of Life*, (Durham: University of North Carolina Press, 2002), P. 55-78.

Burke, Peter: Eyewitnessing: *The Uses of Images as Historical Evidence*, (Ithaca: Cornell University Press, 2001).

Cawelti, John G.: *Adventure, Mystery, and Romance: Formula Stories as Art and Popular Culture*, (Chicago: University of Chicago Press, 1976).

Cheesman, Tom: *The Shocking Ballad Picture Show: German Popular Literature and Cultural History*, (Oxford: Berg, 1994).

Christian, William A.: *Visionaries: The Spanish Republic and the Reign of Christ*, (Berkeley: University of California Press, 1996).

Crehan, Kate: *Gramsci, Culture and Anthropology*, (Berkeley: University of California Press, 2002).

Dalton, Margaret Stieg: *Catholicism, Popular Culture, and the Arts in Germany, 1880-1933*, (Notre Dame: Notre Dame University Press, 2005).

Denning, Michael: *Mechanic Accents: Dime Novels and Working-Class Culture in America*, (New York: Verso, 1998)

Diehl, Paula (Ed.): *Körper im Nationalsozialismus*, (München: Wilhelm Fink, 2006).

Ermarth, Michael. "Girls Gone Wild in Weimar Germany: Siegfried Kracauer on Girlkultur and the Un-Kultur of Americanism," in Modernism/modernity (vol. 19, No. 1, January 2012), P. 1-18.

Galle, Heinz J.: *Volksbücher und Heftromane*, Bd. 2, (Lüneburg: Dieter von Reeken, 2006).

Georgieff, Andrey: *Nacktheit und Kultur*, (Wien: Passagen Verlag, 2005).

Gross, Raphael: *Anständig Geblieben: Nationalsozialistische Moral*, (Frankfurt: Fischer Verlag, 2012).
Grunert, Frank and Dorothee Kimmrich (Eds.): *Denken durch die Dinge: Siegfried Kracauer im Kontext*, (München: Wilhelm Fink, 2009).
Hau, Michael: *The Cult of Health and Beauty in Germany: A Social History, 1890-1930*, (Chicago: University of Chicago Press, 2003).
King, Lynda J.: *Best-Sellers by Design: Vicki Baum and the House of Ullstein*, (Detroit: Wayne State Univeristy Press, 1988).
Körner, Daniel: *Die Wunderheiler der Weimarer Republik*, (Freiburg: Centaurus, 2012).
Kosch, Günther and Manfred Nagl: *Der Kolportageroman*, (Stuttgart: Metzler, 1993).
Kurlander, Eric: *Hitler's Monsters: A Supernatural History of the Third Reich*, (New Haven: Yale University Press, 2017).
Linse, Ulrich: *Barfüssige Propheten*, (Berlin: Siedler, 1983).
Linse, Ulrich: *Geisterseher und Wunderwirker*, (Frankfurt: Fischer, 1996).
Maase, Kaspar und Wolfgang Kaschuba: *Schund und Schönheit: Populäre Kultur um 1900*, (Köln: Böhlau, 2001).
Mellinkoff, Ruth: *Outcasts: Signs of Otherness in North European Art of the Late Middle Ages*, (Berkeley: University of California Press, 1993).
Meyer, Joachim (Ed.): *Berlin – Provinz: Marbacher Magazin 35*, (Marbach: Schillergesellschaft, 1985).
Midgley, David: *Writing Weimar: Critical Realism in German Literature 1918-1933*, (Oxford: Oxford University Press, 2000).
Möhring, Maren: *Marmorleiber: Körperbildung in der deutschen Nacktkultur (1890-1930)*, (Köln: Böhlau, 2004).
Monaco, Paul: *Cinema and Society*, (New York: Elsevier, 1976).
Mosse, George: *Nationalism and Sexuality: Middle-Class Morality and Sexual Norms in Modern Europe*, (Madison: University of Wisconsin Press, 1985).
Mülder, Inka: *Siegfried Kracauer: Grenzgänger zwischen Theorie und Literatur, Seine frühen Schriften 1913-1933*, (Stuttgart: Metzler, 1985).
Neuhaus, Volker: *Der Zeitgeschichtliche Sensationsroman in Deutschland 1855-1878: "Sir John Retcliffe" und seine Schule*, (Berlin: Erich Schmidt, 1980).
O'Sullivan, Michael: *Disruptive Power: Catholic Women, Miracles, and Politics in Modern Germany, 1918-1965*, (Toronto: University of Toronto Press, 2018).
Petersen, Klaus: *Zensur in der Weimarer Republik*, (Stuttgart: Metzler, 1995).
Radway, Janice: *Reading the Romance: Women, Patriarchy, and Popular Literature*, (Chapel Hill: University of North Carolina Press, 1984).
Reuveni, Gideon: *Reading Germany: Literature and Consumer Culture in Germany before 1933*, (New York: Berghahn, 2006).
Ritzheimer, Kara L.: *"Trash," Censorship, and National Identity in Early Twentieth-Century Germany*, (New York: Cambridge University Press, 2016).
Ross, Chad: *Naked Germany: Health, Race, and the Nation*, (Oxford: Berg, 2005).

Schäfer, Julia: *Vermessen – gezeichnet – verlacht: Judenbilder in populären Zeitschriften 1918-1933*, (Frankfurt: Campus, 2004).

Schenda, Rudolf: *Die Lesestoffe der kleinen Leute*, (Munich: Beck, 1976).

Schuster, Ingrid: *Das Forsthaus am Rhein: Studien zu einem Kolportageroman in 90 Heften aus dem Jahre 1906* (Bonn: Bouvier, 1977).

Singer, Ben: *Melodrama and Modernity: Early Sensational Cinema and Its Contexts*, (New York: Columbia University Press, 2001).

Stalder, Helmut: *Siegfried Kracauer: Das journalistische Werk in der Frankfurter Zeitung 1921-1933*, (Würzburg: Königshausen und Neumann, 2003).

Strieder, Carola: *Melodramatik und Sozialkritik in Werken Eugène Sues*, (Erlangen: V. Palm und Enke, 1986).

Tatar, Maria: *Lustmord: Sexual Murder in Weimar Germany*, (Princeton: Princeton University Press, 1995).

Toepfer, Karl: *Empire of Ecstasy: Nudity and Movement in German Body Culture, 1910-1935*, (Berkeley: University of California Press, 1997).

Treitel, Corinna: *A Science for the Soul: Occultism and the Genesis of the German Modern*, (Baltimore: The Johns Hopkins University Press, 2004).

Treitel, Corinna: *Eating Nature in Modern Germany: Food, Agriculture, and Environment, c. 1870 to 2000* (Cambridge: Cambridge University Press, 2017).

Tytler, Graeme: *Physiognomy in the European Novel*, (Princeton: Princeton University Press, 1982).

Wanjek, Peter: *Bibliographie der deutschen Heftromane 1900-1945*, (Wilferdorf: K. Ganzbiller, 1993).

Williams, John Alexander: *Turning to Nature in Germany: Hiking, Nudism, and Conservation, 1900-1940* (Stanford: Stanford University Press, 2007).

Wolffram, Heather: The *Stepchildren of Science: Psychical Research and Parapsychology In Germany, c. 1870-1939*, (Amsterdam: Rodopi, 2009).

Index

A
Adam, Christian 206
Adenauer, Konrad 189
Adolf Ander Verlag 129
America and Americans 30, 39, 67-68, 73, 82-83, 87-88, 91-93, 125, 132, 136, 143, 154, 156
Andreu-Rivels (clowns) 18
Antisemitism 38, 50, 53, 101-102, 115, 121-122, 133, 157-158, 160, 186, 194, 202
Argentina 124-125, 128, 133, 135

B
Baker, Josephine 221
Balzac, Honore de 131
Bäumer, Gertrud 106
Benjamin, Walter 19, 148
Berlin 14-15, 26, 28, 36, 57-58, 67, 72, 78, 89, 92-93, 102, 105, 116, 145-146, 154-158, 160, 162, 165, 173, 175, 177, 180, 192, 193, 195-198, 202-202, 204-206, 217-224
Bernfeld, Siegfried 113-114
Bildungsbürgertum (the educated classes) 24, 75, 111, 146
Blacks 133, 149, 151-152, 156, 166, 184-185, 194, 221
Blonde and blue-eyed 81-82, 86-89, 92, 132, 175
Bohm-Schuch, Clara 216
Bracht, Franz 191, 193, 195, 205
Braun, Otto 53
Brecht, Bertolt 156
Breitscheid, Rudolf 104-105, 108
Brentano, Bernard von 103
Brooks, Peter 134
Brüning, Heinrich 53, 191
Brunner, Karl 74, 78
Bry, Carl Christian 49-51, 53, 60
Buckler, Julie 84

C
Catholics 12-13, 15, 26, 39-48, 57, 59, 78, 100, 103, 115, 173-175, 180-181, 184-191, 196, 201, 203, 217
Censorship 13-15, 72, 74, 81, 91, 99, 103-104, 107-108, 111-112, 116-117, 119, 122, 129, 149-150, 158, 164-168, 196, 206, 214-215, 222
Center Party 12-15, 26, 39-43, 45-48, 57, 59, 78, 100, 103, 173-175, 180-181, 184-191, 196, 201, 203, 217
Chaplin, Charlie 18, 71
Christian, William A. 14, 47
Colporteur 11, 72, 74
Communists 33, 48-49, 53, 103, 106-107, 175, 190, 195-196, 202, 206, 213
Cooper, James Fenimore 150
Crisis 19, 47-48, 106, 163-164, 190-191, 221
Cultural underdog 14, 47

D

Darré, Walther 206
Degeneration 86, 89, 91, 153, 156, 182, 193, 199, 218
Denning, Michael 134
Dessoir, Max 35-38
Deutsch, Josef 41
DDP (Deutsche Demokratische Partei) 73, 102, 105-108, 196, 213
Dickens, Charles 131
Diebel, Paul 57
Dietrich, Marlene 223
Dinter, Artur 105, 114
DNVP (Deutschnationale Volkspartei) 99-101, 108, 217
Döblin, Alfred 223
Drost, August 20-31, 37-38, 214, 218
DVP (Deutsche Volkspartei) 108, 166

E

Ebertin, Elsbeth 51-52, 55, 60
Eckert, Erwin 101
Eichler, Alwin 143
Ellerbek, Ellegaard 115
Emigrants and exiles 59, 85, 92, 125, 128
England 75, 85, 181
Epstein, Hans 151-153, 214
Ethics, morality 13, 81, 86-87, 92-93, 109, 126, 130, 134, 140, 149-150, 166, 175, 181, 187-188, 191, 193, 195-197, 203, 217, 220, 222, 224

F

Falk, Viktor von (Heinrich Socheczewsky) 117
Feher, Friedrich and Hans 94-95
Fenkohl, Gustav 165
Fiedler, Kuno 150-151
Film 11-12, 28, 67-71, 78, 84, 88-90, 93-95, 99, 101-102, 107-108, 111-113, 147, 157, 165-167, 176, 196, 214-215, 218, 220, 222-223
France 60, 72, 81, 123, 136, 156, 158-159, 185, 189
Freya Verlag 122, 129, 216
Fuhrmann, Georg 176-177, 180

G

Gensch, Willy 145-146
Gertz, Jenny 200-201
Goebbels, Joseph 56
Graaz, Hans 198-199, 204, 218
Gramsci, Antonio 14, 36
Grock (Charles Wettach) 17-18
Gronau, Heinz 124, 216
Grossmann, Stefan 114
Günther-Geffers, Elsbeth 12, 30-38, 51-52, 56, 214-215
"Gypsy" stereotypes 30, 131-133

H

Hanussen, Jan Erik (Hermann Steinschneider) 19-20, 51, 57-58
Haspinger, Alois 122
Hass, Hermann 220-223
Hauesser, Ludwig C. 39
Heidecke, Gustav 199
Hellwig, Albert 20, 22-30, 33, 35, 37-38, 108-112, 119, 148, 214
Hess, Rudolf 56
Heuss, Theodor 105-107, 213
Hildebrand, Paul 203
Hildebrecht, Paul 21-22, 26
Himmler, Heinrich 56
Hindenburg, Paul von 28, 205
Hirschfeld, Magnus 175, 216
Hitler, Adolf 17, 48, 51, 53-55, 58-60, 101, 129-130, 206
Hoernle, Edwin 103-104
Hoffmann, Walter 110-111

Homosexuals 178, 219, 221, 224
Hugenberg, Alfred 101
Hyne, Stanley 148

K

Kabel, Walther 148-149, 154-172, 206, 214
Karpeles, Benno 47-48
Keun von Hoogerwoerd, Harald 53
Kieslich, H.E. 175-176
Kinderrepublik 190, 217
Koch, Adolf 174-175, 177, 182, 193, 197-206
Koenen, Wilhelm 100
Költzsch, Franz 99-100
Kosch, Günter 117
Kracauer, Siegfried 11-13, 15, 17-19, 26, 47, 50, 57, 67-71, 88, 90, 93-95, 111-112, 146-148, 166, 173-178, 192-194, 199-200, 204, 213-215, 220, 222-224
Krieck, Ernst 151-154
Krishnamurti 48, 51
Kröner, Walter 32, 35-36, 51
Kube, Wilhelm 102-103, 106
Küble, Philip 184-190, 192, 194
Kulturbolschewismus (cultural Bolshevism) 190, 196, 221
Külz, Wilhelm 73, 107-108, 196
Kunze, Richard 202
Kurfürstendamm 15, 57, 67, 156, 205, 213, 218, 222-224

L

Lambert, Rudolf 32-34, 36
Lang, Fritz 11, 71, 84-85
Lavater, Johann Casper 91, 129, 132
Lending library 146, 176, 220
Lewandowski, Herbert 149
Leyendecker, Peter 195-197
Lombroso, Cesare 129, 132
Löwenstein, Kurt 102, 104-105, 165-166, 216-217
Ludendorff, Erich 48
Luft, Margarete 59

M

Mädchenhändler 92-93, 143
Mager, Alois 43
Maikowsky, Hans 216
Mann, Heinrich 223
Marien Verlag 79, 93, 122, 129
Marx, Wilhelm 108
Matz, Else 166, 217
Maurus, Gerda 223
Mausbach, Joseph 188-191, 217
Mellinkoff, Ruth 131
Melodrama 38, 74, 79, 81, 84-85, 112, 117, 123, 134, 159
Midgley, David 160
Mignon Verlag 116-117, 119-120, 127, 129
Möckel, Erich 21-22, 26
Moecke, Max 51
Muck-Lamberty, Friedrich 39
Müller-Fraureth, Carl 129
Mumm, Reinhard 100-104, 106-107
Münchmeyer Verlag 83, 94, 129

N

Nagl, Manfred 117
National character or traits 132, 165, 199, 220
Nationalist 28, 91, 100, 102-104, 112-113, 134, 151-154, 156, 185, 195, 199, 203, 206, 213-214, 216, 218, 221, 223-224
NSDAP (Nazi Party) 15, 48, 50-60, 65-66, 78, 91, 95, 98, 101-105, 112, 114-115, 151-156, 158, 160-161, 164, 166, 175, 191, 194-196, 202, 204-206, 213-214, 216, 220-221
Neues Verlagshaus für Volksliteratur 216

Neumann, Marie 20-23, 26
Neumann, Therese 35, 37, 39-47, 50, 57
Norkus, Herbert 216

O
Oestreich, Paul 112-113
Olden, Rudolf 46-49, 60
O'Sullivan, Michael 39, 41

P
Paola Rost, Franz de 150
Papen, Franz von 53, 191, 194-197, 205
Parry, Lee 223
Paulsen, Wilhelm 201-202
Pelz, Carl 32-35, 56-59, 66
Petzet, Wolfgang 111-112
Pfeil, Ellmar 117
Pfülf, Toni 102
Physiognomy 55, 91, 129-132, 194
Piel, Harry 12, 69-71, 78, 176
Pinkert, Ernst Friedrich 77-78, 80-95, 98, 111, 117, 119-120, 123, 157
Popert, Hermann 105-106
Protestants 12, 39, 48, 100-103, 115, 129, 203-204
Province 14, 22, 24, 29, 36, 57, 154, 156, 189, 198, 217-219, 225
Pudor, Heinrich 178
Putz zu Adlersthurn, Anton 179-182

R
Red hair 87, 131
Reuter, Wilhelm 124
Rosenberg, Alfred 56
Roth, Joseph 215
Russia 82, 84-85, 92, 117, 133

S
Salardenne, Roger 189
Salomon, Ernst von 113

Schenda, Rudolf 72
Schendell, Wilhelm 165
Schermann, Rafael 51
Schiller, Friedrich 123, 158
Schleicher, Kurt von 53, 195
Schumacher, Artur 54-55
Seeling, Otto 38
Seitz, Josef 187-189
Seydewitz, Max 104
Siemering, Hertha 123
Skladanowsky, Max 71
Sling (Paul Schlesinger) 22-29, 37, 41
Social Darwinism 129, 178, 182
SPD (Social Democratic Party) 13, 27-28, 47, 59-60, 73, 103-107, 144, 165-166, 175, 190, 195-196, 201, 206, 217-218
Spandrel Edict (Zwickelerlass) 191, 195-196
Stapel, Wilhelm 191-194, 213, 218-219
Stites, Richard 81
Stöcker, Adolf 100-101
Strasser, Gregor 54-55
Streicher, Julius 114
Subaltern 36, 38, 41, 63, 133-134, 166, 178, 217
Sue, Eugène 72, 158
Suren, Hans 182-184, 187, 191, 199, 206, 216, 222

T
Tausend, Franz 48
Thieme, Reinhold 166
Toepfer, Karl 201
Toller, Ernst 223
Treitel, Corinna 38, 59

U
Ungewitter, Richard 178, 180

V

Viebig, Clara 123
Vulpius, Christian August 123

W

Wallace, Ernst 159
Walter, Paul 134
Wandervogel 92, 197
Weber, Helene 106
Weber, Matthias 121
Weimar coalition 15, 203
Weimar Constitution 13, 56, 99-100, 115, 188, 195
Weissenberg, Joseph 39, 48, 51
Wessel, Horst 216
Weyl, Richard 202
Wingender, Hans 115
Winterberg, Richard 35-36
Wolff, Theodor 213
Wunderle, Georg 43-44

Y

Yogananda, Paramhansa 39
Youth 13-15, 47, 49-50, 69, 71, 73-81, 99, 102-123, 134-135, 143-151, 165-166, 175, 177, 183-185, 188, 190-191, 197-199, 205, 214, 217, 220-224

Z

Zach, Lorenz 174-175
Zeileis, Valentin 48
Zobeltitz, Fedor von 77, 149-150
Zschokke, Heinrich 123

Cultural Studies

Elisa Ganivet
Border Wall Aesthetics
Artworks in Border Spaces

2019, 250 p., hardcover, ill.
79,99 € (DE), 978-3-8376-4777-8
E-Book: 79,99 € (DE), ISBN 978-3-8394-4777-2

Jocelyne Porcher, Jean Estebanez (eds.)
Animal Labor
A New Perspective on Human-Animal Relations

2019, 182 p., hardcover
99,99 € (DE), 978-3-8376-4364-0
E-Book: 99,99 € (DE), ISBN 978-3-8394-4364-4

Andreas Sudmann (ed.)
The Democratization of Artificial Intelligence
Net Politics in the Era of Learning Algorithms

2019, 334 p., pb., col. ill.
49,99 € (DE), 978-3-8376-4719-8
E-Book: 49,99 € (DE), ISBN 978-3-8394-4719-2

**All print, e-book and open access versions of the titles in our list
are available in our online shop www.transcript-verlag.de/en!**

Cultural Studies

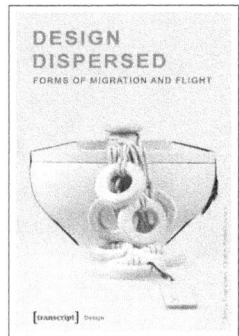

Burcu Dogramaci, Kerstin Pinther (eds.)
Design Dispersed
Forms of Migration and Flight

2019, 274 p., pb., col. ill.
34,99 € (DE), 978-3-8376-4705-1
E-Book: 34,99 € (DE), ISBN 978-3-8394-4705-5

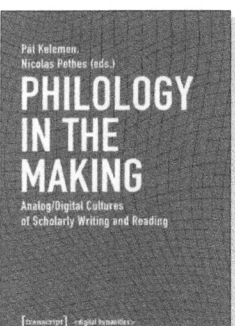

Pál Kelemen, Nicolas Pethes (eds.)
Philology in the Making
Analog/Digital Cultures of Scholarly Writing and Reading

2019, 316 p., pb., ill.
34,99 € (DE), 978-3-8376-4770-9
E-Book: 34,99 € (DE), ISBN 978-3-8394-4770-3

Chris Goldie, Darcy White (eds.)
Northern Light
Landscape, Photography and Evocations of the North

2018, 174 p., hardcover, ill.
79,99 € (DE), 978-3-8376-3975-9
E-Book: 79,99 € (DE), ISBN 978-3-8394-3975-3

**All print, e-book and open access versions of the titles in our list
are available in our online shop www.transcript-verlag.de/en!**

GPSR Authorized Representative: Easy Access System Europe, Mustamäe tee 50, 10621 Tallinn, Estonia, gpsr.requests@easproject.com

www.ingramcontent.com/pod-product-compliance
Lightning Source LLC
Chambersburg PA
CBHW051538020426
42333CB00016B/1995